Jean-Claude Corbeil • Ariane Archambault

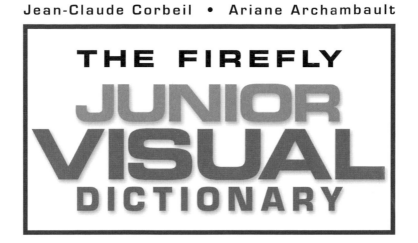

THE FIREFLY
JUNIOR
VISUAL
DICTIONARY

FIREFLY BOOKS

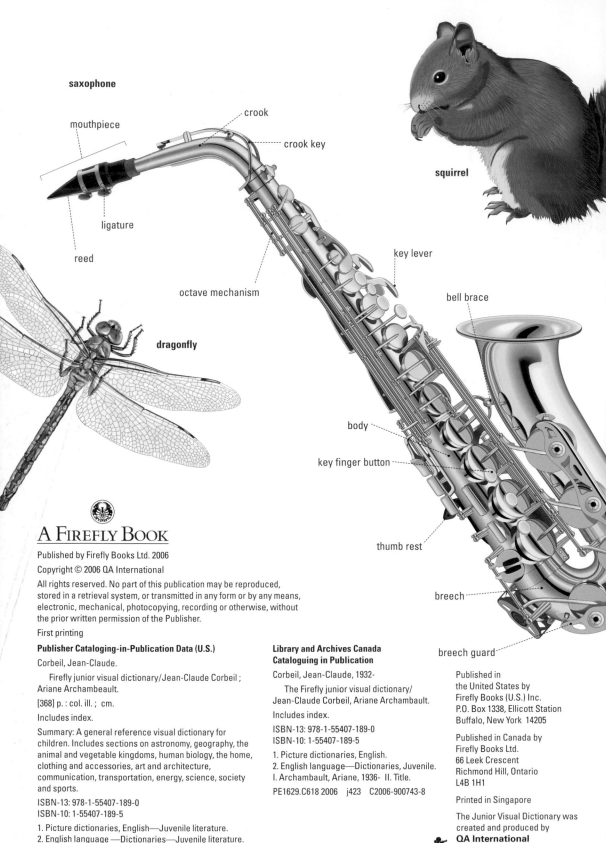

saxophone

mouthpiece

crook

crook key

squirrel

ligature

reed

octave mechanism

key lever

bell brace

dragonfly

body

key finger button

thumb rest

breech

breech guard

A FIREFLY BOOK

Published by Firefly Books Ltd. 2006

Copyright © 2006 QA International

First printing

Publisher Cataloging-in-Publication Data (U.S.)

Corbeil, Jean-Claude.

Firefly junior visual dictionary/Jean-Claude Corbeil ; Ariane Archambeault.

[368] p. : col. ill. ; cm.

Includes index.

Summary: A general reference visual dictionary for children. Includes sections on astronomy, geography, the animal and vegetable kingdoms, human biology, the home, clothing and accessories, art and architecture, communication, transportation, energy, science, society and sports.

ISBN-13: 978-1-55407-189-0
ISBN-10: 1-55407-189-5

1. Picture dictionaries, English—Juvenile literature.
2. English language —Dictionaries—Juvenile literature.
I. Archambeault, Ariane. II.Title.

423.1 dc22   PE1629.C6736 2006

Library and Archives Canada Cataloguing in Publication

Corbeil, Jean-Claude, 1932-

The Firefly junior visual dictionary/ Jean-Claude Corbeil, Ariane Archambault.

Includes index.

ISBN-13: 978-1-55407-189-0
ISBN-10: 1-55407-189-5

1. Picture dictionaries, English.
2. English language—Dictionaries, Juvenile.
I. Archambault, Ariane, 1936- II. Title.

PE1629.C618 2006   j423   C2006-900743-8

Published in
the United States by
Firefly Books (U.S.) Inc.
P.O. Box 1338, Ellicott Station
Buffalo, New York 14205

Published in Canada by
Firefly Books Ltd.
66 Leek Crescent
Richmond Hill, Ontario
L4B 1H1

Printed in Singapore

The Junior Visual Dictionary was created and produced by

QA International
329, rue de la Commune Ouest, 3ᵉ étage
Montréal (Québec) H2Y 2E1 Canada
T 514.499.3000 F 514.499.3010
www.qa-international.com

Jean-Claude Corbeil • Ariane Archambault

THE FIREFLY
JUNIOR
VISUAL
DICTIONARY

EDITORIAL STAFF
Publisher: Jacques Fortin
Editorial Director: François Fortin
Editorial Director, Junior Edition: Caroline Fortin
Editor-in-Chief: Serge D'Amico
Editor-in-Chief, Junior Edition: Martine Podesto
Associate Editor, Junior Edition: Johanne Champagne
Graphic Designer: Josée Noiseux
Scholastic Canada Ltd. Editor: Jennifer MacKinnon

TERMINOLOGY
Jean Beaumont
Catherine Briand
Nathalie Guillo

ILLUSTRATIONS
Art Director: Jocelyn Gardner
Art Director, Junior Edition: Anouk Noël
Jean-Yves Ahern
Rielle Lévesque
Alain Lemire
Mélanie Boivin
Yan Bohler
Claude Thivierge
Pascal Bilodeau
Michel Rouleau
Carl Pelletier

LAY-OUT
Jean-François Nault
Jean-Philippe Bouchard
Nathalie Gignac
Kien Tang

DOCUMENTATION
Gilles Vézina
Kathleen Wynd
Stéphane Batigne
Sylvain Robichaud
Jessie Daigle

DATA MANAGEMENT
Programmer: Daniel Beaulieu

PROOFREADING
Veronica Schami Editorial Services

PRODUCTION
Guylaine Houle

PREPRESS
Sophie Pellerin
Tony O'Riley
Karine Lévesque
Kien Tang

CONTRIBUTORS
Jean-Louis Martin, Marc Lalumière, Jacques Perrault, Stéphane Roy,
Alice Comtois, Michel Blais, Christiane Beauregard, Mamadou Togola,
Annie Maurice, Charles Campeau, Mivil Deschênes, Jonathan Jacques,
Martin Lortie, Raymond Martin, Frédérick Simard, Yan Tremblay,
Mathieu Blouin, Sébastien Dallaire, Hoang Khanh Le, Martin Desrosiers,
Nicolas Oroc, François Escalmel, Danièle Lemay, Pierre Savoie, Benoît
Bourdeau, Marie-Andrée Lemieux, Caroline Soucy, Yves Chabot,
Anne-Marie Ouellette, Anne-Marie Villeneuve, Anne-Marie Brault,
Nancy Lepage, Daniel Provost, François Vézina.

CONTENTS

5

SOLAR SYSTEM

The solar system is our own little corner of the universe. It consists of a single star, the Sun, and all the astral bodies that orbit it: nine planets, more than 100 natural satellites, thousands of asteroids and millions of comets. Completing the procession circling around our star are billions of pebbles, dust particles and gases.

PLANETS AND SATELLITES

ORBITS OF THE PLANETS

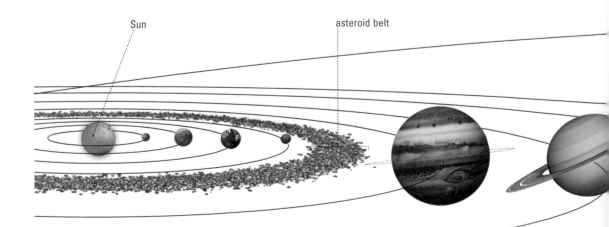

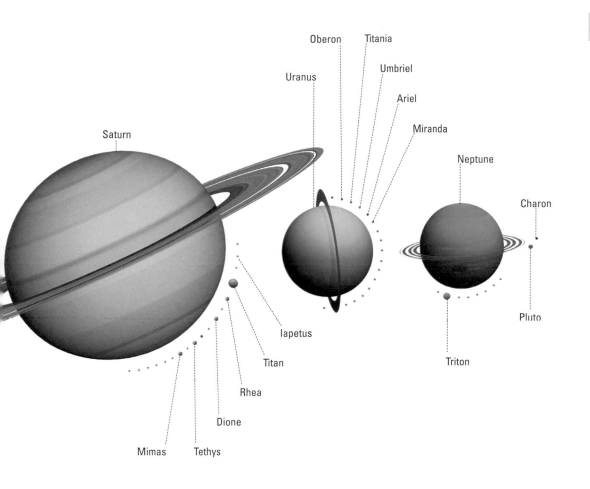

Oberon
Titania
Umbriel
Uranus
Ariel
Miranda
Saturn
Neptune
Charon
Iapetus
Titan
Triton
Pluto
Rhea
Dione
Mimas
Tethys

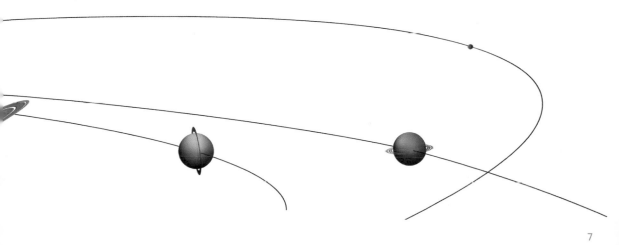

ASTRONOMY

SUN

structure of the Sun

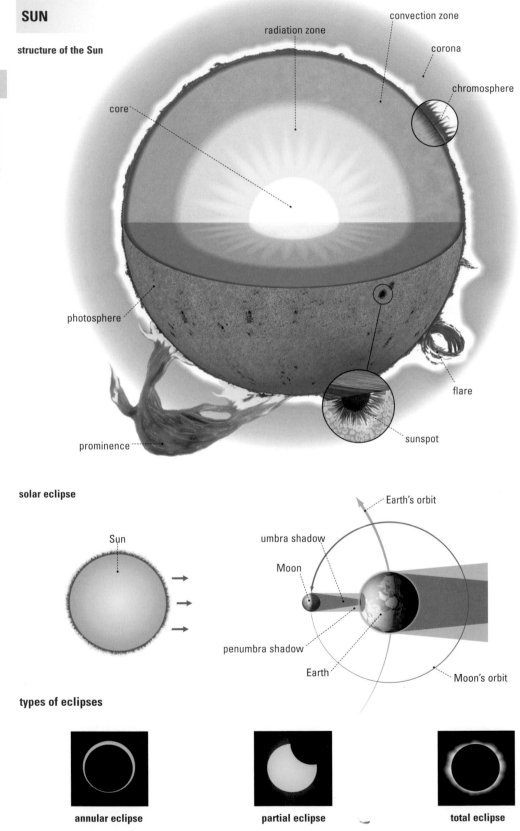

radiation zone

convection zone

corona

chromosphere

core

photosphere

flare

prominence

sunspot

solar eclipse

Sun

Earth's orbit

umbra shadow

Moon

penumbra shadow

Earth

Moon's orbit

types of eclipses

annular eclipse

partial eclipse

total eclipse

lunar features

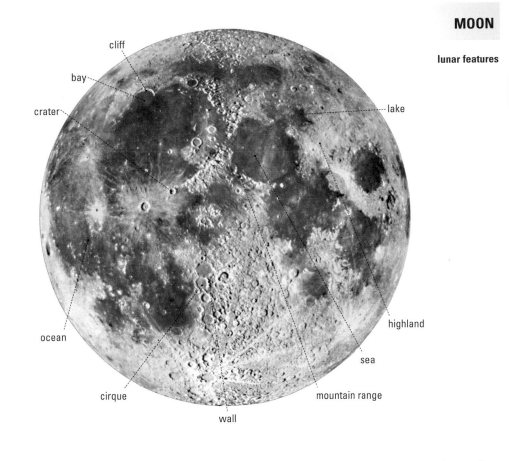

cliff

bay

crater

lake

ocean

highland

cirque

sea

wall

mountain range

lunar eclipse

penumbra shadow

Earth's orbit

umbra shadow

Sun

Earth

Moon's orbit

Moon

types of eclipses

partial eclipse

total eclipse

ASTRONOMY

phases of the Moon

new moon

new crescent

first quarter

waxing gibbous

full moon

waning gibbous

last quarter

old crescent

COMET

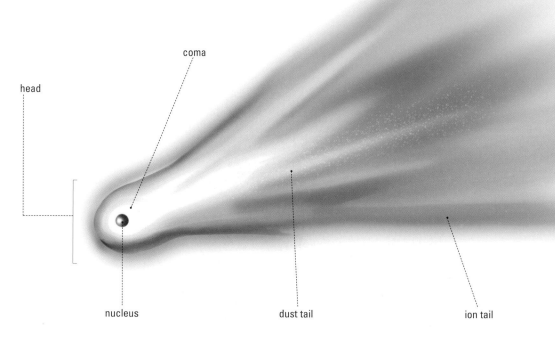

coma

head

nucleus

dust tail

ion tail

The universe contains approximately 100 billion galaxies, each one made up of several billion stars, gases and dust particles. Our solar system is located at the edge of a galaxy called the Milky Way. Seen from Earth, the Milky Way looks like a bright ribbon spread across the night sky. The whitish trail comes from the light of its 200 to 300 billion stars.

MILKY WAY

Milky Way (seen from above)

nucleus

spiral arm

Milky Way (side view)

disk

halo

globular cluster

bulge

ASTRONOMICAL OBSERVATION

The invention of the refracting telescope and the reflecting telescope has truly revolutionized our vision of the universe. These instruments collect the light coming from a celestial object and use lenses or mirrors to concentrate it. With them, the stars and planets were observed enlarged and in detail for the first time. Today specialists are developing increasingly advanced models of telescopes.

REFRACTING TELESCOPE

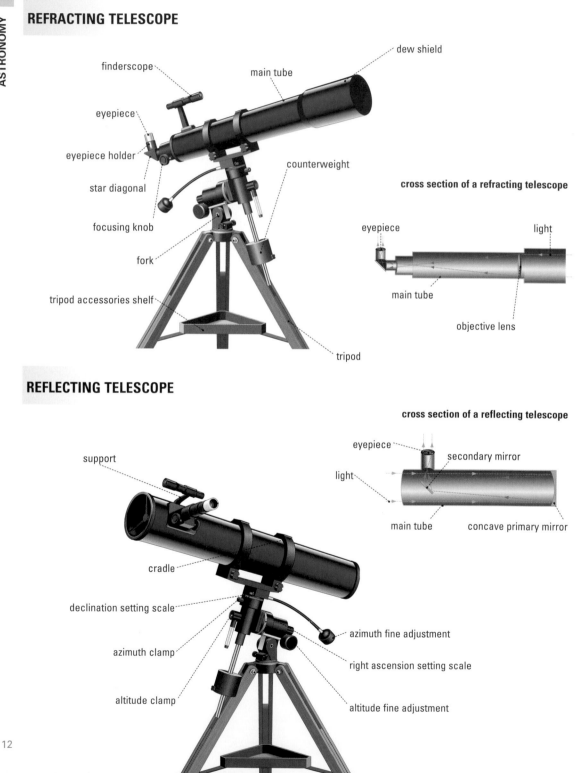

dew shield

finderscope

main tube

eyepiece

eyepiece holder

star diagonal

counterweight

cross section of a refracting telescope

eyepiece

light

focusing knob

fork

main tube

objective lens

tripod accessories shelf

tripod

REFLECTING TELESCOPE

cross section of a reflecting telescope

eyepiece

secondary mirror

support

light

main tube

concave primary mirror

cradle

declination setting scale

azimuth fine adjustment

azimuth clamp

right ascension setting scale

altitude clamp

altitude fine adjustment

Space probes explore planets and areas in space where no human being can go. Sent up by a space shuttle or by a space launcher, these ingenious robots are modern-day explorers. Unlike rockets, which can only be used once, the space shuttle is a reusable vehicle. Among its many missions is the transportation of modules for the International Space Station.

SPACE PROBES

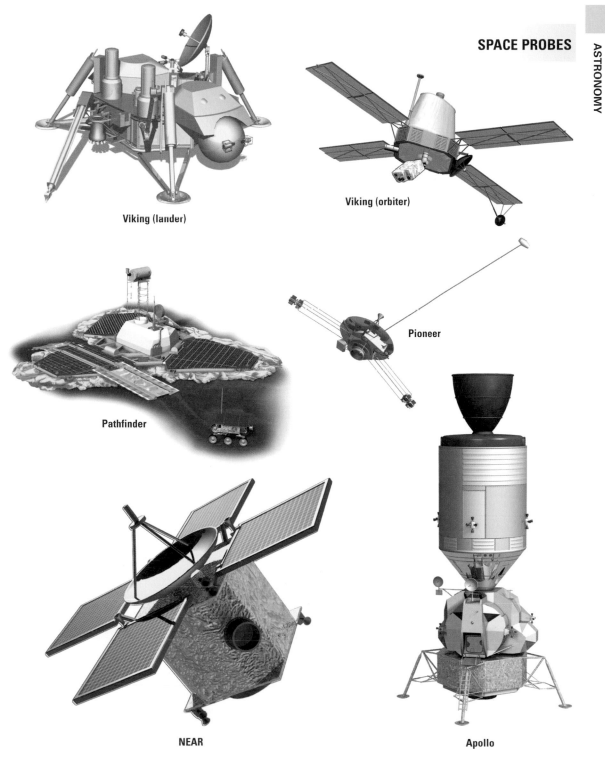

Viking (lander)

Viking (orbiter)

Pioneer

Pathfinder

NEAR

Apollo

INTERNATIONAL SPACE STATION

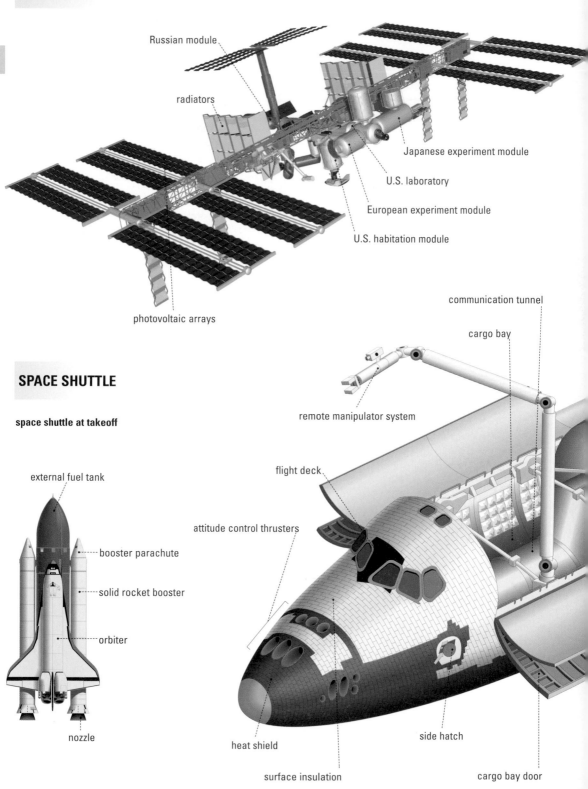

Russian module

radiators

Japanese experiment module

U.S. laboratory

European experiment module

U.S. habitation module

photovoltaic arrays

communication tunnel

cargo bay

SPACE SHUTTLE

space shuttle at takeoff

remote manipulator system

flight deck

external fuel tank

attitude control thrusters

booster parachute

solid rocket booster

orbiter

nozzle

heat shield

side hatch

surface insulation

cargo bay door

orbiter

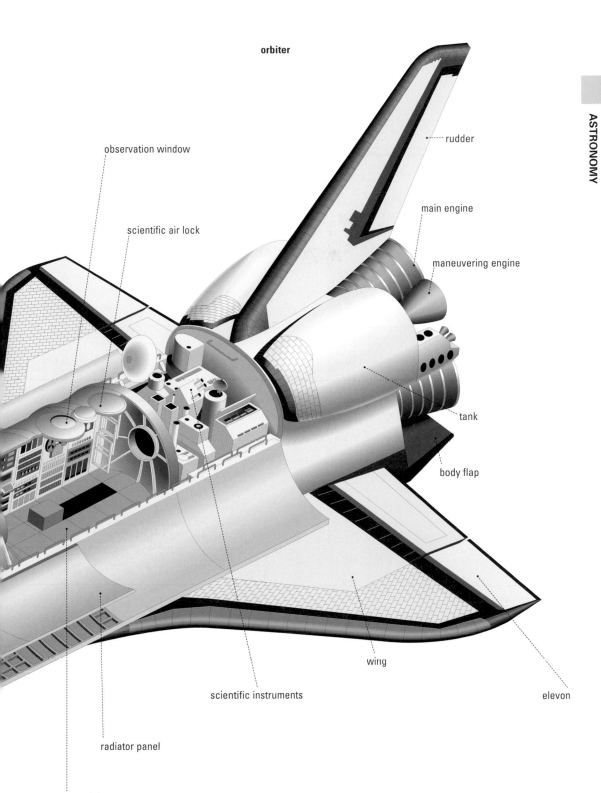

observation window

scientific air lock

rudder

main engine

maneuvering engine

tank

body flap

spacelab

radiator panel

scientific instruments

wing

elevon

SPACE LAUNCHER

cross section of a space launcher (Ariane V)

examples of space launchers

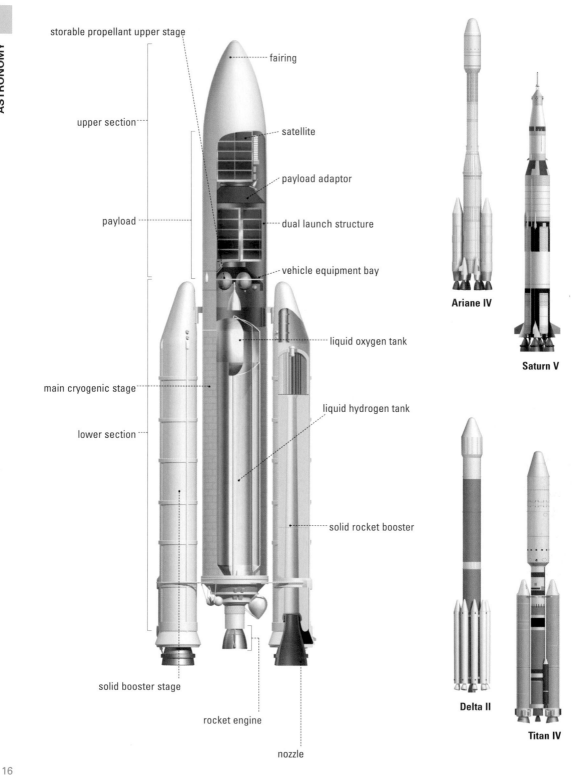

storable propellant upper stage

fairing

upper section

satellite

payload adaptor

payload

dual launch structure

vehicle equipment bay

liquid oxygen tank

main cryogenic stage

liquid hydrogen tank

lower section

solid rocket booster

solid booster stage

rocket engine

nozzle

Ariane IV

Saturn V

Delta II

Titan IV

SPACESUIT

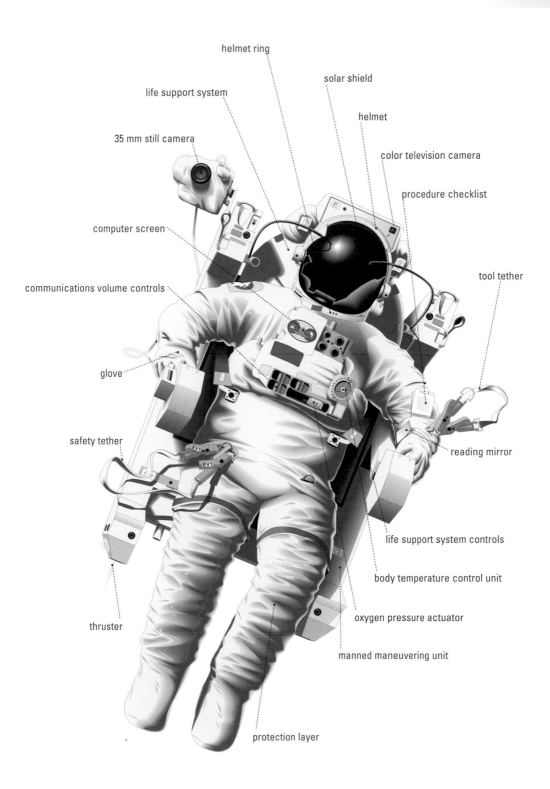

helmet ring

solar shield

life support system

helmet

35 mm still camera

color television camera

procedure checklist

computer screen

tool tether

communications volume controls

glove

reading mirror

safety tether

EV1

EV1

life support system controls

body temperature control unit

thruster

oxygen pressure actuator

manned maneuvering unit

protection layer

CONFIGURATION OF THE CONTINENTS

Our world is divided into seven huge areas of land surrounded by water, which are called continents. Eurasia is the body of land formed by Europe and Asia together. Even though the two territories are not separated by water, they are considered two distinct continents for historical reasons. Together, the seven continents cover approximately one-third of the surface of the globe. With the exception of Antarctica, they are all inhabited.

PLANISPHERE

Arctic

Arctic Ocean

North America

Atlantic Ocean

Pacific Ocean

Central America

Caribbean Sea

South America

Eurasia

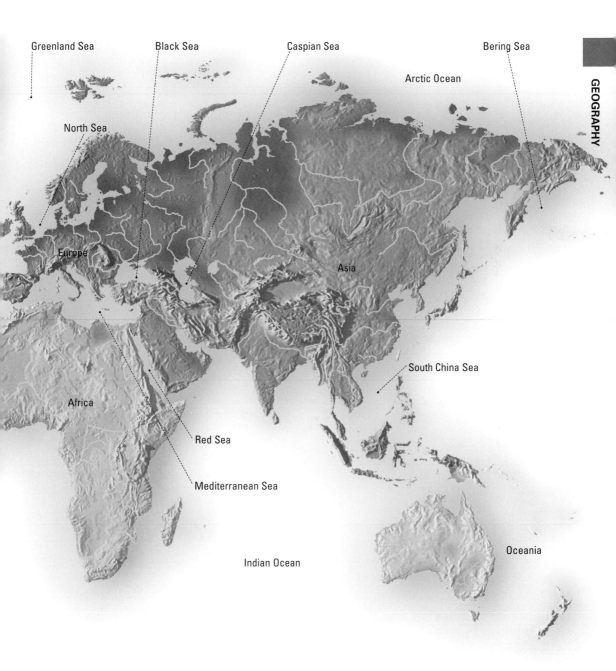

Greenland Sea

Black Sea

Caspian Sea

Bering Sea

Arctic Ocean

North Sea

Europe

Asia

Africa

South China Sea

Red Sea

Mediterranean Sea

Oceania

Indian Ocean

Antarctica

CARTOGRAPHY

To represent the Earth's surface, cartographers draw geographical maps that show, in detail, the different features of a given region. Creating the maps requires much research and gathering of information. Cartographers also have to select a system of projection that will allow three-dimensional reality to be shown as a flat, two-dimensional map.

EARTH'S COORDINATES AND GRID SYSTEMS

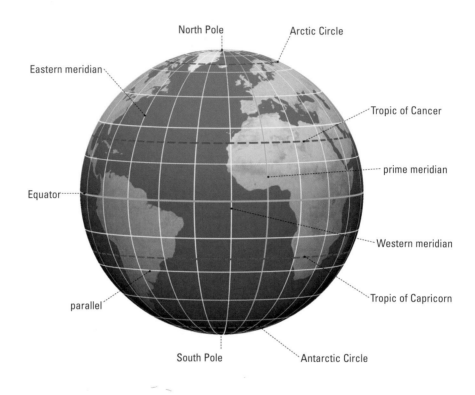

North Pole

Arctic Circle

Eastern meridian

Tropic of Cancer

prime meridian

Equator

Western meridian

Tropic of Capricorn

parallel

South Pole

Antarctic Circle

Northern hemisphere

Southern hemisphere

Western hemisphere   **Eastern hemisphere**

MAP PROJECTIONS

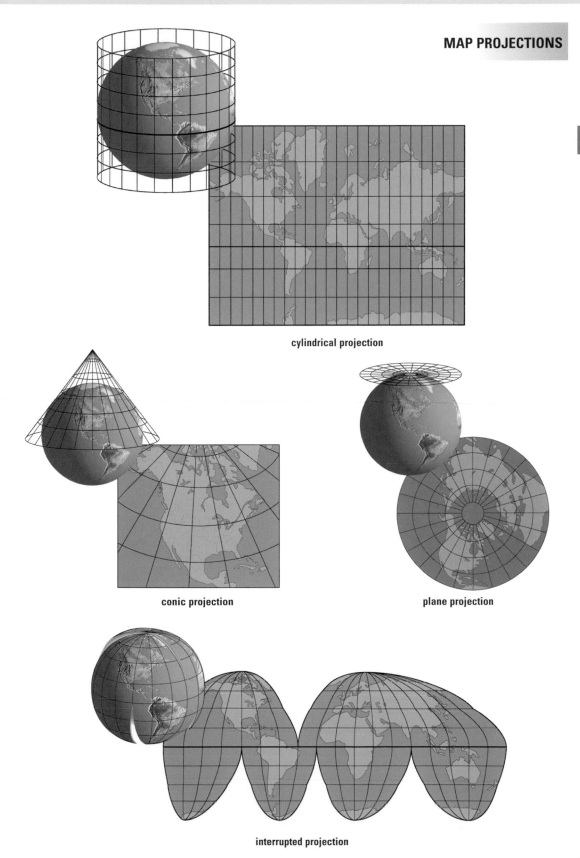

cylindrical projection

conic projection

plane projection

interrupted projection

GEOGRAPHY

MAPS

physical map

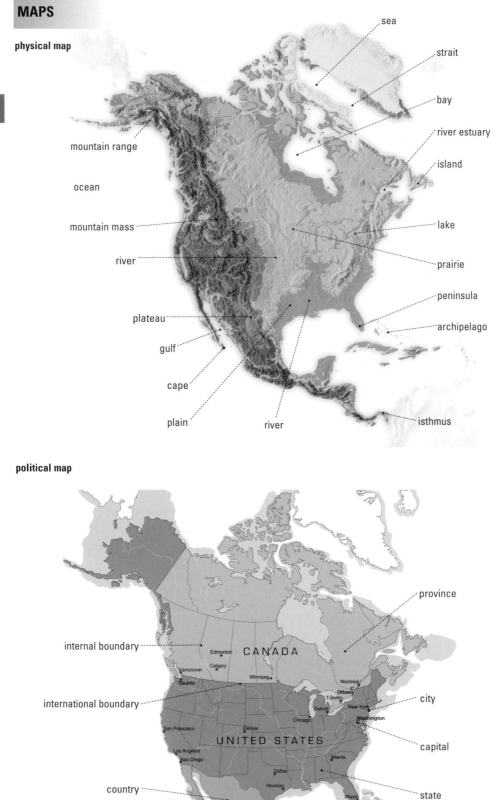

sea

strait

bay

river estuary

mountain range

island

ocean

mountain mass

lake

river

prairie

peninsula

plateau

archipelago

gulf

cape

plain

river

isthmus

political map

province

internal boundary

CANADA

Edmonton

Calgary

Vancouver

Winnipeg

Seattle

Montréal

Ottawa

Toronto

international boundary

Detroit

New York

city

Chicago

San Francisco

Denver

Washington

UNITED STATES

capital

Los Angeles

San Diego

Atlanta

Dallas

country

Houston

Miami

state

Monterrey

MEXICO

Guadalajara

Ciudad de México

road map

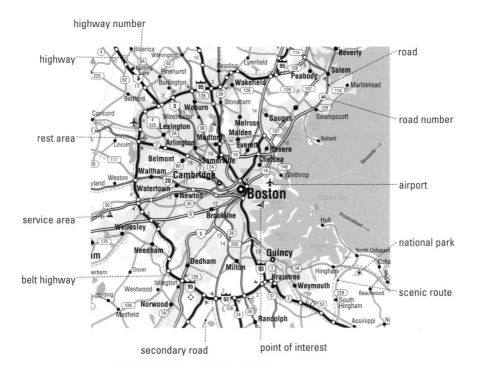

highway number

highway

rest area

service area

belt highway

secondary road

point of interest

road

road number

airport

national park

scenic route

COMPASS ROSE

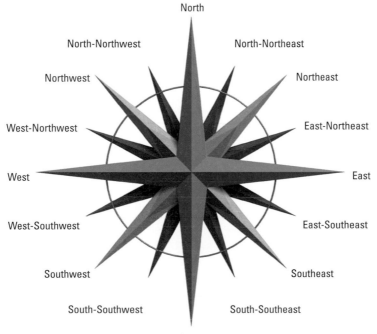

North

North-Northwest

North-Northeast

Northwest

Northeast

West-Northwest

East-Northeast

West

East

West-Southwest

East-Southeast

Southwest

Southeast

South-Southwest

South-Southeast

South

STRUCTURE OF THE EARTH

Even if it is impossible to explore the Earth's interior, geologists have been able to figure out what the planet is made of by studying the way seismic waves spread underground. Seismic waves are the vibrations that accompany earthquakes. Because these waves move differently according to the rocks and materials that they encounter, geologists have determined that Earth is made up of three principal layers: the crust, the mantle and the core.

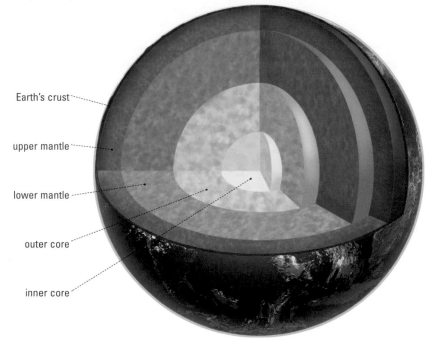

- Earth's crust
- upper mantle
- lower mantle
- outer core
- inner core

section of the Earth's crust

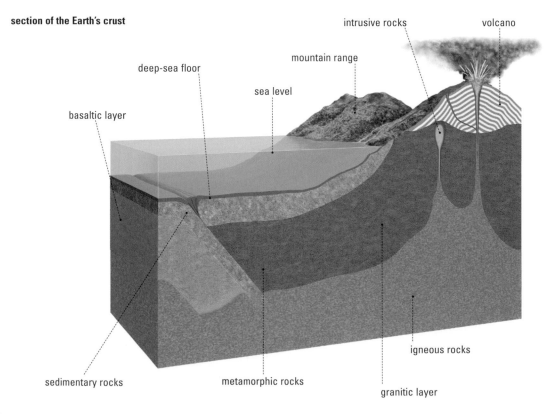

- intrusive rocks
- volcano
- deep-sea floor
- mountain range
- sea level
- basaltic layer
- sedimentary rocks
- metamorphic rocks
- granitic layer
- igneous rocks

The Earth's crust is made up of rocks of various origins. All rocks are composed of different kinds of minerals. Granite, for example, is a very hard rock containing several minerals, including quartz. There are about 3,500 different minerals that can be distinguished, among other ways, by their color and their hardness. Many minerals, such as gold and diamonds, are sought after for their value.

minerals

quartz

silver

gold

diamond

graphite

mica

malachite

rocks

rock salt

sandstone

chalk

coal

limestone

marble

slate

basalt

granite

GEOLOGICAL PHENOMENA

Volcanoes and earthquakes are spectacular geological phenomena that demonstrate Earth's continuous activity. Similar to a jigsaw puzzle, the Earth's crust is made up of about a dozen pieces, called tectonic plates. Earthquakes occur regularly at the meeting point of two plates that are in movement. Most of the volcanoes likely to cause violent eruptions are found at the edges of these plates.

EARTHQUAKE

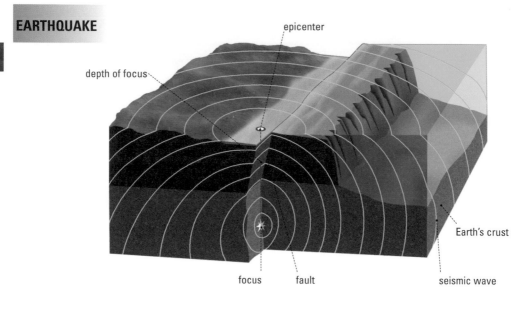

epicenter

depth of focus

Earth's crust

focus   fault   seismic wave

seismographs

vertical seismograph

spring   pen

mass

rotating drum

pillar

seismogram

stand

vertical ground movement

bedrock

horizontal seismograph

mass

pen

rotating drum

seismogram

horizontal ground movement

VOLCANO

volcano during eruption

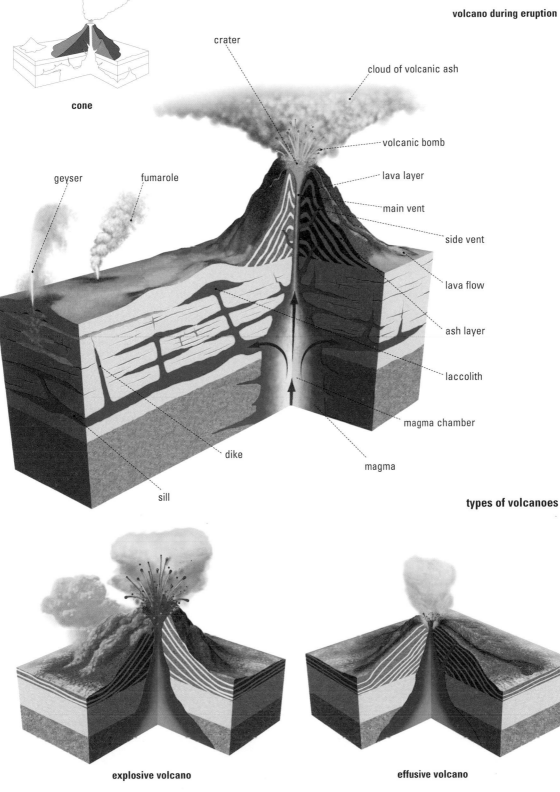

cone

crater

cloud of volcanic ash

volcanic bomb

lava layer

main vent

side vent

lava flow

ash layer

laccolith

magma chamber

magma

geyser

fumarole

dike

sill

types of volcanoes

explosive volcano

effusive volcano

EARTH'S FEATURES

Since the birth of our planet, some oceans have formed while others have disappeared. Chains of mountains have risen from Earth's surface and eventually flattened out. Although the landscape around us seems unchanging, it is constantly evolving. The transformation may be radical, as in a seismic event, or slow, as in seawater gradually altering the shape of a country's coastline.

MOUNTAIN

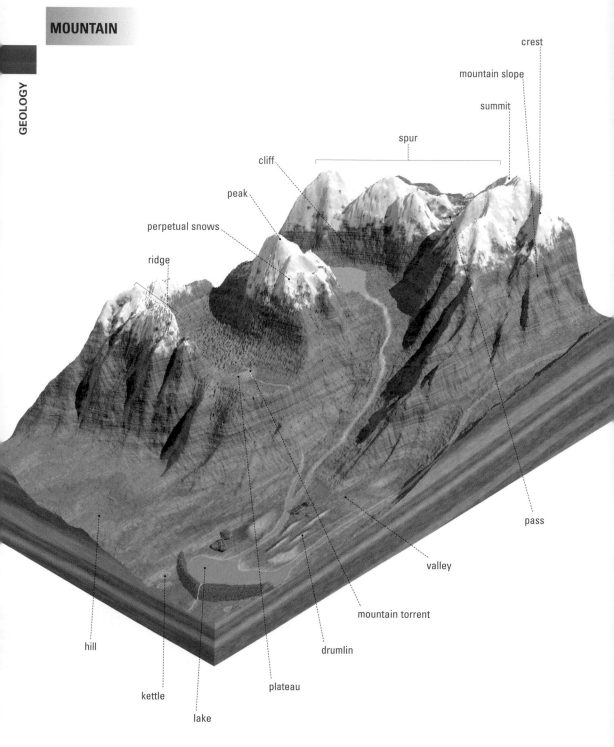

crest

mountain slope

summit

spur

cliff

peak

perpetual snows

ridge

pass

valley

mountain torrent

hill

drumlin

plateau

kettle

lake

GLACIER

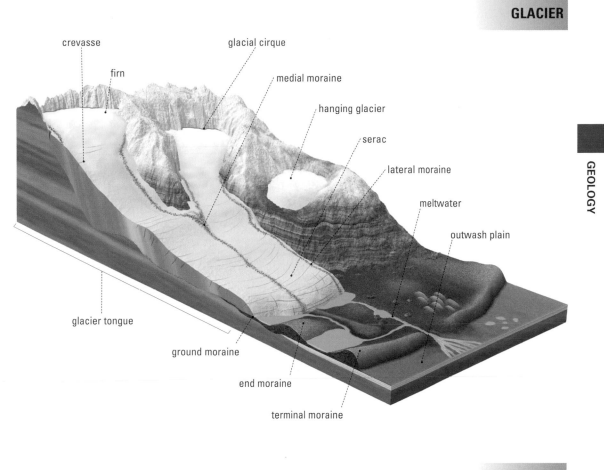

crevasse

firn

glacial cirque

medial moraine

hanging glacier

serac

lateral moraine

meltwater

outwash plain

glacier tongue

ground moraine

end moraine

terminal moraine

DESERT

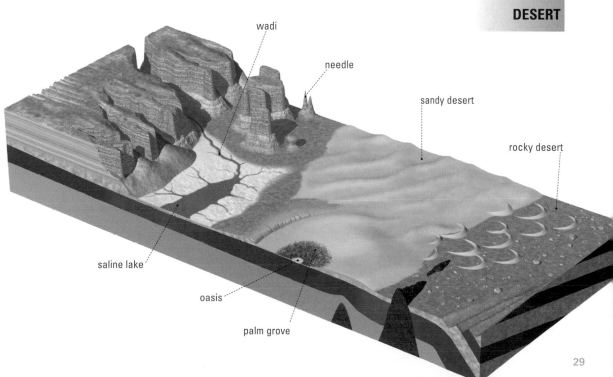

wadi

needle

sandy desert

rocky desert

saline lake

oasis

palm grove

WATERCOURSE

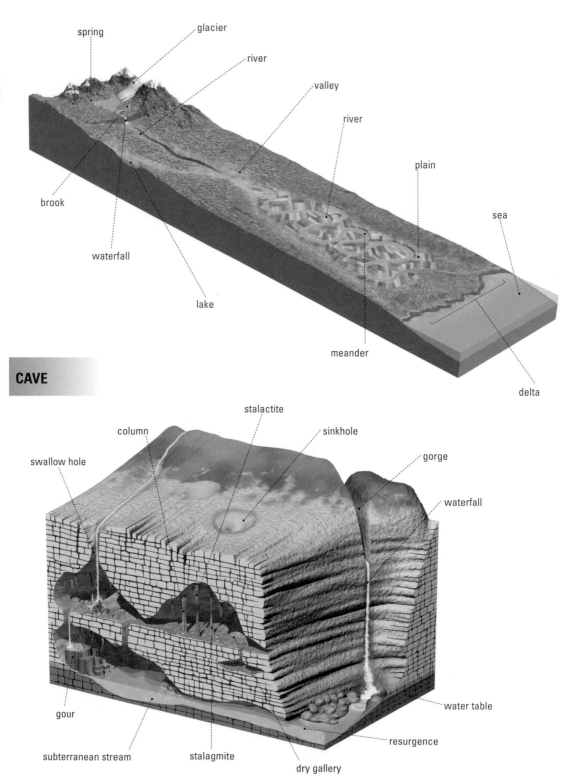

spring

glacier

river

valley

river

plain

sea

brook

waterfall

lake

meander

delta

CAVE

column

stalactite

sinkhole

gorge

swallow hole

waterfall

gour

water table

subterranean stream

stalagmite

dry gallery

resurgence

COMMON COASTAL FEATURES

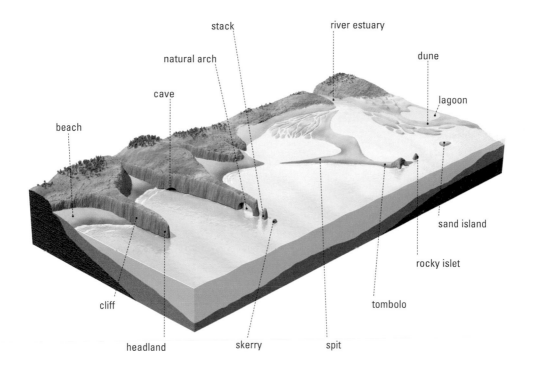

- stack
- river estuary
- natural arch
- dune
- cave
- lagoon
- beach
- sand island
- rocky islet
- cliff
- tombolo
- headland
- skerry
- spit

examples of shorelines

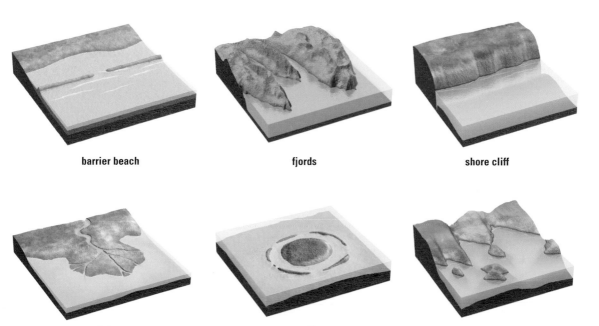

barrier beach

fjords

shore cliff

delta

atoll

rias

Earth's atmosphere is the envelope of gases that surround the planet. The atmosphere is made up of a successive series of layers, each of which play a role in maintaining life on our planet. For example, the layer closest to the ground, the troposphere, contains the air we breathe. It is also in this layer that most meteorological phenomena, such as winds and tornadoes, are produced.

PROFILE OF THE EARTH'S ATMOSPHERE

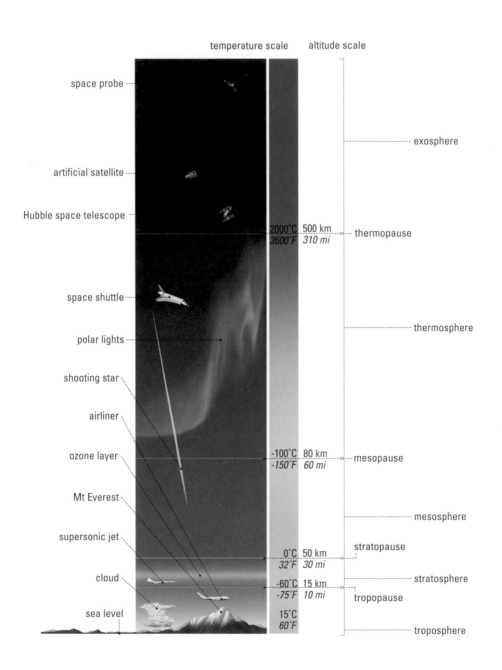

temperature scale   altitude scale

space probe

artificial satellite

Hubble space telescope

space shuttle

polar lights

shooting star

airliner

ozone layer

Mt Everest

supersonic jet

cloud

sea level

2000°C 500 km
3600°F 310 mi

-100°C 80 km
-150°F 60 mi

0°C 50 km
32°F 30 mi

-60°C 15 km
-75°F 10 mi

15°C
60°F

exosphere

thermopause

thermosphere

mesopause

mesosphere

stratopause

stratosphere

tropopause

troposphere

Climate is the set of meteorological conditions that are common to a given region. The amount of solar energy that a part of the world receives is mostly responsible for its climate. Because Earth travels around the Sun in a slightly tilted position, either its northern or its southern half is heated more intensely, depending on the time of year. This phenomenon creates the Earth's seasons, which are opposite in the Northern and Southern hemispheres.

SEASONS OF THE YEAR

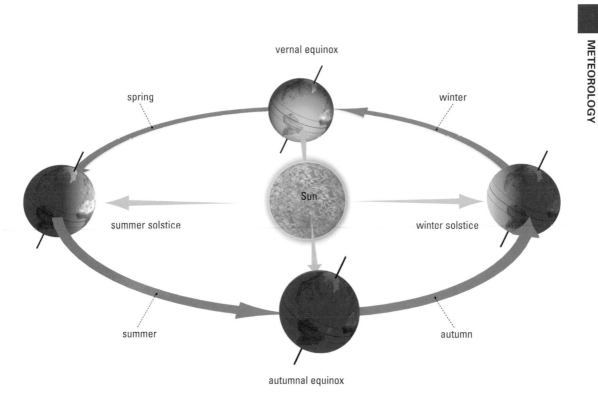

vernal equinox

spring

winter

summer solstice

Sun

winter solstice

summer

autumn

autumnal equinox

seasons in the cold temperate climates

spring **summer** **autumn** **winter**

METEOROLOGY

CLIMATES OF THE WORLD

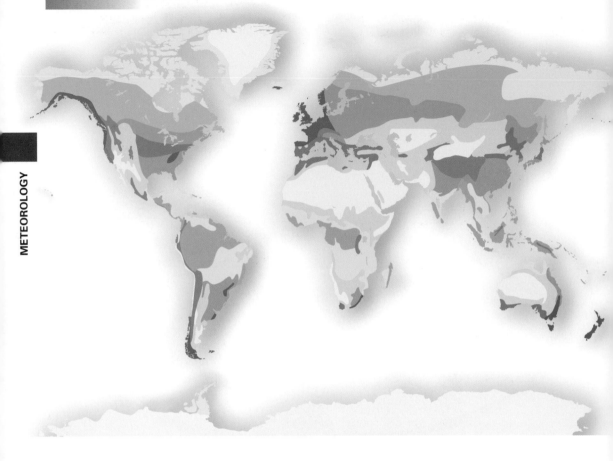

cold temperate climates

 humid continental—hot summer

humid continental—warm summer

subarctic

tropical climates

tropical rain forest

tropical wet-and-dry (savanna)

dry climates

steppe

desert

warm temperate climates

humid subtropical

Mediterranean subtropical

marine

polar climates

polar tundra

polar ice cap

highland climates

highland

Whether it is liquid like rain or solid like snow, precipitation often accompanies storms. Some atmospheric disturbances, such as cyclones and tornadoes, are distinguished by violent winds and can cause considerable damage. Unfortunately, the most devastating of these storms, tornadoes, are difficult to predict because little is known about the mechanisms that drive them.

CLOUDS

high clouds

cirrostratus

cirrocumulus

cirrus

middle clouds

altostratus

altocumulus

low clouds

stratocumulus

nimbostratus

cumulus

stratus

cumulonimbus

clouds of vertical development

METEOROLOGY

PRECIPITATION

drizzle

rain

heavy rain

dew

sleet

snow

freezing rain

mist

fog

THUNDERSTORM

lightning   cloud   rain   rainbow

TROPICAL CYCLONE

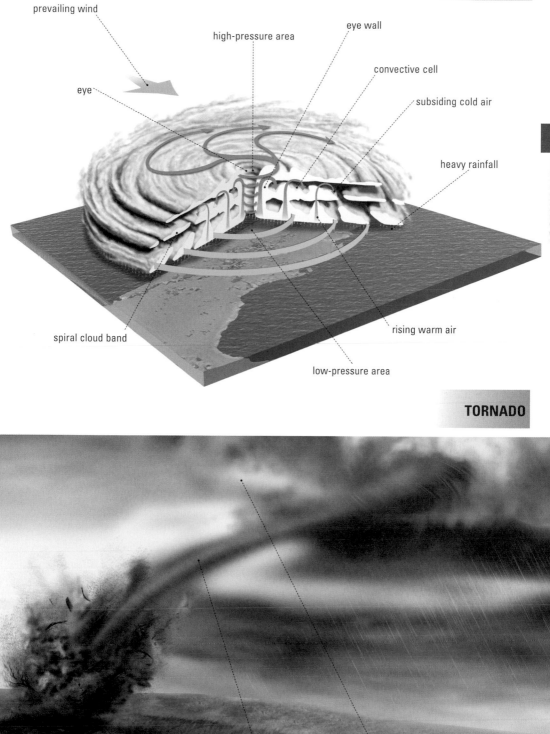

prevailing wind

high-pressure area

eye wall

convective cell

subsiding cold air

eye

heavy rainfall

spiral cloud band

rising warm air

low-pressure area

TORNADO

debris

funnel cloud

wall cloud

METEOROLOGICAL FORECAST

There are approximately 12,000 weather stations around the world. They are equipped with instruments that take many measurements on a daily basis and record wind speed and direction, temperature, and rainfall. All the observations are then sent to the World Meteorological Organization. With the help of these data, which are fed into computer models, meteorologists can fairly accurately predict the weather.

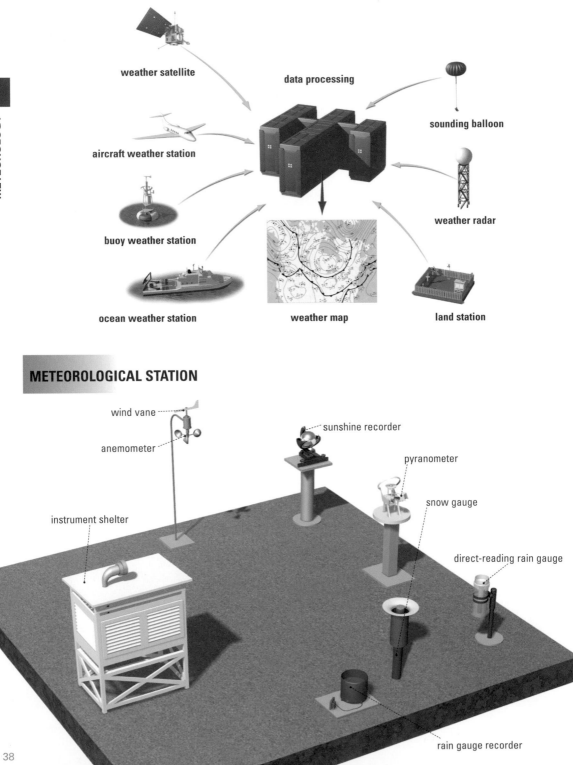

weather satellite

data processing

sounding balloon

aircraft weather station

buoy weather station

weather radar

ocean weather station

weather map

land station

METEOROLOGICAL STATION

wind vane

anemometer

sunshine recorder

pyranometer

snow gauge

instrument shelter

direct-reading rain gauge

rain gauge recorder

METEOROLOGICAL MEASURING INSTRUMENTS

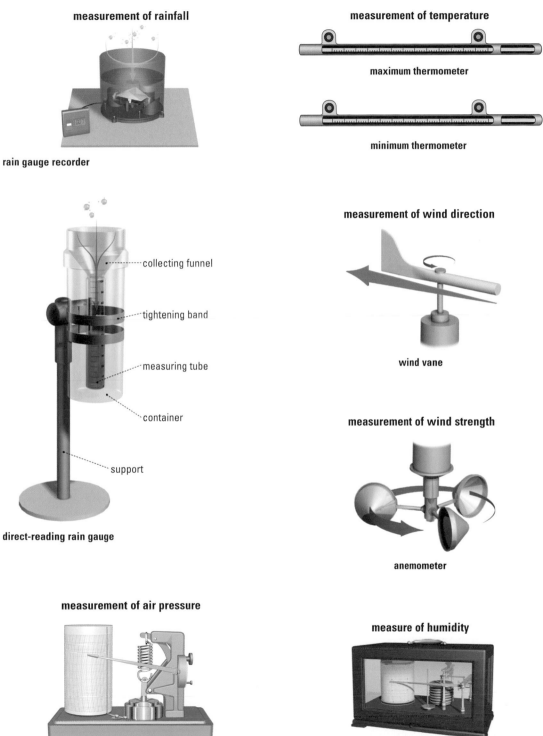

measurement of rainfall

rain gauge recorder

collecting funnel

tightening band

measuring tube

container

support

direct-reading rain gauge

measurement of temperature

maximum thermometer

minimum thermometer

measurement of wind direction

wind vane

measurement of wind strength

anemometer

measurement of air pressure

barograph

measure of humidity

hygrograph

BIOSPHERE

Living organisms inhabit many different kinds of environments on Earth. However, no life-forms are found outside the very thin layer of earth, air and water we call the biosphere. This habitable part of our planet is a complex world where all species live in very close relationship to their environment. All living things draw the energy they need to survive from their food. The feeding pattern can be looked at as a series of links that form a chain, called the food chain.

VEGETATION AND BIOSPHERE

vegetation regions

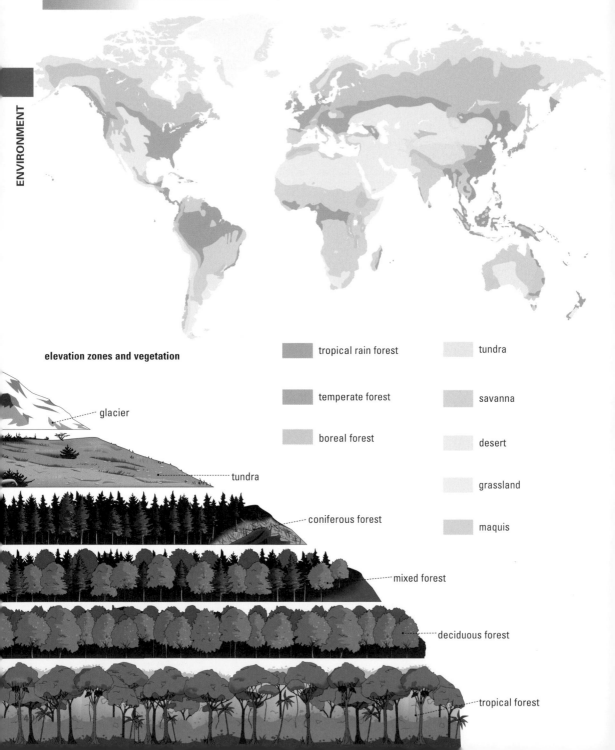

elevation zones and vegetation

- glacier
- tundra
- coniferous forest
- mixed forest
- deciduous forest
- tropical forest

- tropical rain forest
- temperate forest
- boreal forest

- tundra
- savanna
- desert
- grassland
- maquis

structure of the biosphere

atmosphere

hydrosphere

lithosphere

FOOD CHAIN

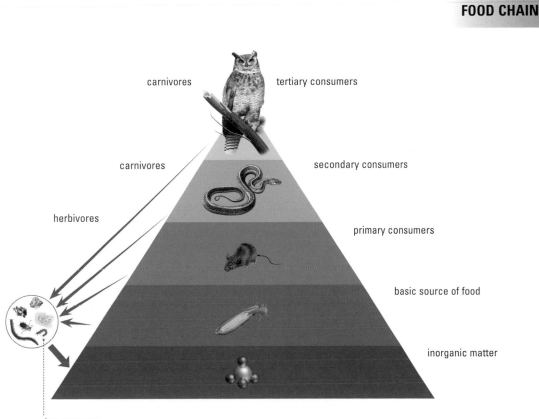

carnivores — tertiary consumers

carnivores — secondary consumers

herbivores — primary consumers

basic source of food

inorganic matter

decomposers

The Sun's heat creates a constant exchange between the oceans and the atmosphere. Water vapor, condensed in the clouds, falls toward Earth as rain or snow. When it lands on a continent, the water penetrates the ground, runs into lakes and rivers and eventually returns to the ocean. Some of the water evaporates over the oceans and rises once again into the atmosphere. This process is called the water cycle.

ENVIRONMENT

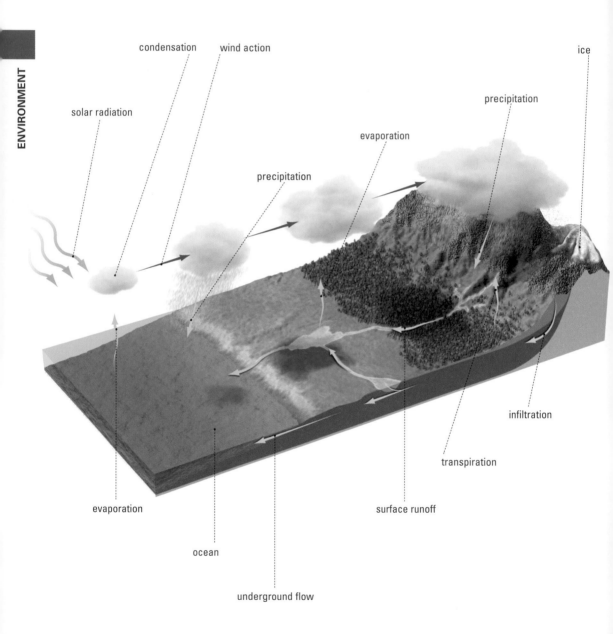

condensation

wind action

ice

solar radiation

precipitation

evaporation

precipitation

evaporation

infiltration

transpiration

surface runoff

ocean

underground flow

Some of the Sun's rays are absorbed by the ground and thrown back into the atmosphere in the form of heat. Certain gases in the atmosphere have the ability to trap this heat. Because of this natural phenomenon, called the "greenhouse effect," temperatures on Earth are suitable for supporting life. For over 150 years, however, human activity has increased the amount of greenhouse gases released into the atmosphere, contributing to global warming.

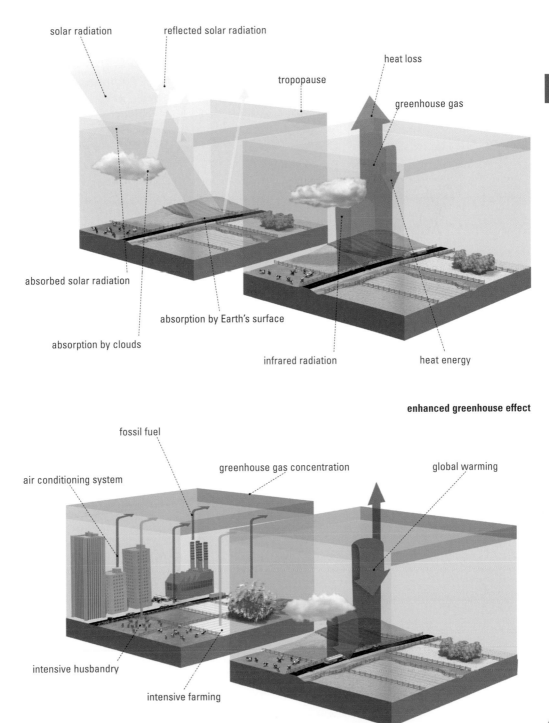

natural greenhouse effect

solar radiation

reflected solar radiation

heat loss

tropopause

greenhouse gas

absorbed solar radiation

absorption by Earth's surface

absorption by clouds

infrared radiation

heat energy

enhanced greenhouse effect

fossil fuel

greenhouse gas concentration

global warming

air conditioning system

intensive husbandry

intensive farming

POLLUTION

Industries release large quantities of chemical waste into the environment. Some of it is extremely toxic. Thermal power stations and motorized vehicles also do their share of polluting. Fortunately, more and more people are beginning to realize that natural resources are not inexhaustible and that we cannot continue to pollute the air, earth and water without affecting the future of our planet.

ENVIRONMENT

LAND POLLUTION

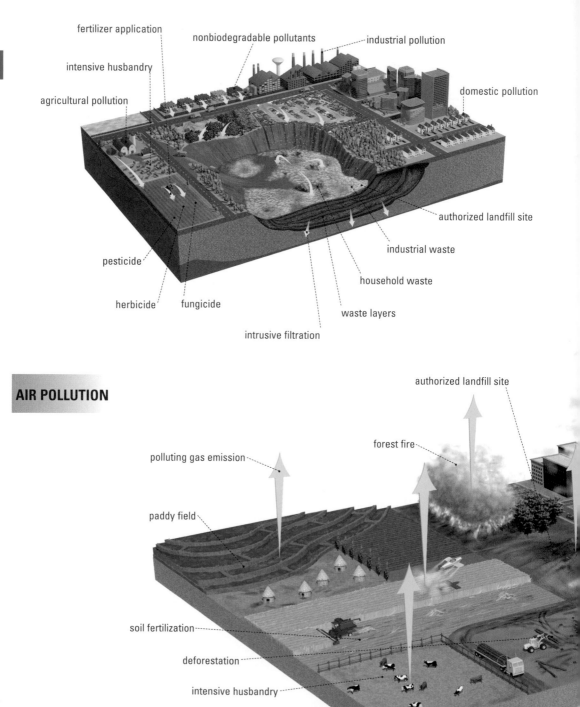

fertilizer application
nonbiodegradable pollutants
industrial pollution
intensive husbandry
domestic pollution
agricultural pollution
authorized landfill site
industrial waste
pesticide
household waste
herbicide
fungicide
waste layers
intrusive filtration

AIR POLLUTION

authorized landfill site
forest fire
polluting gas emission
paddy field
soil fertilization
deforestation
intensive husbandry

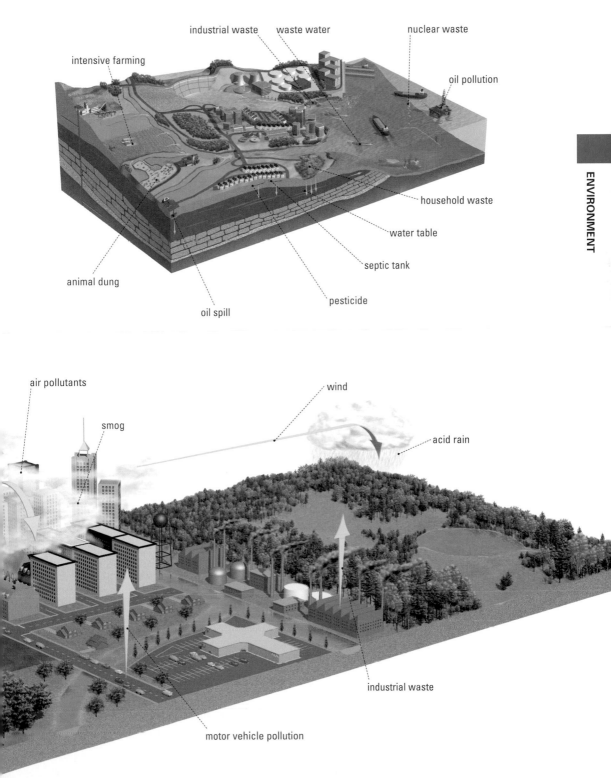

intensive farming

industrial waste

waste water

nuclear waste

oil pollution

household waste

water table

septic tank

animal dung

oil spill

pesticide

air pollutants

wind

smog

acid rain

industrial waste

motor vehicle pollution

SELECTIVE SORTING OF WASTE

A large portion of the household waste produced in industrialized countries can be recycled. More and more cities have a system for the selective sorting of waste. Garbage is brought to sorting plants where workers and machines separate recyclable materials like glass, metal, plastic and paper. These materials then go through a number of cleaning operations and transformations.

ENVIRONMENT

sorting plant

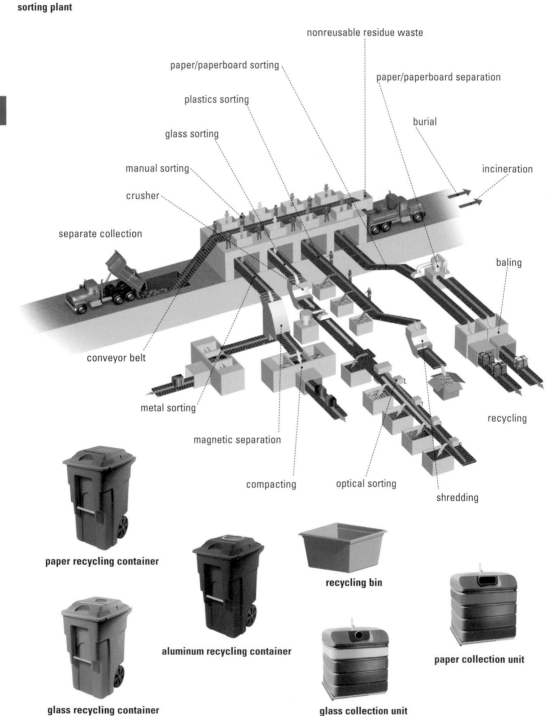

nonreusable residue waste

paper/paperboard sorting

paper/paperboard separation

plastics sorting

burial

glass sorting

incineration

manual sorting

crusher

separate collection

baling

conveyor belt

recycling

metal sorting

magnetic separation

compacting

optical sorting

shredding

paper recycling container

recycling bin

aluminum recycling container

paper collection unit

glass recycling container

glass collection unit

Although all vegetables are made up of plant cells, they do not all have the same structure. The simplest vegetables, such as algae, lichens, mosses, ferns and mushrooms, have no leaves, flowers or seeds. Mushrooms do not even have chlorophyll, the pigment that gives plants their green color. This is why biologists classify mushrooms in a separate kingdom.

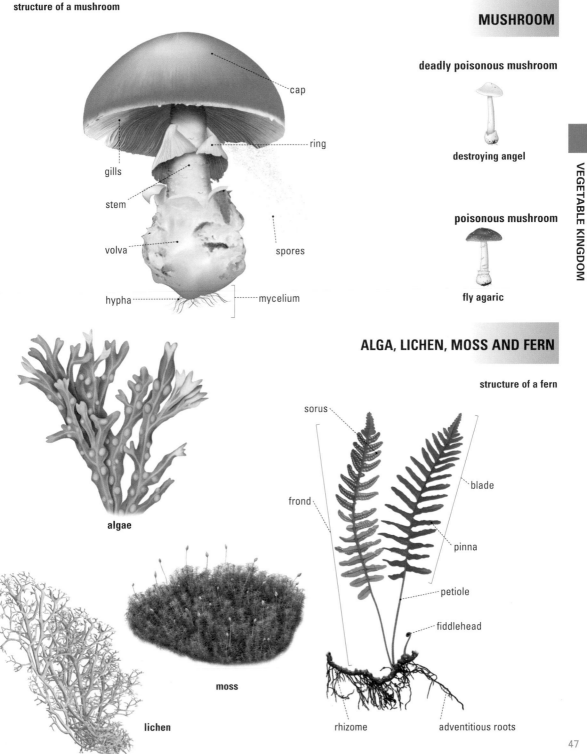

structure of a mushroom

cap

ring

gills

stem

volva

spores

hypha

mycelium

MUSHROOM

deadly poisonous mushroom

destroying angel

poisonous mushroom

fly agaric

ALGA, LICHEN, MOSS AND FERN

structure of a fern

sorus

blade

frond

pinna

petiole

fiddlehead

algae

moss

lichen

rhizome

adventitious roots

FLOWERING PLANTS

Reproduction in flowering plants is ensured, in part, by the seed that protects the tiny plant embryo. During germination, the embryo develops by taking in nutritive substances (food) contained in the seed, and it quickly becomes a new, independent plant. The majority of plants familiar to us belong to this very varied group, which includes more than 235,000 species.

STRUCTURE OF A PLANT AND GERMINATION

structure of a plant

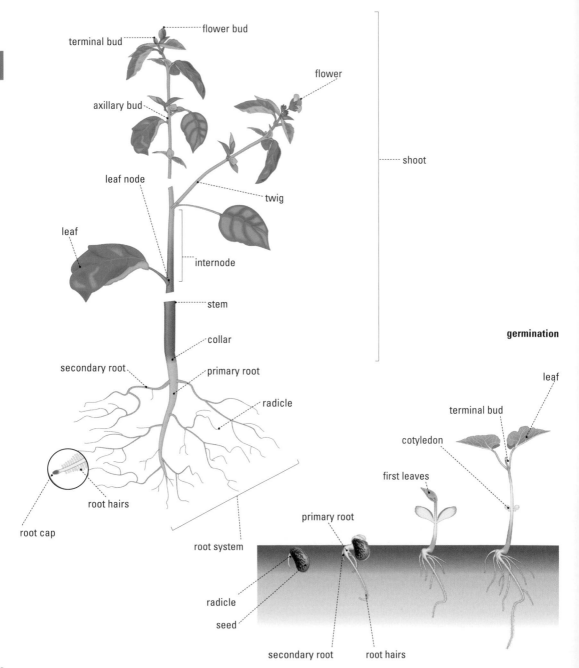

flower bud

terminal bud

flower

axillary bud

shoot

leaf node

twig

leaf

internode

stem

collar

germination

secondary root

primary root

leaf

radicle

terminal bud

cotyledon

first leaves

root hairs

primary root

root cap

root system

radicle

secondary root

root hairs

seed

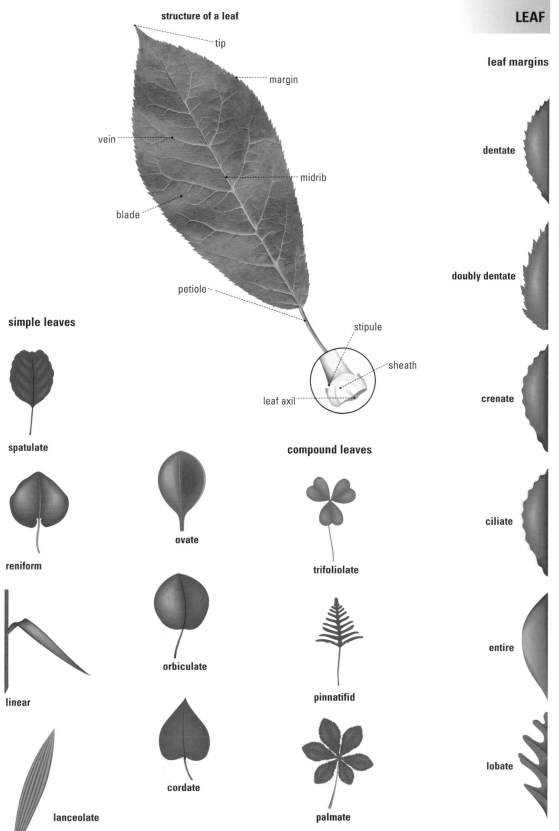

structure of a leaf

tip

margin

vein

midrib

blade

petiole

stipule

sheath

leaf axil

leaf margins

dentate

doubly dentate

crenate

ciliate

entire

lobate

simple leaves

spatulate

reniform

linear

lanceolate

ovate

orbiculate

cordate

compound leaves

trifoliolate

pinnatifid

palmate

FLOWER

structure of a flower

stigma

anther

filament

petal

style

receptacle

ovary

peduncle

sepal

ovule

corolla

calyx

pistil

stamen

examples of flowers

orchid

lily

daffodil

tulip

primrose

begonia

daisy

buttercup

violet

thistle

lily of the valley

poppy

dandelion

carnation

sunflower

crocus

rose

TREE

Trees are plants that can reach considerable size. There are two principal categories: broadleaved trees, which grow fairly large leaves, and conifers, which have narrow leaves in the form of needles or scales. Conifers are said to be evergreen because, with just a few exceptions, they keep their leaves throughout the year. Broadleaved trees are called deciduous, which means "falling-off" in Latin, because their leaves generally fall before winter.

STRUCTURE OF A TREE

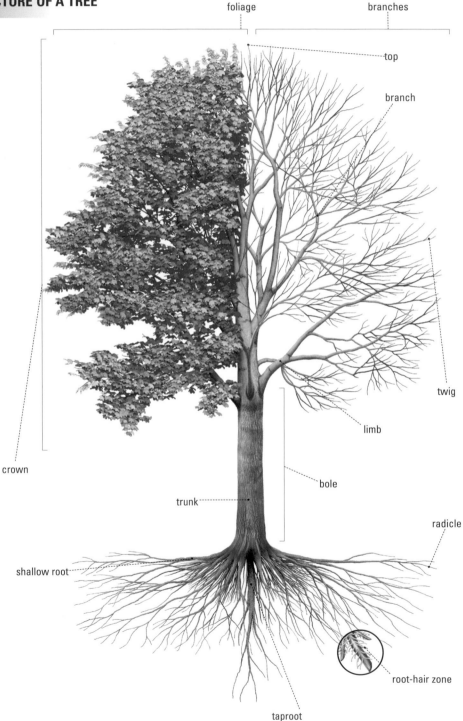

foliage

branches

top

branch

twig

limb

crown

bole

trunk

radicle

shallow root

root-hair zone

taproot

52

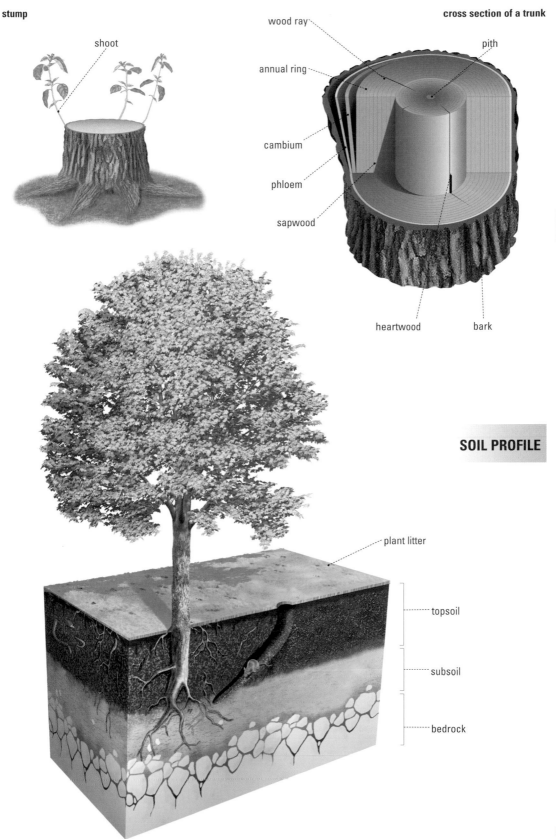

stump

shoot

cross section of a trunk

wood ray

pith

annual ring

cambium

phloem

sapwood

heartwood

bark

SOIL PROFILE

plant litter

topsoil

subsoil

bedrock

EXAMPLES OF BROADLEAVED TREES

maple

willow

oak

palm tree

walnut

poplar

beech

birch

EXAMPLES OF CONIFERS

branch

pine seeds

pinecone

cedar of Lebanon

larch

spruce

fir

pine

SIMPLE ORGANISMS AND ECHINODERMS

Whether they consist of a single cell, like the amoeba or the paramecium, or billions of cells, like the blue whale, all animals are made of animal cells. Excluding unicellulars, now classified in a separate kingdom, there are two principal groups: the verte-brates, which have a spine (vertebral column), and the invertebrates, which do not. If sponges are the most primitive of invertebrates, echinoderms are among the most highly evolved.

ANIMAL KINGDOM

ANIMAL CELL

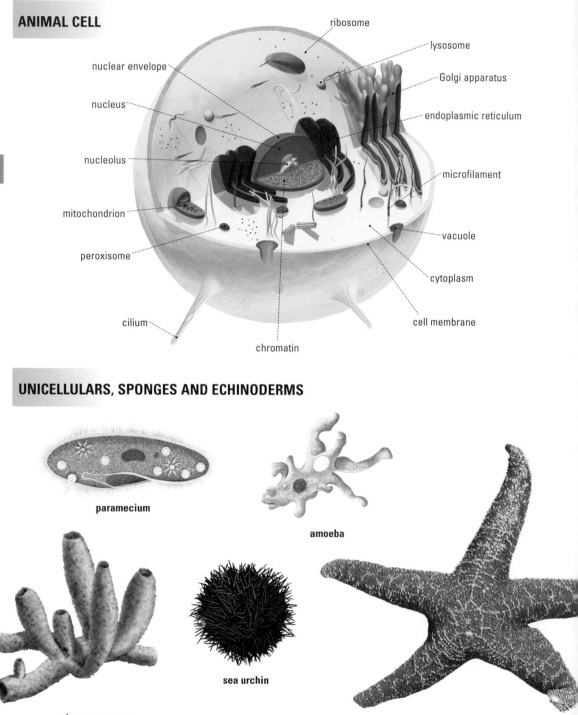

ribosome

lysosome

nuclear envelope

Golgi apparatus

nucleus

endoplasmic reticulum

nucleolus

microfilament

mitochondrion

peroxisome

vacuole

cytoplasm

cilium

cell membrane

chromatin

UNICELLULARS, SPONGES AND ECHINODERMS

paramecium

amoeba

calcareous sponge

sea urchin

starfish

Mollusks are named after the Latin *molluscus*, which means "soft." These soft-bodied animals have no skeleton, but they usually have a shell. The majority of the 100,000 species are aquatic and breathe with the help of gills. Land mollusks, such as the snail and the slug, breathe using lungs. Some of these invertebrates are both male and female at the same time. They are called hermaphrodites.

SNAIL

morphology of a snail

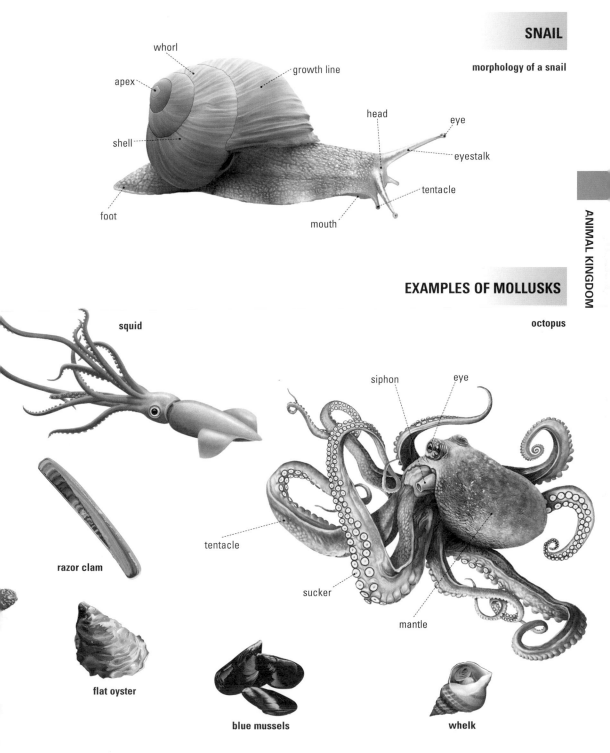

whorl

apex

shell

foot

growth line

head

eye

eyestalk

tentacle

mouth

EXAMPLES OF MOLLUSKS

squid

octopus

siphon

eye

tentacle

sucker

mantle

razor clam

flat oyster

blue mussels

whelk

ANIMAL KINGDOM

CRUSTACEANS

Like insects and spiders, crustaceans belong to the arthropods, a group of invertebrates characterized by the presence of jointed legs. In front of the legs, which are used for walking or swimming, are pincers that help crustaceans pick up food. The 30,000 species of crustaceans are distinguished by, among other things, two pairs of antennae, ten legs and a body covered by a protective shell.

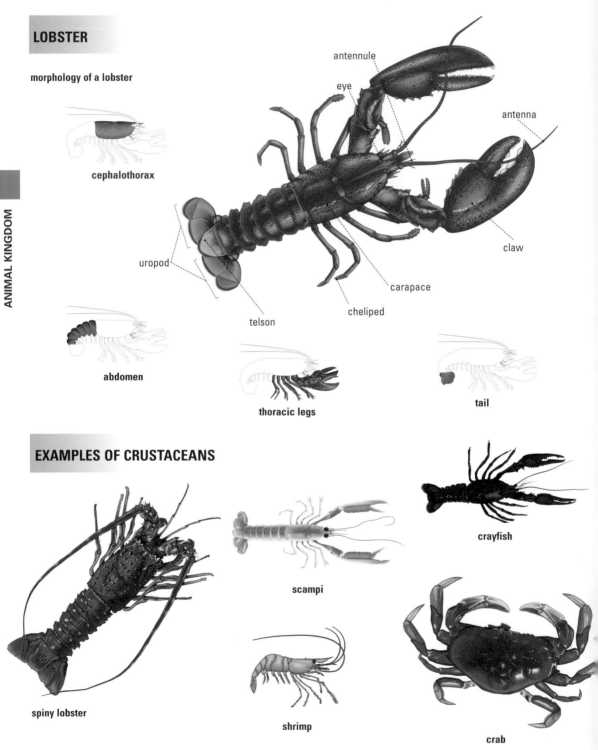

LOBSTER

morphology of a lobster

cephalothorax

antennule

eye

antenna

claw

uropod

carapace

cheliped

telson

abdomen

thoracic legs

tail

EXAMPLES OF CRUSTACEANS

crayfish

scampi

spiny lobster

shrimp

crab

Spiders are the best known of the arachnids, a principal group of invertebrates that includes more than 50,000 species. All the members of this group have a pair of pincers in front of their mouth, in which they hold their prey. Unlike insects and crustaceans, arachnids do not have antennae. They are also distinguished by their eight legs.

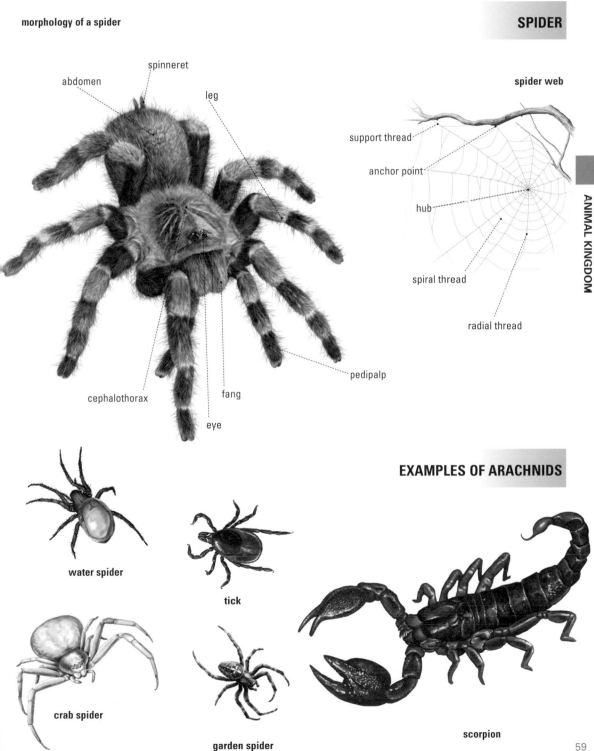

morphology of a spider

SPIDER

abdomen

spinneret

leg

cephalothorax

fang

eye

pedipalp

spider web

support thread

anchor point

hub

spiral thread

radial thread

EXAMPLES OF ARACHNIDS

water spider

tick

crab spider

garden spider

scorpion

ANIMAL KINGDOM

INSECTS

Insects are the most numerous and most varied group of land animals. Today, there are more than one million species of insects, which abound in every environment. Insects are distinguished from other arthropods by their six legs and, in most cases, by the presence of wings. They are the only invertebrates capable of flying.

ANIMAL KINGDOM

HONEYBEE

morphology of a honeybee (worker)

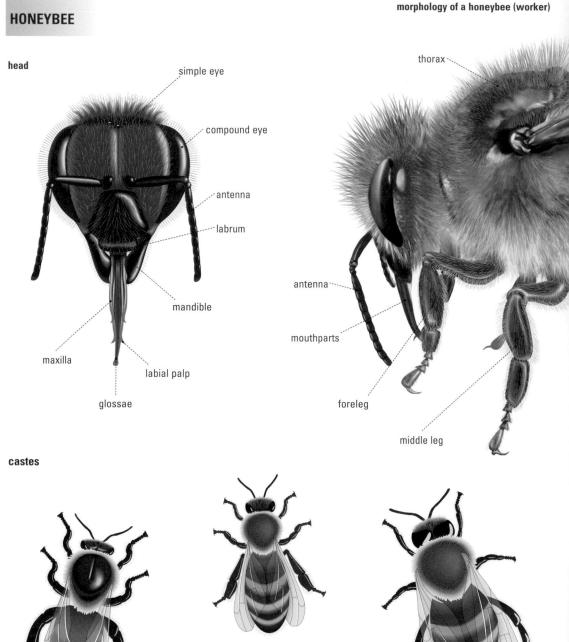

head

simple eye

compound eye

antenna

labrum

mandible

maxilla

labial palp

glossae

thorax

antenna

mouthparts

foreleg

middle leg

castes

queen

worker

drone

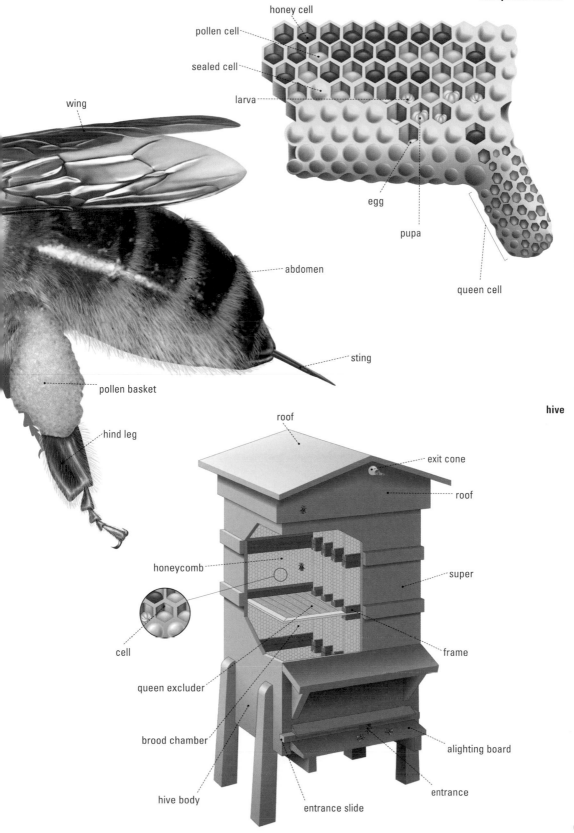

honeycomb section

honey cell

pollen cell

sealed cell

larva

wing

abdomen

egg

pupa

queen cell

sting

pollen basket

hind leg

hive

roof

exit cone

roof

honeycomb

super

cell

frame

queen excluder

brood chamber

alighting board

hive body

entrance

entrance slide

BUTTERFLY

morphology of a butterfly

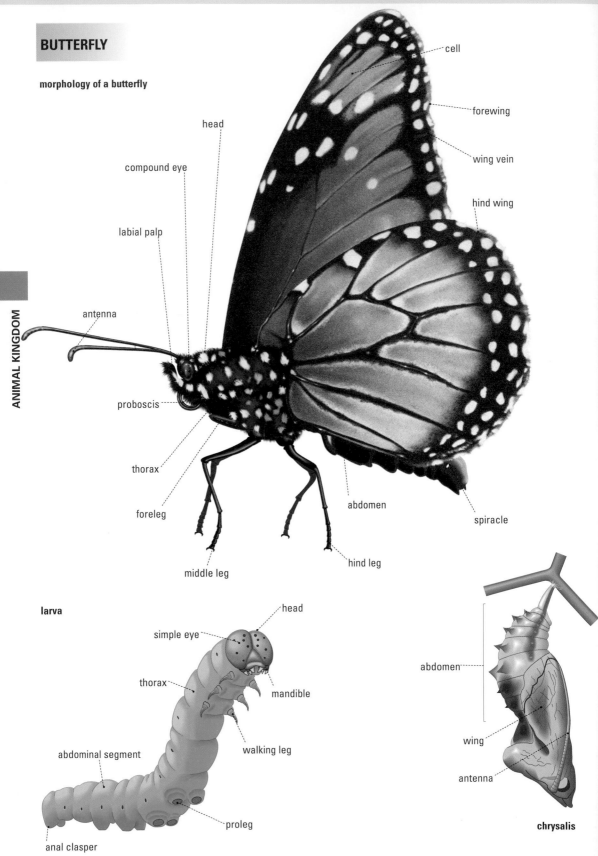

cell

forewing

wing vein

hind wing

head

compound eye

labial palp

antenna

proboscis

thorax

foreleg

middle leg

hind leg

abdomen

spiracle

larva

head

simple eye

thorax

mandible

walking leg

abdominal segment

proleg

anal clasper

abdomen

wing

antenna

chrysalis

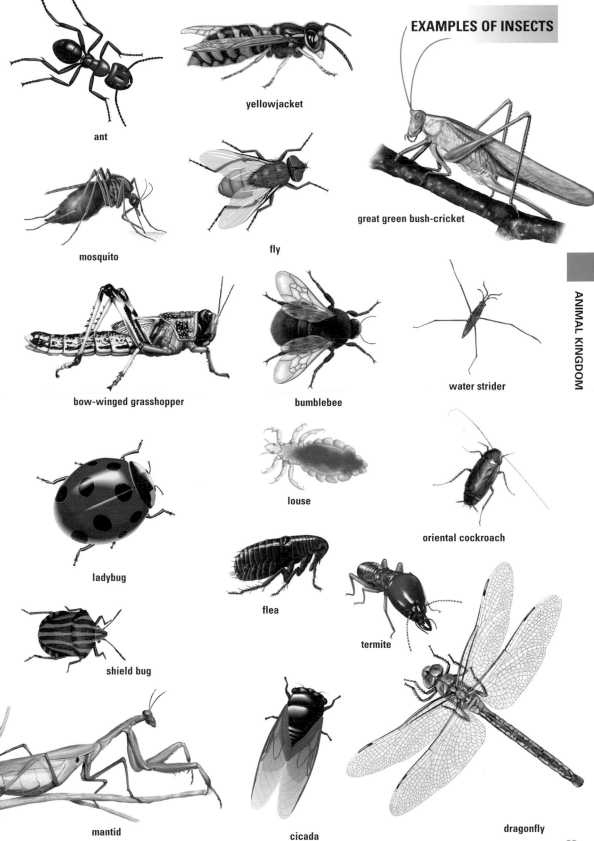

EXAMPLES OF INSECTS

yellowjacket

ant

mosquito

fly

great green bush-cricket

bow-winged grasshopper

bumblebee

water strider

ladybug

louse

oriental cockroach

shield bug

flea

termite

mantid

cicada

dragonfly

CARTILAGINOUS FISHES

Fish are the oldest vertebrate animals. The majority of modern species are divided into two groups: bony fish and cartilaginous fish. This second group, which is distinguished by the presence of a skeleton made of cartilage, is mainly represented by rays and sharks. All fish, whether cartilaginous or bony, are perfectly adapted to aquatic life and have tapering bodies, fins and gills.

SHARK

ANIMAL KINGDOM

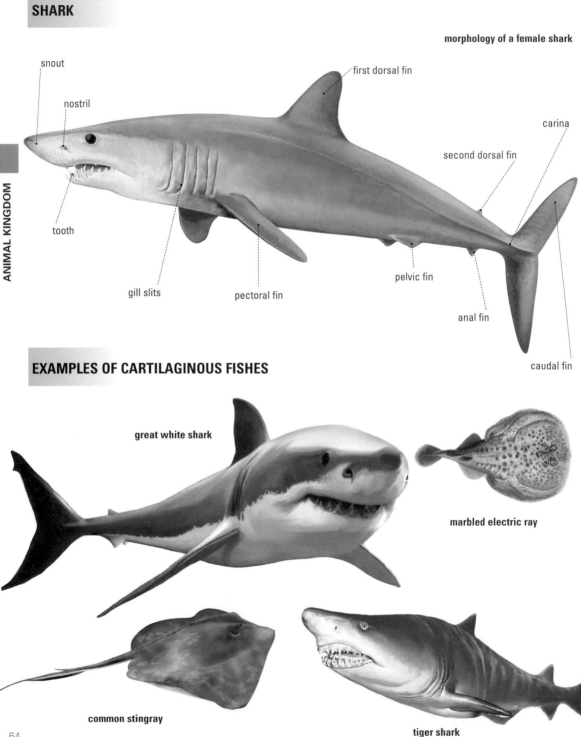

morphology of a female shark

snout

nostril

tooth

gill slits

pectoral fin

first dorsal fin

second dorsal fin

carina

pelvic fin

anal fin

caudal fin

EXAMPLES OF CARTILAGINOUS FISHES

great white shark

marbled electric ray

common stingray

tiger shark

As their name suggests, bony fish possess a skeleton made entirely or partially of bone. Appearing on Earth 150 million years after the cartilaginous fish, the more highly evolved bony fish are represented today by more than 20,000 species as varied as the eel, the seahorse, the tiny sardine and the spiny-finned perch. Bony fish are found in most aquatic environments on the planet.

morphology of a perch

PERCH

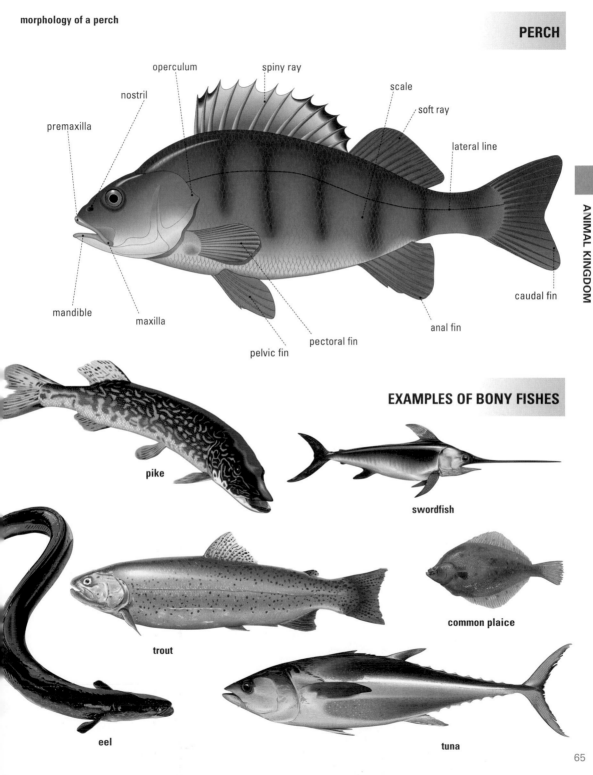

- operculum
- spiny ray
- nostril
- scale
- soft ray
- premaxilla
- lateral line
- mandible
- maxilla
- pelvic fin
- pectoral fin
- anal fin
- caudal fin

EXAMPLES OF BONY FISHES

pike

swordfish

trout

common plaice

eel

tuna

AMPHIBIANS

Amphibians are characterized by their ability to live as happily in water as on land. Without losing their swimming skills, they were the first vertebrates to leave their aquatic environment and reach solid ground, thanks to their legs and their lungs. The great majority of the 3,000 known species live in humid land environments or in freshwater.

FROG

morphology of a frog

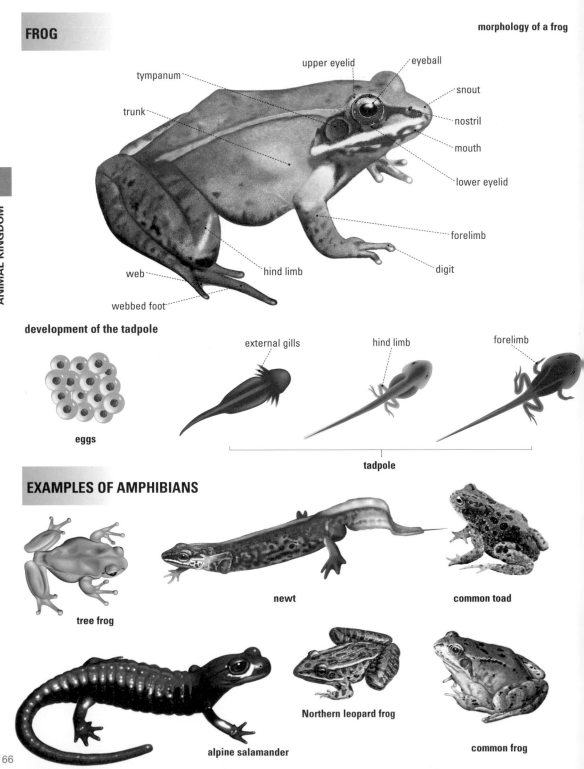

tympanum

trunk

upper eyelid

eyeball

snout

nostril

mouth

lower eyelid

forelimb

web

hind limb

digit

webbed foot

development of the tadpole

external gills

hind limb

forelimb

eggs

tadpole

EXAMPLES OF AMPHIBIANS

tree frog

newt

common toad

alpine salamander

Northern leopard frog

common frog

Reptiles were the first vertebrates to completely adapt to living on land, with well-developed lungs and a shell or scaly skin that prevents them from losing water. These cold-blooded animals owe their popularity to certain families that have long been extinct: the dinosaurs. Today there are some 6,500 known species of reptiles, living mainly in tropical regions.

morphology of a turtle

TURTLE

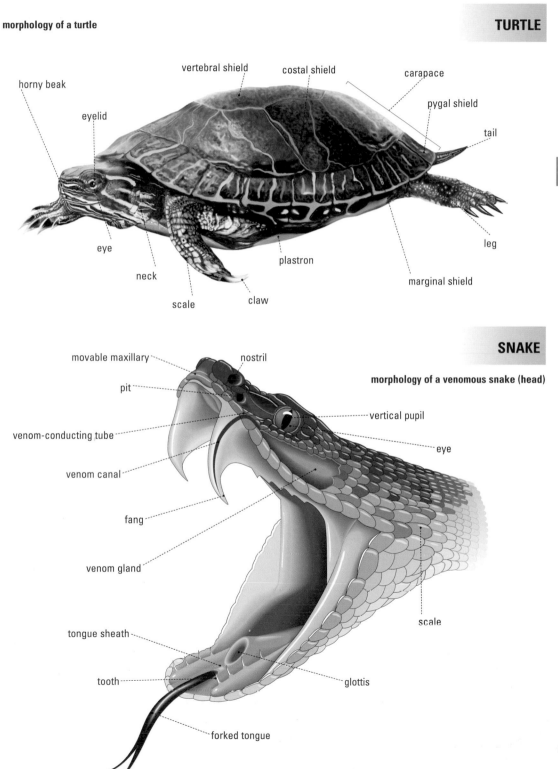

- vertebral shield
- costal shield
- carapace
- horny beak
- pygal shield
- eyelid
- tail
- eye
- leg
- neck
- plastron
- marginal shield
- scale
- claw

SNAKE

morphology of a venomous snake (head)

- movable maxillary
- nostril
- pit
- vertical pupil
- venom-conducting tube
- eye
- venom canal
- fang
- venom gland
- scale
- tongue sheath
- tooth
- glottis
- forked tongue

EXAMPLES OF REPTILES

python

leatherback turtle

garter snake

cobra

coral snake

rattlesnake

boa

viper

monitor lizard

chameleon

lizard

iguana

alligator

caiman

crocodile

DINOSAURS

stegosaurus

spinosaurus

allosaurus

parasauroloph

hadrosaurus

diplodocus

tyrannosaurus

pachycephalosaurus

ankylosaurus

deinonychus

triceratops

brachiosaurus

BIRDS

With the exception of the bat, birds are the only vertebrates capable of flying. Their light skeleton and feather-covered wings make them the best aviators in the animal kingdom. The scientific classification of birds is based on characteristics that can be difficult to recognize, such as the structure of their feathers. This is why the 10,000 known species are often divided into two groups: aquatic and shorebirds and terrestrial birds.

BIRD

morphology of a bird

nostril

bill

nape

chin

throat

wing covert

breast

abdomen

wing

inner toe

claw

middle toe

outer toe

bird feeder

birdhouse

nest

egg

blastodisc

shell

air space

yolk

albumen

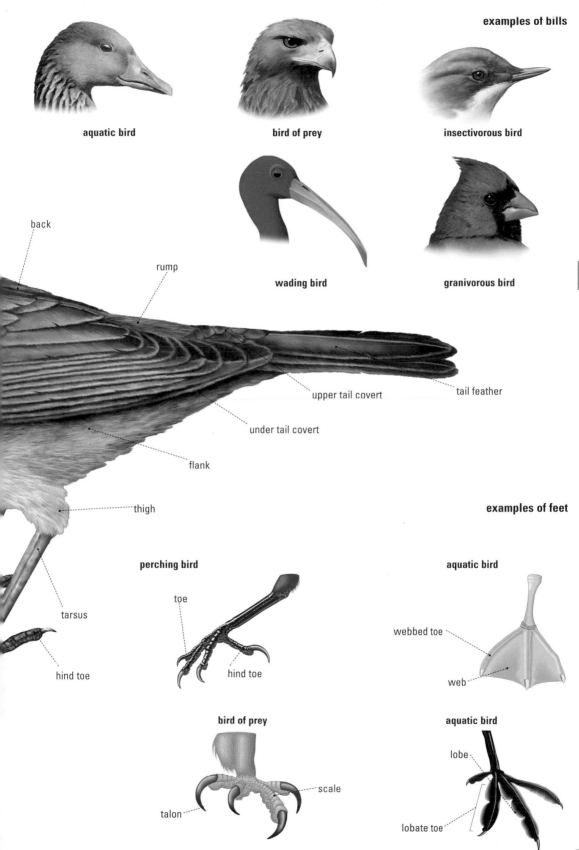

examples of bills

aquatic bird

bird of prey

insectivorous bird

wading bird

granivorous bird

back

rump

upper tail covert

tail feather

under tail covert

flank

thigh

examples of feet

perching bird

toe

hind toe

tarsus

hind toe

aquatic bird

webbed toe

web

bird of prey

scale

talon

aquatic bird

lobe

lobate toe

EXAMPLES OF TERRESTRIAL BIRDS

cardinal

jay

goldfinch

hummingbird

swallow

starling

finch

raven

sparrow

great horned owl

pigeon

partridge

toucan

eagle

macaw

falcon

peacock

rooster

chick

turkey

hen

goose

ostrich

EXAMPLES OF AQUATIC AND SHOREBIRDS

penguin

stork

kingfisher

tern

flamingo

oystercatcher

duck

pelican

75

MAMMALS

Most of the 4,600 species of mammals are recognized at first glance by their hair-covered skin. All females feed their young with milk produced by their mammary glands, which is where the name "mammal" comes from. They are the most highly evolved vertebrates. Along with birds, they are the only animals able to maintain a constant internal body temperature.

MARSUPIAL MAMMALS

morphology of a female kangaroo

examples of marsupials

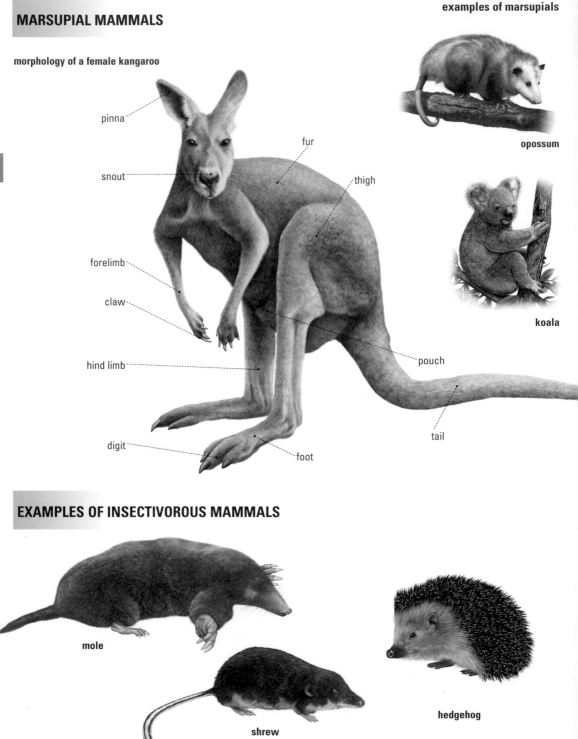

pinna

snout

fur

thigh

forelimb

claw

hind limb

pouch

digit

foot

tail

opossum

koala

EXAMPLES OF INSECTIVOROUS MAMMALS

mole

shrew

hedgehog

RODENTS

morphology of a rat

pinna

fur

whisker

nose

digit

claw

tail

ANIMAL KINGDOM

examples of rodents

field mouse

porcupine

beaver

hamster

squirrel

guinea pig

chipmunk

groundhog

LAGOMORPHS

hare

pika

rabbit

CARNIVOROUS MAMMALS (DOG)

morphology of a dog

stop   cheek

muzzle   withers   back

dog's forepaw   thigh

flews   tail

claw

digital pad   shoulder

toe   elbow

palmar pad   forearm   knee

hock

dew pad   wrist   toe

carpal pad

dewclaw

examples of dog breeds

Saint Bernard

bulldog

poodle

collie   Great Dane   Dalmatian

CARNIVOROUS MAMMALS (CAT)

morphology of a cat

head

ear

tail

eye

fur

pupil

eyelashes

whisker

upper eyelid

nictitating membrane

lower eyelid

whisker

nose leather

lip

muzzle

examples of cat breeds

Abyssinian

Manx

Maine coon

American shorthair

Persian

Siamese

EXAMPLES OF CARNIVOROUS MAMMALS

badger

river otter

weasel

mongoose

mink

hyena

fennec

raccoon

wolf

fox

skunk

black bear

polar bear

jaguar

lynx

leopard

lion

tiger

cheetah

FLYING MAMMALS

morphology of a bat

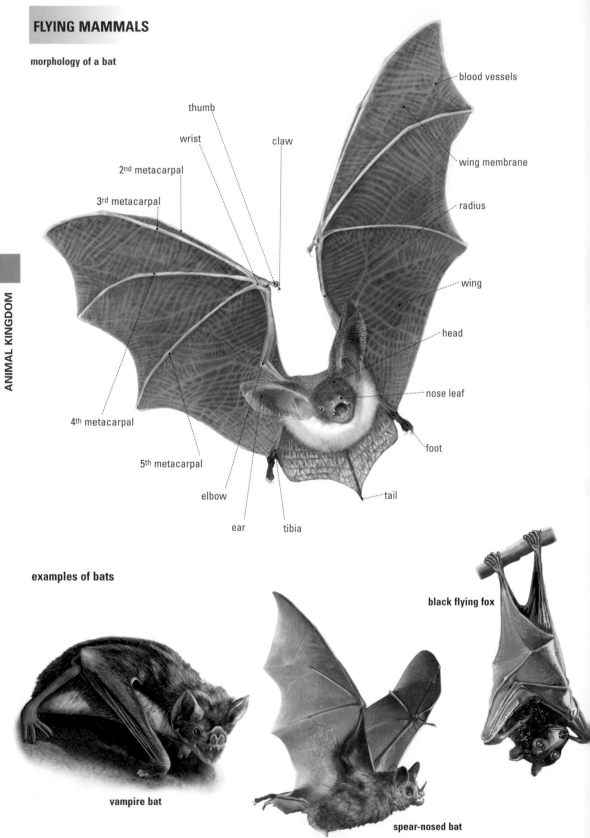

blood vessels

thumb

wrist

claw

wing membrane

2nd metacarpal

radius

3rd metacarpal

wing

head

nose leaf

4th metacarpal

foot

5th metacarpal

elbow

tail

ear

tibia

examples of bats

black flying fox

vampire bat

spear-nosed bat

PRIMATE MAMMALS

morphology of a gorilla

face

fur

arm

hand

prehensile digit

leg

opposable thumb

foot

examples of primates

lemur

orangutan

gibbon

baboon

macaque

chimpanzee

UNGULATE MAMMALS

morphology of a horse

horse's hoof

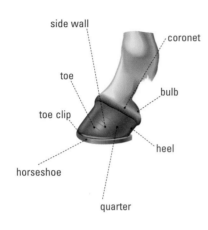

- side wall
- coronet
- toe
- bulb
- toe clip
- heel
- horseshoe
- quarter

horseshoe

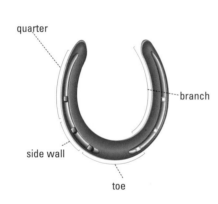

- quarter
- branch
- side wall
- toe

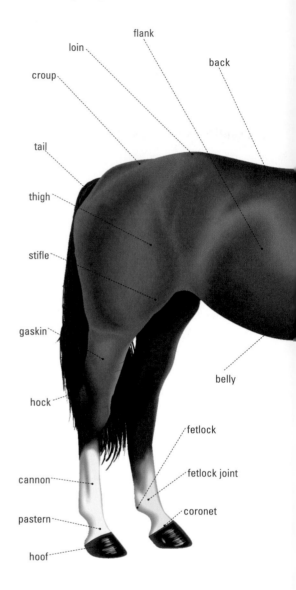

- flank
- loin
- back
- croup
- tail
- thigh
- stifle
- gaskin
- belly
- hock
- fetlock
- fetlock joint
- cannon
- coronet
- pastern
- hoof

gaits

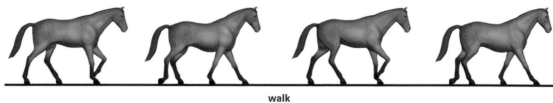

walk

trot

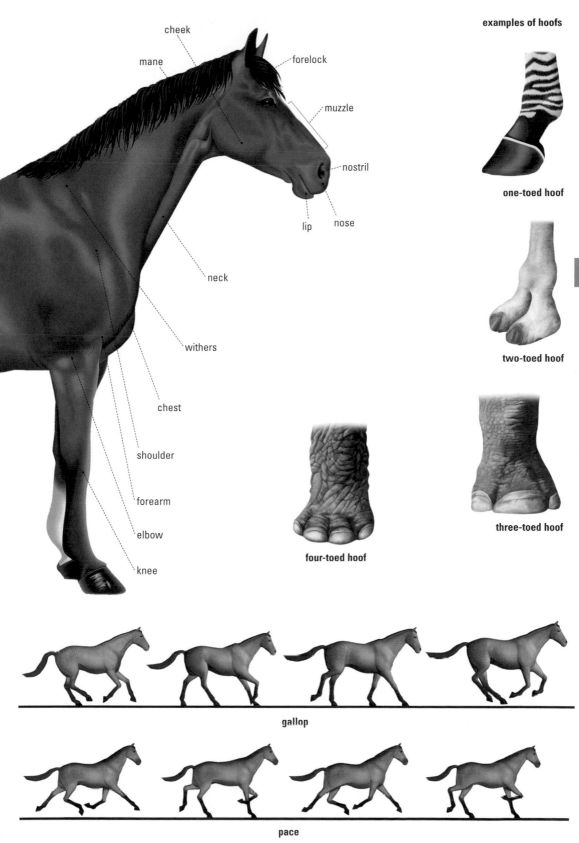

cheek

mane

forelock

muzzle

nostril

lip

nose

neck

withers

chest

shoulder

forearm

elbow

knee

examples of hoofs

one-toed hoof

two-toed hoof

three-toed hoof

four-toed hoof

gallop

pace

examples of ungulate mammals

pig

cow

yak

bison

white-tailed deer

mouflon

goat

sheep

rhinoceros

dromedary camel

bactrian camel

donkey

zebra

llama

hippopotamus

giraffe

elephant

okapi

MARINE MAMMALS

morphology of a dolphin

dorsal fin

blowhole

tail

beak

pectoral fin

eye

caudal fin

examples of marine mammals

seal

sea lion

walrus

northern right whale

narwhal

dolphin

porpoise

humpback whale

beluga whale

killer whale

sperm whale

HUMAN BODY

Like the body of most animals, that of humans presents a bilateral symmetry. This means that most parts are duplicated on both the left and the right sides of the body. Even if they are based on the same model, every body is unique. The shape, height and proportions of the human body vary greatly from one individual to another.

body (front view)

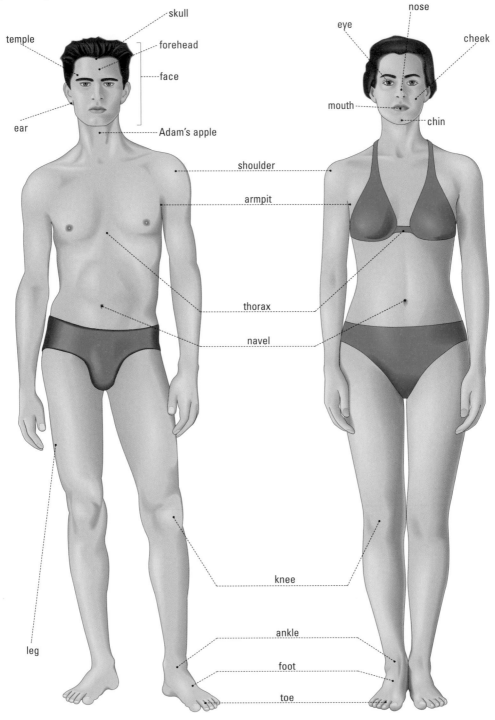

skull

temple

forehead

face

ear

Adam's apple

nose

eye

cheek

mouth

chin

shoulder

armpit

thorax

navel

knee

leg

ankle

foot

toe

body (back view)

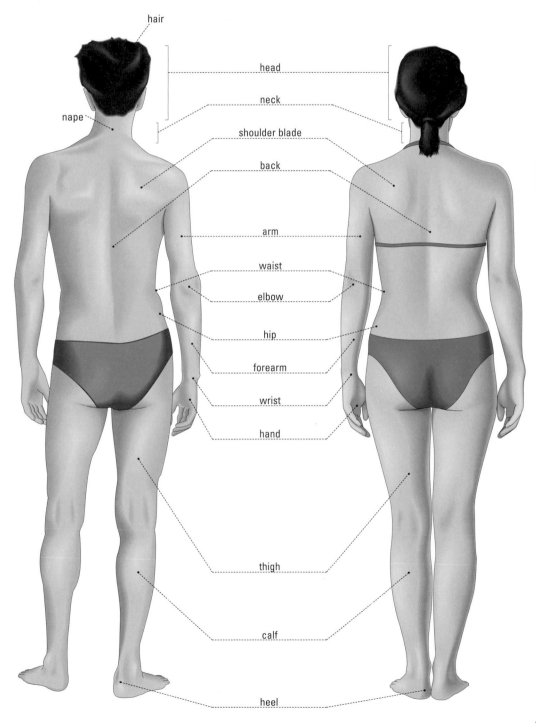

hair

head

neck

nape

shoulder blade

back

arm

waist

elbow

hip

forearm

wrist

hand

thigh

calf

heel

SKELETON

The skeleton is the framework of the body. Its 206 bones support and protect the organs. The bones of the skull, for example, protect the brain. The skeleton has three types of bones, categorized according to their form: short, long and flat. Most bones are linked together by joints. With the help of the muscles that put them into action, bones allow the body to remain standing and to move around.

principal bones

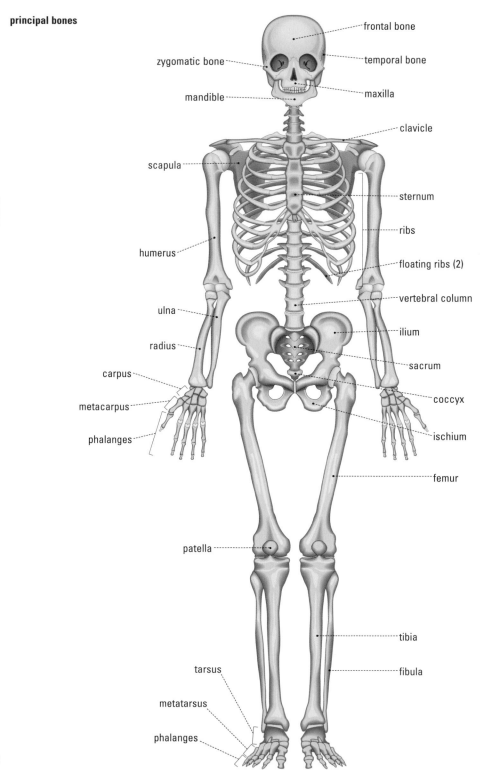

- frontal bone
- zygomatic bone
- temporal bone
- mandible
- maxilla
- clavicle
- scapula
- sternum
- ribs
- floating ribs (2)
- humerus
- vertebral column
- ulna
- ilium
- radius
- sacrum
- carpus
- coccyx
- metacarpus
- ischium
- phalanges
- femur
- patella
- tibia
- tarsus
- fibula
- metatarsus
- phalanges

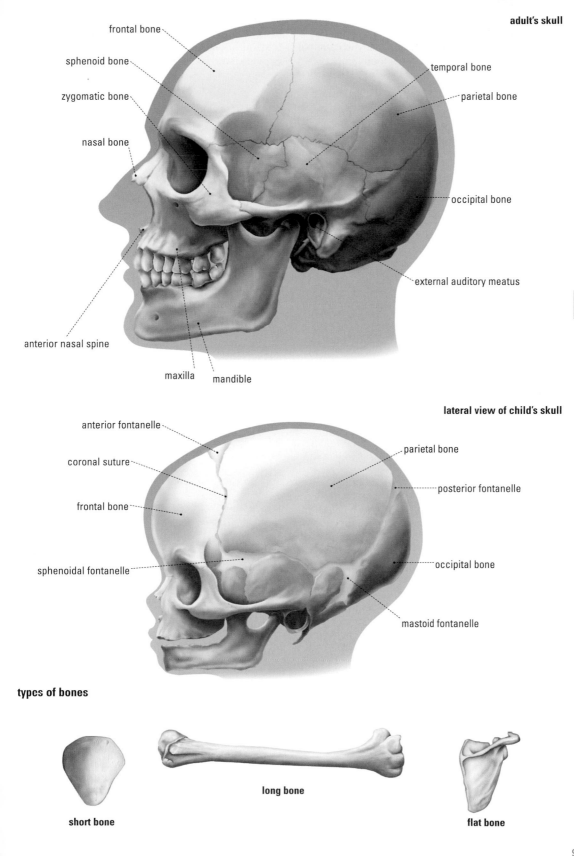

adult's skull

frontal bone

sphenoid bone

zygomatic bone

nasal bone

temporal bone

parietal bone

occipital bone

external auditory meatus

anterior nasal spine

maxilla   mandible

lateral view of child's skull

anterior fontanelle

coronal suture

frontal bone

sphenoidal fontanelle

parietal bone

posterior fontanelle

occipital bone

mastoid fontanelle

HUMAN BEING

types of bones

short bone

long bone

flat bone

TEETH

Solidly inserted in the bones of the jaw, teeth play a very important role in chewing, the first step in the process of digestion. Each type of tooth participates in the transformation of food into small pieces that are easy to swallow. The cutting incisors, located at the front of the mouth, slice the food, the pointed canines tear it up, and the large premolars and molars grind it up.

human denture

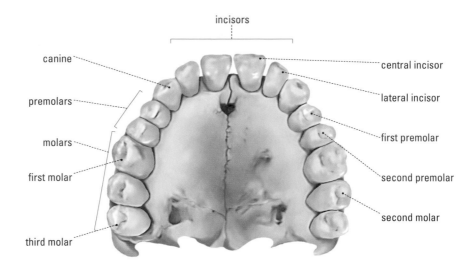

incisors

canine
central incisor
lateral incisor

premolars
first premolar

molars
second premolar

first molar

third molar
second molar

cross section of a molar

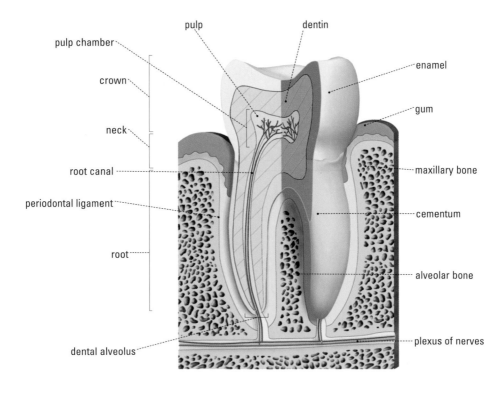

pulp
dentin

pulp chamber
enamel

crown

gum

neck

root canal
maxillary bone

periodontal ligament
cementum

root

alveolar bone

dental alveolus
plexus of nerves

Without muscles, the body would be nothing more than an immobile mass of bones and organs. All the body's movements are produced by skeletal muscles. Under orders from the brain, these muscles contract and lift the bones, thus allowing the body to move. Some muscles, like the 15 or so that go into action when we smile, do not act on the bones but on the skin.

principal muscles

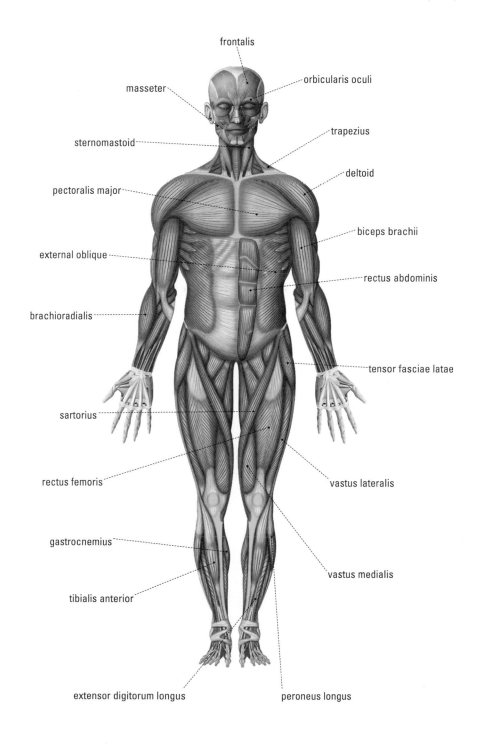

frontalis

orbicularis oculi

masseter

trapezius

sternomastoid

deltoid

pectoralis major

biceps brachii

external oblique

rectus abdominis

brachioradialis

tensor fasciae latae

sartorius

rectus femoris

vastus lateralis

gastrocnemius

vastus medialis

tibialis anterior

extensor digitorum longus

peroneus longus

HUMAN BEING

The human body possesses 11 different systems made up of organs. Although each organ system plays a particular role, they all work together to ensure the body functions correctly. The lungs, one of the organs in the respiratory system, fill the body with oxygen. However, it is the vessels in the circulatory system that distribute the oxygen to every cell in the body.

DIGESTIVE SYSTEM

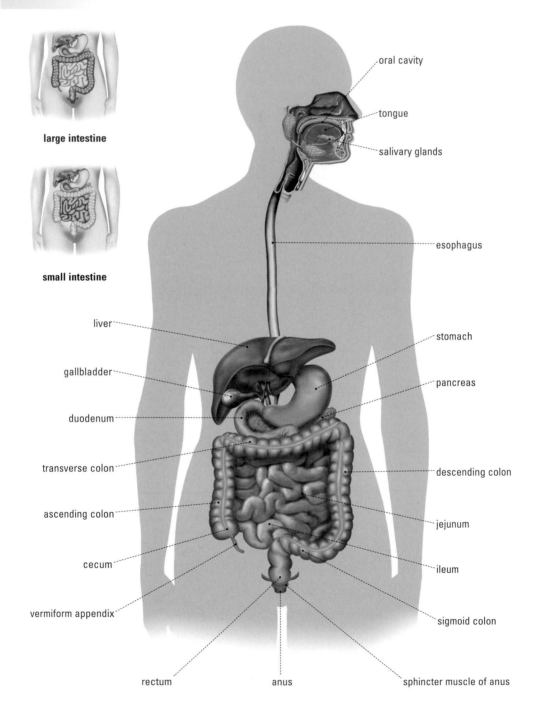

large intestine

small intestine

oral cavity

tongue

salivary glands

esophagus

liver

stomach

gallbladder

pancreas

duodenum

transverse colon

descending colon

ascending colon

jejunum

cecum

ileum

vermiform appendix

sigmoid colon

rectum

anus

sphincter muscle of anus

RESPIRATORY SYSTEM

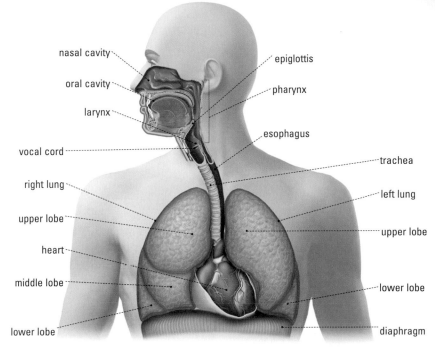

nasal cavity

oral cavity

larynx

vocal cord

right lung

upper lobe

heart

middle lobe

lower lobe

epiglottis

pharynx

esophagus

trachea

left lung

upper lobe

lower lobe

diaphragm

NERVOUS SYSTEM

central nervous system

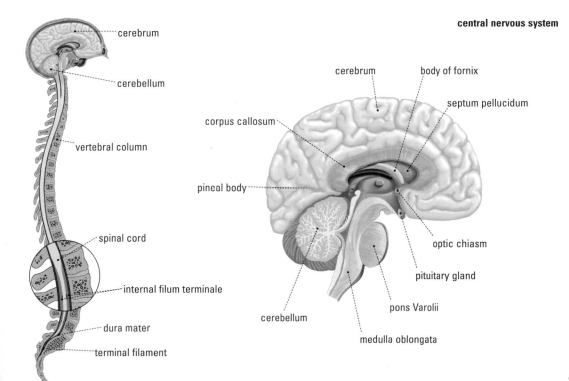

cerebrum

cerebellum

vertebral column

spinal cord

internal filum terminale

dura mater

terminal filament

cerebrum

corpus callosum

pineal body

cerebellum

body of fornix

septum pellucidum

optic chiasm

pituitary gland

pons Varolii

medulla oblongata

CIRCULATORY SYSTEM

heart

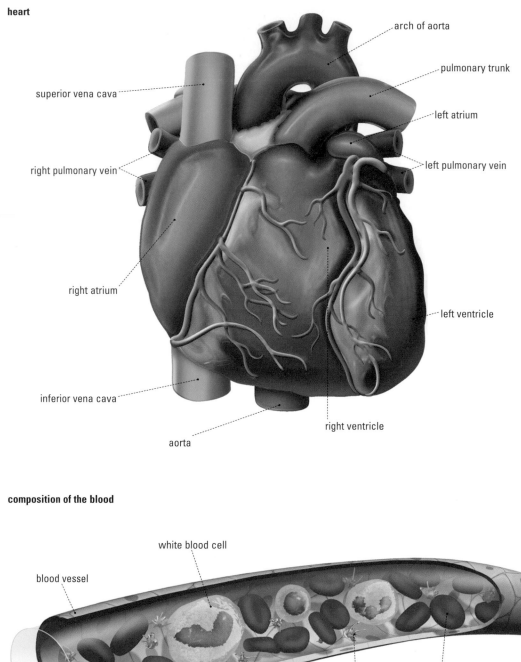

arch of aorta

pulmonary trunk

superior vena cava

left atrium

right pulmonary vein

left pulmonary vein

right atrium

left ventricle

inferior vena cava

right ventricle

aorta

composition of the blood

white blood cell

blood vessel

platelet

red blood cell

plasma

principal veins and arteries

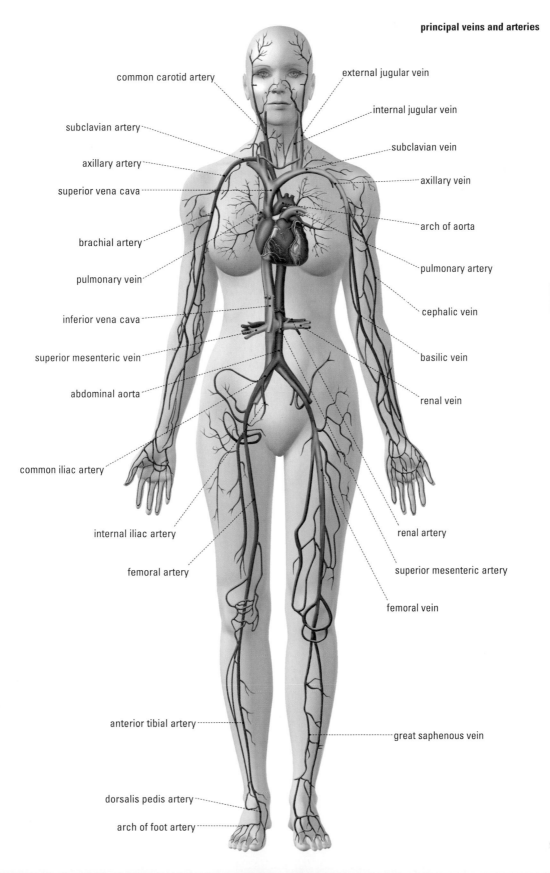

common carotid artery

external jugular vein

internal jugular vein

subclavian artery

subclavian vein

axillary artery

axillary vein

superior vena cava

arch of aorta

brachial artery

pulmonary artery

pulmonary vein

cephalic vein

inferior vena cava

basilic vein

superior mesenteric vein

abdominal aorta

renal vein

common iliac artery

internal iliac artery

renal artery

femoral artery

superior mesenteric artery

femoral vein

anterior tibial artery

great saphenous vein

dorsalis pedis artery

arch of foot artery

HUMAN BEING

99

The five senses inform a human being of what is going on around him or her. The sense organs are equipped with special cells called sensory receptors. These cells collect information and transmit it to the nerves, which then send the information to the brain. In translating these signals into sensations like sound, images or odors, the brain permits the body to react to the world surrounding it.

HEARING

auditory ossicles

structure of the ear

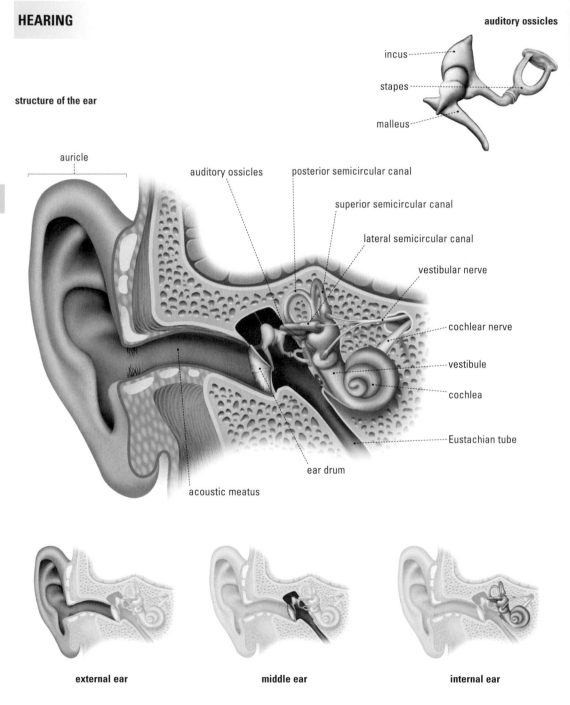

auditory ossicles

incus

stapes

malleus

auricle

auditory ossicles

posterior semicircular canal

superior semicircular canal

lateral semicircular canal

vestibular nerve

cochlear nerve

vestibule

cochlea

Eustachian tube

ear drum

acoustic meatus

external ear

middle ear

internal ear

HUMAN BEING

TOUCH

skin

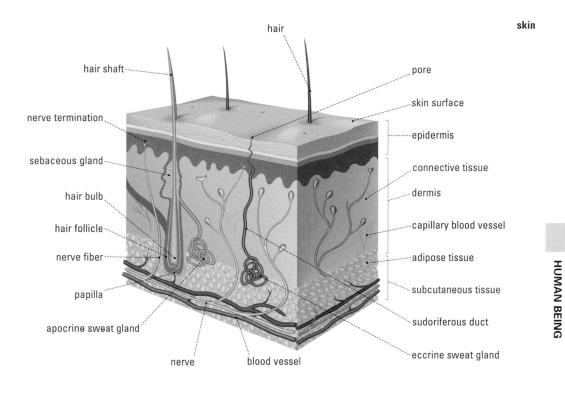

- hair
- hair shaft
- nerve termination
- sebaceous gland
- hair bulb
- hair follicle
- nerve fiber
- papilla
- apocrine sweat gland
- nerve
- blood vessel
- pore
- skin surface
- epidermis
- connective tissue
- dermis
- capillary blood vessel
- adipose tissue
- subcutaneous tissue
- sudoriferous duct
- eccrine sweat gland

HUMAN BEING

hand

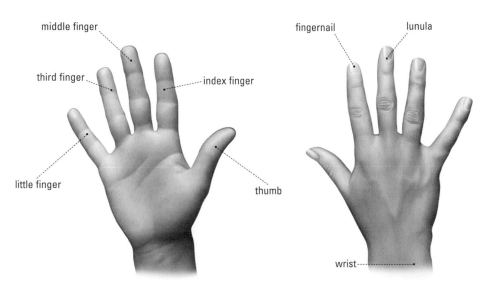

- middle finger
- third finger
- index finger
- little finger
- thumb
- fingernail
- lunula
- wrist

palm

back

SIGHT

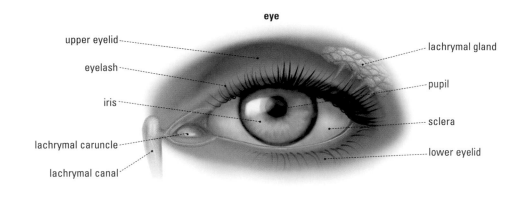

eye

upper eyelid

eyelash

iris

lachrymal caruncle

lachrymal canal

lachrymal gland

pupil

sclera

lower eyelid

SMELL AND TASTE

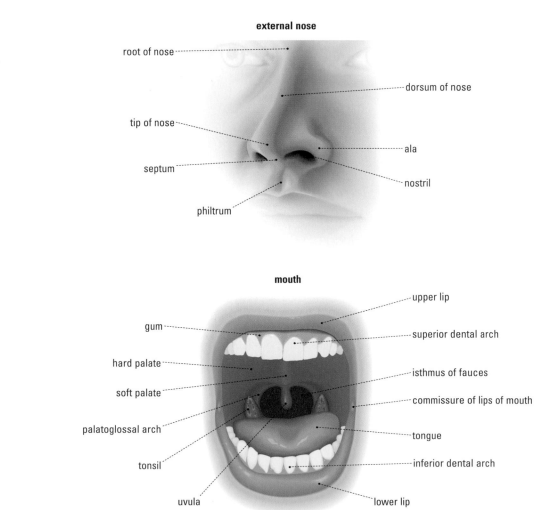

external nose

root of nose

tip of nose

septum

philtrum

dorsum of nose

ala

nostril

mouth

upper lip

gum

hard palate

soft palate

palatoglossal arch

tonsil

uvula

superior dental arch

isthmus of fauces

commissure of lips of mouth

tongue

inferior dental arch

lower lip

Vegetables are the group of edible garden plants included in the human diet. They are classified according to the part of the plant that is eaten. The pepper is considered a fruit vegetable, spinach a leaf vegetable and asparagus a stalk vegetable. Whether eaten as a side dish or as a main dish, vegetables are part of people's diets almost everywhere in the world.

BULB VEGETABLES

section of a bulb

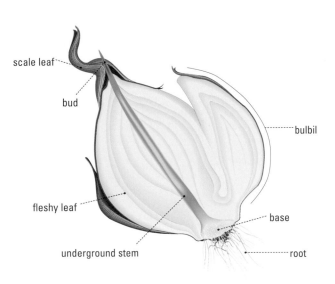

scale leaf

bud

bulbil

fleshy leaf

base

underground stem

root

FOOD

EXAMPLES OF BULB VEGETABLES

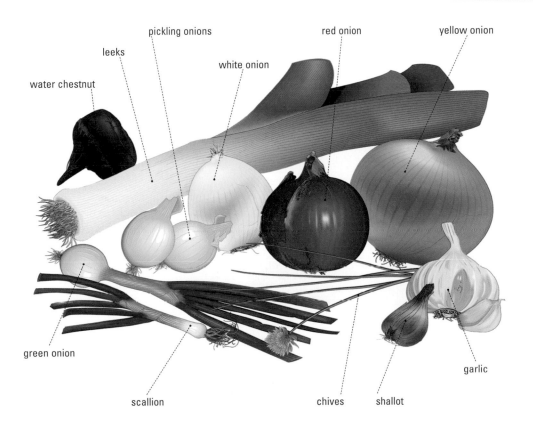

pickling onions

red onion

yellow onion

leeks

white onion

water chestnut

green onion

garlic

scallion

chives

shallot

TUBER VEGETABLES

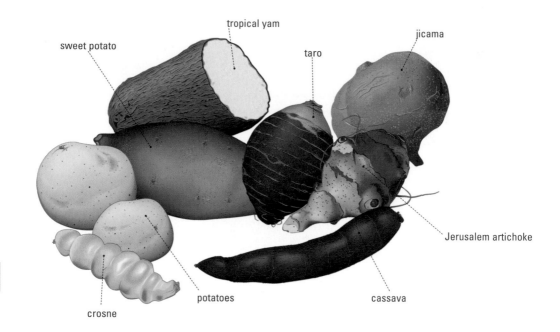

tropical yam

jicama

sweet potato

taro

Jerusalem artichoke

potatoes

cassava

crosne

ROOT VEGETABLES

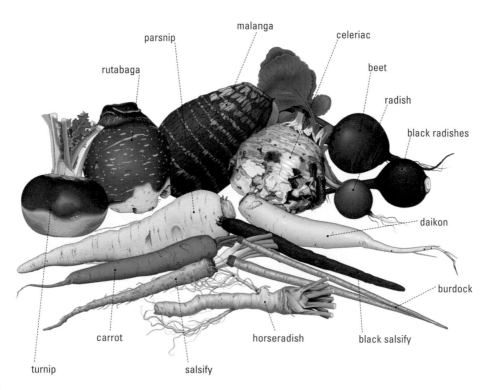

malanga

parsnip

celeriac

rutabaga

beet

radish

black radishes

daikon

burdock

black salsify

carrot

horseradish

turnip

salsify

STALK VEGETABLES

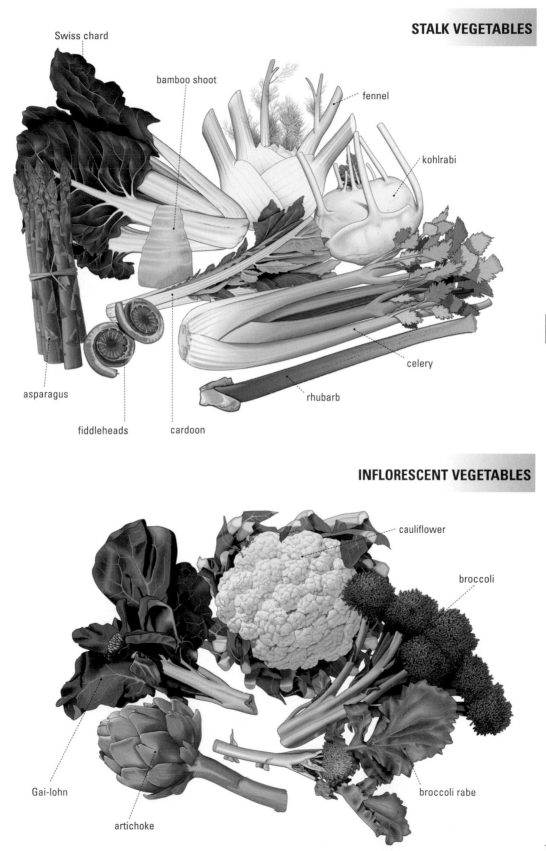

Swiss chard

bamboo shoot

fennel

kohlrabi

celery

asparagus

rhubarb

fiddleheads

cardoon

FOOD

INFLORESCENT VEGETABLES

cauliflower

broccoli

Gai-lohn

broccoli rabe

artichoke

LEAF VEGETABLES

red cabbage

green cabbage

savoy cabbage

white cabbage

Belgian endive

pe-tsai

romaine lettuce

bok choy

collards

sea kale

curly kale

curly endive

escarole

radicchio

ornamental kale

iceberg lettuce

leaf lettuce

celtuce

grape leaves

garden cress

brussels sprouts

garden sorrel

butter lettuce

purslane

nettle

watercress

dandelion

spinach

corn salad

arugula

FRUIT VEGETABLES

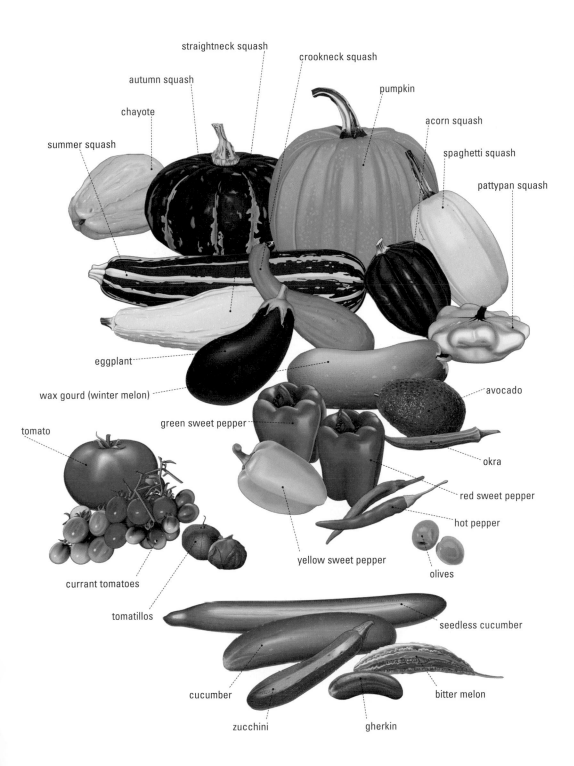

straightneck squash

crookneck squash

autumn squash

pumpkin

chayote

acorn squash

summer squash

spaghetti squash

pattypan squash

eggplant

wax gourd (winter melon)

avocado

green sweet pepper

tomato

okra

red sweet pepper

hot pepper

yellow sweet pepper

olives

currant tomatoes

tomatillos

seedless cucumber

cucumber

bitter melon

zucchini

gherkin

Approximately 13,000 plant species make up the large family of legumes. These vegetables are distinguished by their pod-shaped fruits, which contain many highly nutritious seeds. Lentils, beans and peanuts are a few examples of legumes. In many South American countries, legumes have long been considered a staple food.

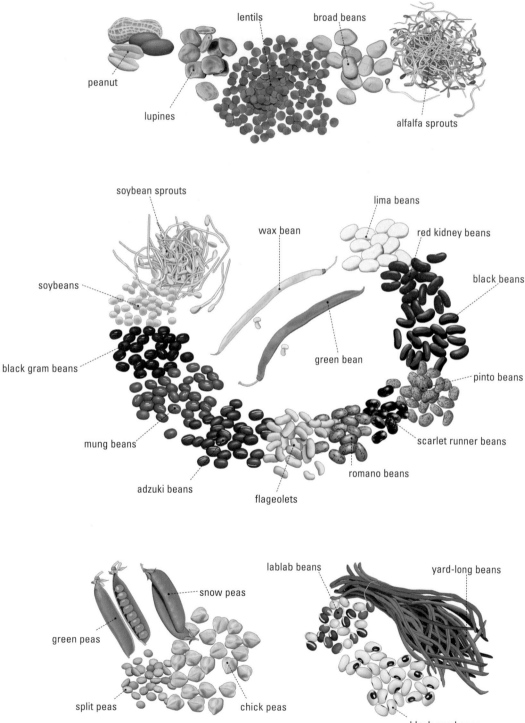

peanut

lupines

lentils

broad beans

alfalfa sprouts

soybean sprouts

wax bean

lima beans

red kidney beans

soybeans

black beans

black gram beans

green bean

pinto beans

mung beans

scarlet runner beans

adzuki beans

romano beans

flageolets

lablab beans

yard-long beans

snow peas

green peas

split peas

chick peas

black-eyed peas

In the botanical sense, the fruit is the organ that contains small plant embryos, or seeds. This means that olives, nuts and cucumbers are fruits. Even the inedible samaras of maple trees are fruits. In every-day practice, fruits are considered sweet foods, like apples and cherries, and are usually eaten as a snack or dessert.

BERRIES

section of a strawberry

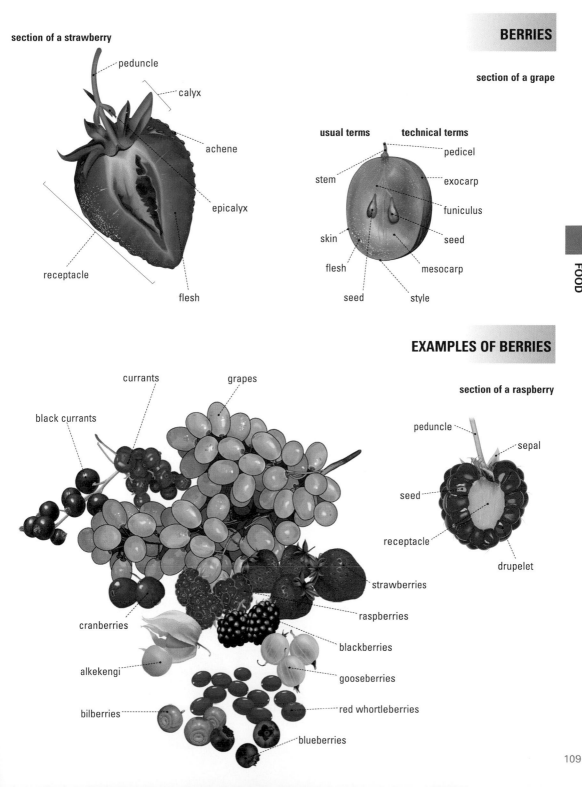

peduncle

calyx

achene

epicalyx

receptacle

flesh

section of a grape

usual terms   technical terms

pedicel

stem

exocarp

funiculus

skin

seed

flesh

mesocarp

seed

style

EXAMPLES OF BERRIES

currants

grapes

black currants

section of a raspberry

peduncle

sepal

seed

receptacle

drupelet

strawberries

raspberries

cranberries

blackberries

alkekengi

gooseberries

bilberries

red whortleberries

blueberries

FOOD

STONE FRUITS

section of a peach

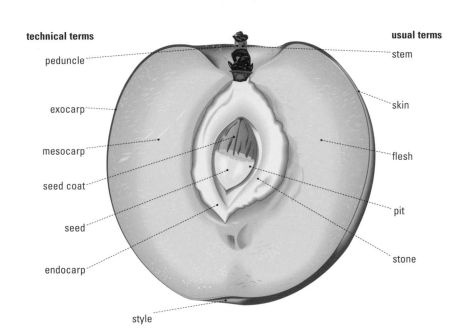

technical terms | usual terms

peduncle | stem
exocarp | skin
mesocarp | flesh
seed coat | pit
seed
endocarp | stone

style

EXAMPLES OF STONE FRUITS

dates

nectarine

peach

plums

cherries

apricot

POME FRUITS

section of an apple

technical terms

usual terms

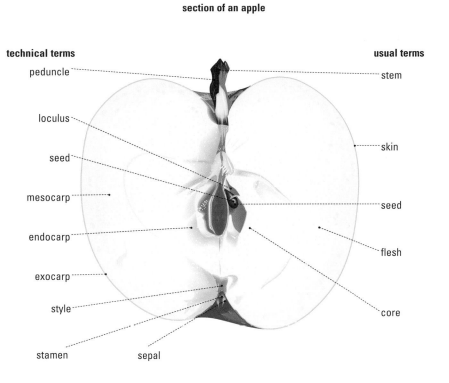

peduncle ---------- stem

loculus

seed

mesocarp

endocarp

exocarp

style

stamen   sepal

skin

seed

flesh

core

EXAMPLES OF POME FRUITS

pear

quince

apple

Japanese plums

CITRUS FRUITS

section of an orange

technical terms   usual terms

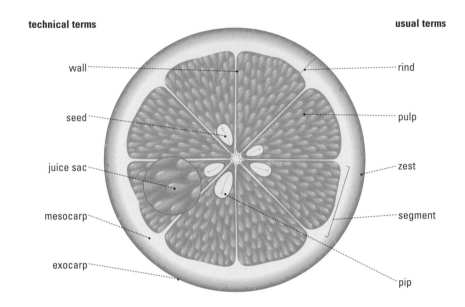

wall·········· ·········· rind

seed·········· ·········· pulp

juice sac·········· ·········· zest

mesocarp·········· ·········· segment

exocarp··········

·········· pip

EXAMPLES OF CITRUS FRUITS

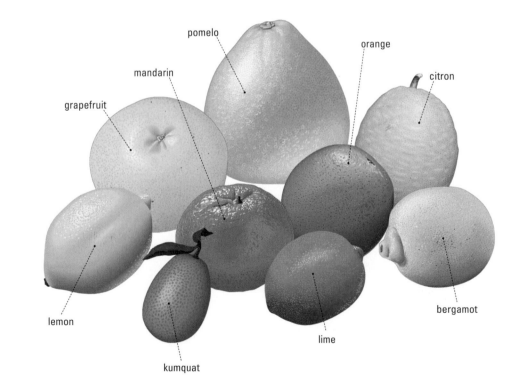

pomelo

mandarin

orange

grapefruit

citron

lemon

kumquat

lime

bergamot

MELONS

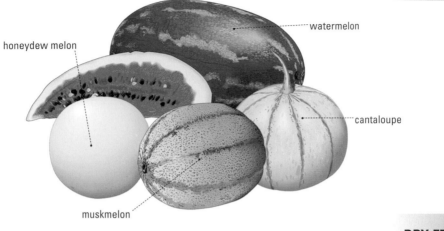

honeydew melon

watermelon

cantaloupe

muskmelon

DRY FRUITS

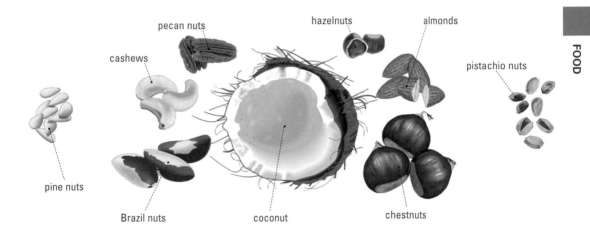

pecan nuts

hazelnuts

almonds

cashews

pistachio nuts

pine nuts

Brazil nuts

coconut

chestnuts

TROPICAL FRUITS

pineapple

pomegranate

papaya

mango

kiwi

litchi

carambola

banana

passion fruit

fig

MISCELLANEOUS FOODS

Meals are made up of foods that vary according to the time of day and the part of the world in which they are consumed. Most foods belong to the principal food groups, like fruits and vegetables, cereal products or dairy products. Because each type of food provides different nutritional elements to the body, a varied diet is the key to staying healthy.

CEREAL PRODUCTS

multigrain bread

white bread

bagel

baguette

croissant

chapati

pasta

rice

tortillas

pita bread

EGGS AND DAIRY PRODUCTS

yogurt

butter

quail egg

hen egg

milk carton

ice cream

cheese

pepperoni

salad

MEALS

turkey

fish

cooked ham

stew

pizza

steak

spaghetti

sandwich

fruit juice

pie

cookies

cake

baby food

Clothing is designed to cover the human body. It can be used to protect, to hide, to warm or to enhance its wearer's appearance. A number of factors determine how people dress: their age, gender and sometimes their occupation. The climate, country and historical period in which a person lives also play important roles. In developed countries, the fashion industry has a strong influence on many people's seasonal wardrobes.

MEN'S CLOTHING

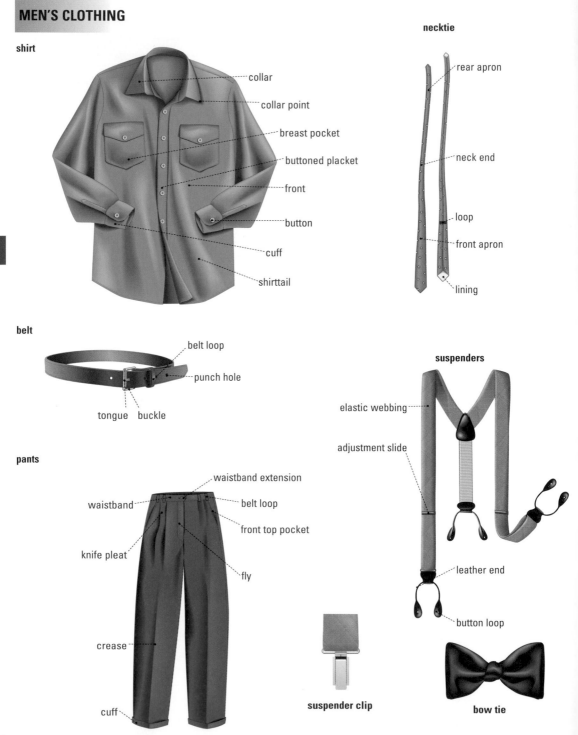

shirt

- collar
- collar point
- breast pocket
- buttoned placket
- front
- button
- cuff
- shirttail

necktie

- rear apron
- neck end
- loop
- front apron
- lining

belt

- belt loop
- punch hole
- tongue
- buckle

suspenders

- elastic webbing
- adjustment slide
- leather end
- button loop

pants

- waistband extension
- waistband
- belt loop
- front top pocket
- knife pleat
- fly
- crease
- cuff

suspender clip

bow tie

hood

frog

duffle coat

toggle fastening

windbreaker

double-breasted jacket

snap fastener

raincoat

elastic waistband

jacket

single-breasted jacket

MEN'S UNDERWEAR

athletic shirt

briefs

waistband

fly

elasticized leg opening

drawers

crotch

boxer shorts

WOMEN'S CLOTHING

suit

jacket

pea jacket

cape

skirt

polo dress

poncho

princess-seamed dress

classic blouse

ski pants

straight skirt

sarong

pleated skirt

pajamas

overcoat

bathrobe

culottes

hose

panty hose

short sock

sock

stocking

WOMEN'S UNDERWEAR

half-slip

body suit

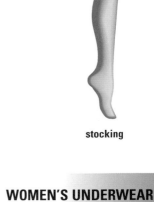

shoulder strap

cup

midriff band

bra

briefs

CLOTHING AND PERSONAL OBJECTS

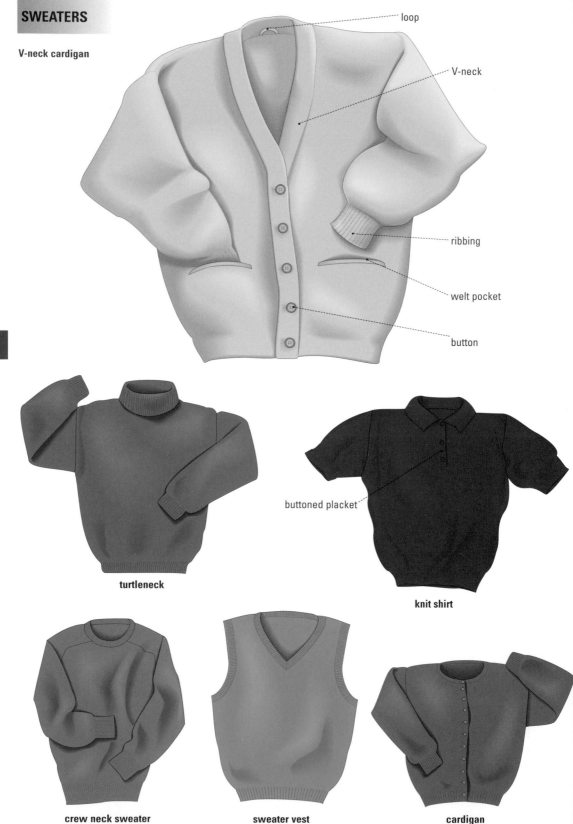

SWEATERS

V-neck cardigan

loop

V-neck

ribbing

welt pocket

button

turtleneck

buttoned placket

knit shirt

crew neck sweater

sweater vest

cardigan

CHILDREN'S CLOTHING

T-shirt dress

jumpsuit

jeans

shorts

pajamas

bunting bag

overalls

adjustable strap

bib

fly

drawstring hood

fly front closing

snowsuit

rompers

sleepers

screen print

snap-fastening front

inside-leg snap-fastening

SPORTSWEAR

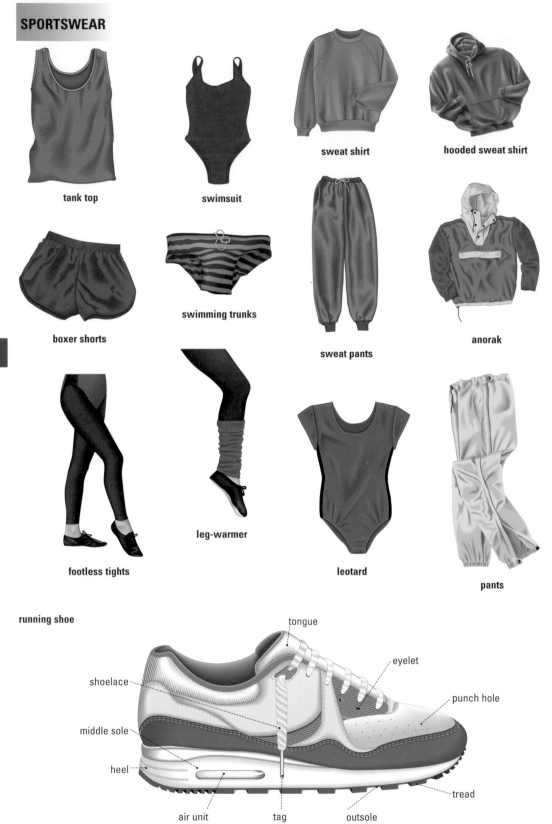

tank top

swimsuit

sweat shirt

hooded sweat shirt

boxer shorts

swimming trunks

sweat pants

anorak

footless tights

leg-warmer

leotard

pants

running shoe

tongue

eyelet

shoelace

punch hole

middle sole

heel

air unit

tag

outsole

tread

Many accessories have a practical use. A wide-brimmed hat, for example, protects the head from the sun, while a pair of gloves or mittens keeps hands warm. Other accessories, such as a belt and matching handbag, serve to complete an outfit in a visually pleasing way. Added to these accessories is a multitude of practical objects used daily to care for the body.

MEN'S GLOVES

mitten

back of a glove

stitching

palm of a glove

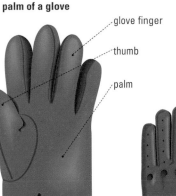

glove finger

thumb

palm

snap fastener

driving glove

WOMEN'S GLOVES

wrist-length glove

short glove

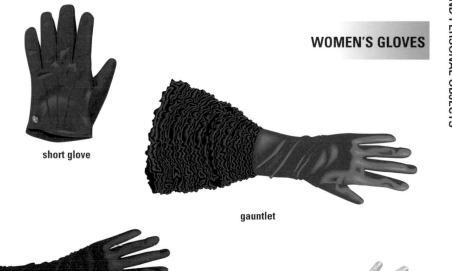

gauntlet

evening glove

mitt

gauntlet

HEADGEAR

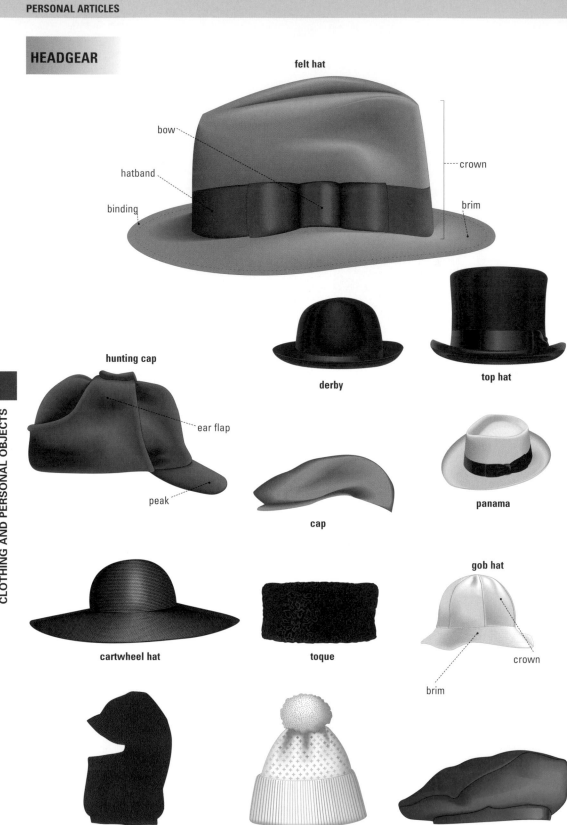

felt hat

bow

hatband

binding

crown

brim

derby

top hat

hunting cap

ear flap

peak

cap

panama

cartwheel hat

toque

gob hat

crown

brim

balaclava

stocking cap

beret

SHOES

parts of a shoe

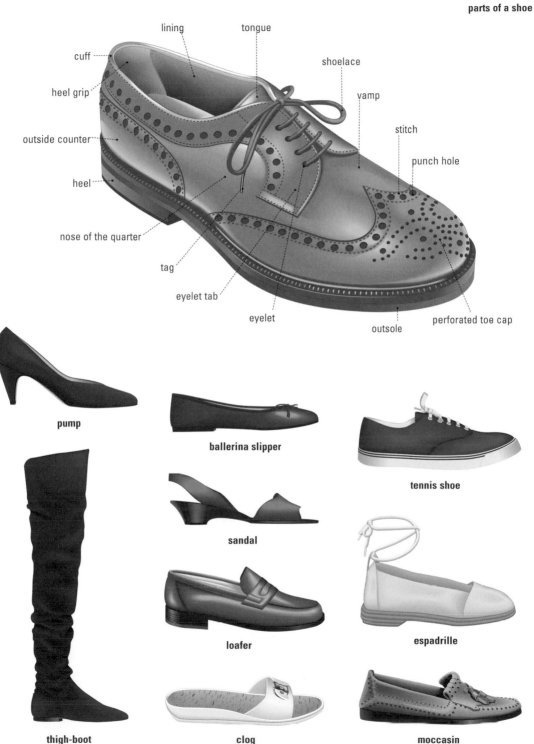

lining

tongue

cuff

shoelace

heel grip

vamp

outside counter

stitch

punch hole

heel

nose of the quarter

tag

eyelet tab

eyelet

perforated toe cap

outsole

pump

ballerina slipper

tennis shoe

sandal

thigh-boot

loafer

espadrille

clog

moccasin

LEATHER GOODS

attaché case

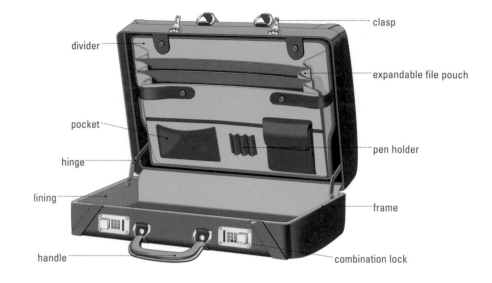

- clasp
- divider
- expandable file pouch
- pocket
- pen holder
- hinge
- lining
- frame
- handle
- combination lock

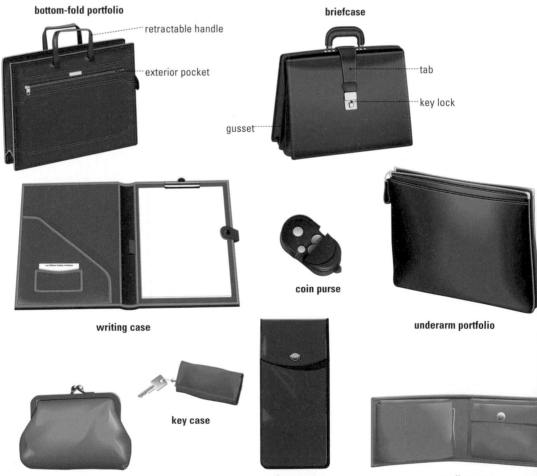

bottom-fold portfolio

- retractable handle
- exterior pocket

briefcase

- tab
- key lock
- gusset

writing case

coin purse

underarm portfolio

key case

purse

eyeglasses case

wallet

LUGGAGE AND HANDBAGS

latch

hasp

trunk

tray

handle

cornerpiece

fittings

zipper

garment bag

Pullman case

handle

frame

pull strap

buckle

shoulder strap

wheel

trim

identification tag

shoulder bag

carrier bag

eyelet

drawstring

front pocket

drawstring bag

men's bag

drawstring bag

CLOTHING AND PERSONAL OBJECTS

EYEGLASSES

eyeglasses parts

bridge · glass lens · bar · temple · bend · rim · pad arm · earpiece

half-glasses

sunglasses

monocle

UMBRELLAS AND WALKING STICKS

spreader

umbrellas

canopy · tie · rib · tip · shank · handle · ring · tab

umbrella stand

telescopic umbrella

cover · push button

stick umbrella

walking stick

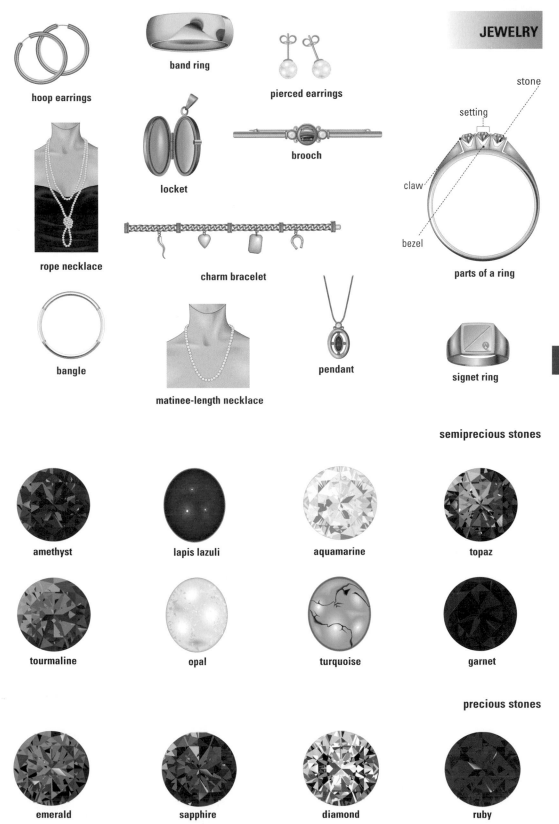

JEWELRY

band ring

pierced earrings

hoop earrings

stone

setting

locket

brooch

claw

bezel

rope necklace

charm bracelet

parts of a ring

bangle

matinee-length necklace

pendant

signet ring

semiprecious stones

amethyst

lapis lazuli

aquamarine

topaz

tourmaline

opal

turquoise

garnet

precious stones

emerald

sapphire

diamond

ruby

HAIRDRESSING

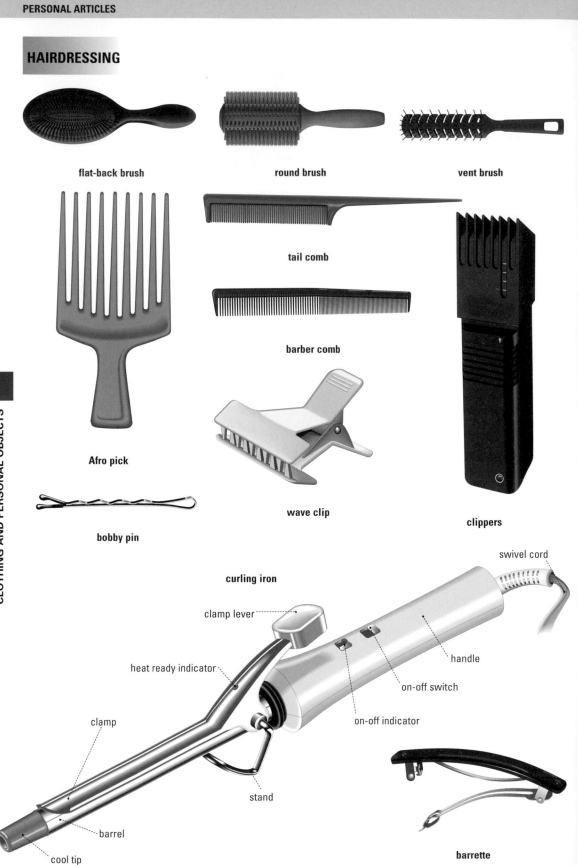

flat-back brush

round brush

vent brush

tail comb

barber comb

Afro pick

bobby pin

wave clip

clippers

curling iron

swivel cord

clamp lever

heat ready indicator

handle

on-off switch

on-off indicator

clamp

stand

barrel

cool tip

barrette

130

hair dryer

fan housing

air-inlet grille

barrel

air-outlet grille

speed selector switch

heat selector switch

on-off switch

handle

air concentrator

hang-up ring

power supply cord

SHAVING

CLOTHING AND PERSONAL OBJECTS

bristle

aftershave

shaving mug

shaving brush

shaving foam

screen

trimmer

closeness setting

housing

charging light

head

on-off switch

collar

handle

charge indicator

blade injector

electric razor

double-edged razor

disposable razor

BODY CARE

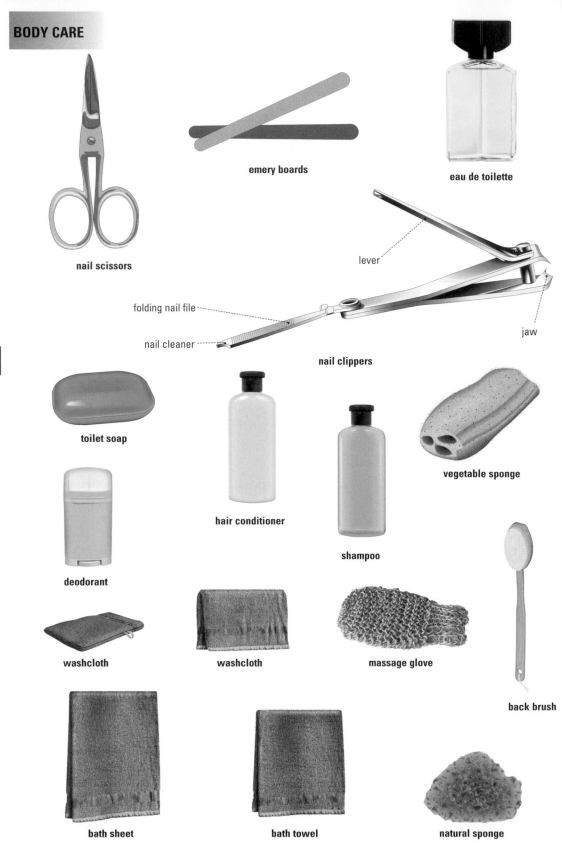

nail scissors

emery boards

eau de toilette

lever

folding nail file

nail cleaner

jaw

nail clippers

toilet soap

hair conditioner

shampoo

vegetable sponge

deodorant

washcloth

washcloth

massage glove

back brush

bath sheet

bath towel

natural sponge

DENTAL CARE

toothbrush

stimulator tip

bristle

row

handle

head

toothpaste

mouthwash

dental floss

MAKEUP

powder blusher

liquid foundation

powder puff

brow brush and lash comb

liquid eyeliner

liquid mascara

eyeshadow

lipstick

pressed powder

133

The materials used to cover the building, the flat or peaked shape of the roof, the addition of a garage and the number of floors are all factors that help to determine the outside appearance of a house. The surrounding land is also an important part of the overall appearance, whether it consists of a narrow flower bed or is large enough for a swimming pool, vegetable garden and tool shed.

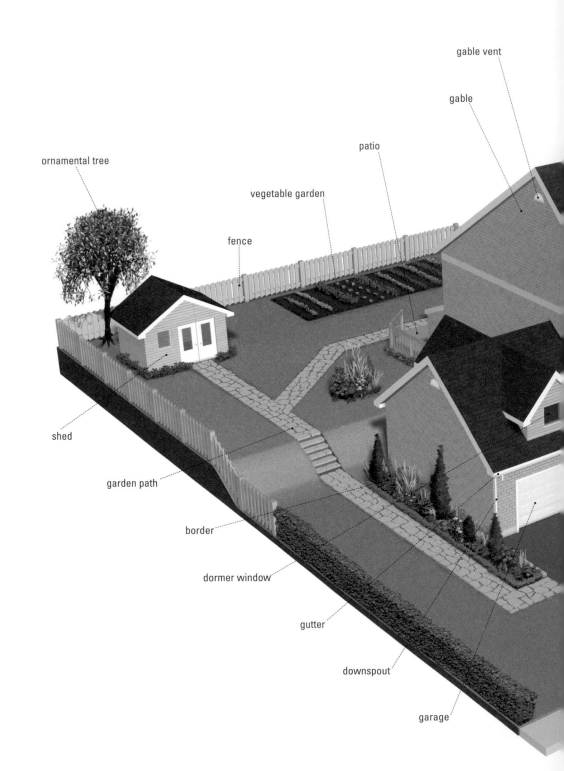

gable vent

gable

patio

ornamental tree

vegetable garden

fence

shed

garden path

border

dormer window

gutter

downspout

garage

above-ground swimming pool

filter

in-ground swimming pool

steps

diving board

lightning rod

chimney

roof

cornice

skylight

steps

hedge

lawn

basement window

flower bed

sidewalk

porch

driveway

site plan

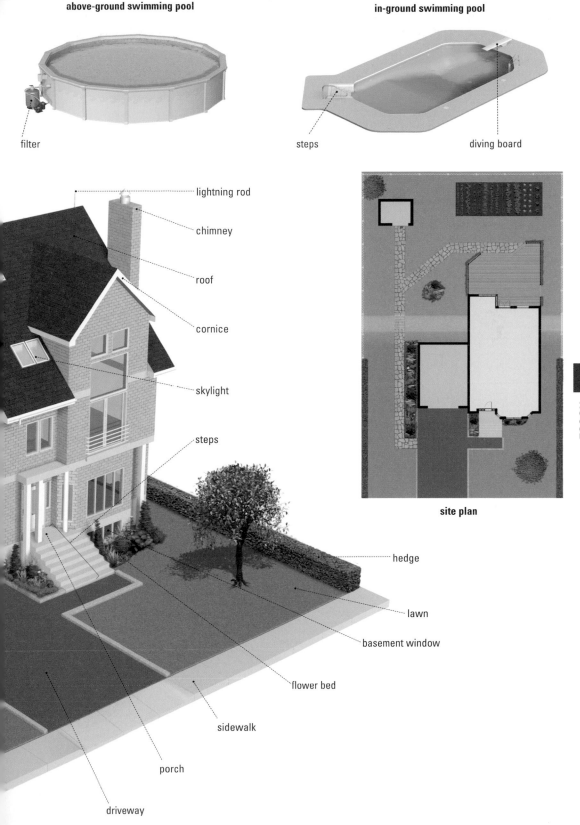

Whether constructed of wood, brick or straw, every house is made up of basic elements, such as a roof and walls. Some walls have a door cut into them to allow people to enter or exit the house. Openings like windows allow light and fresh air to enter. Modern houses have many doors and windows in different styles.

HOUSE

DOOR

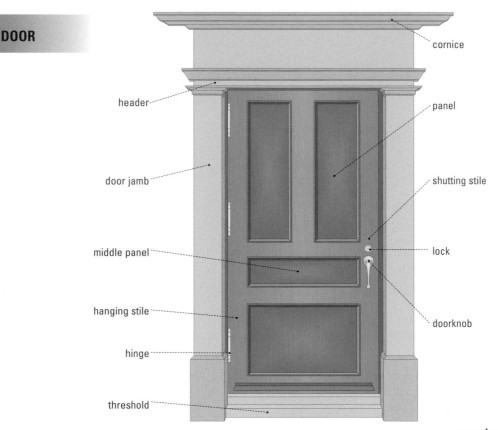

cornice

header

panel

door jamb

shutting stile

middle panel

lock

hanging stile

hinge

doorknob

threshold

lock

examples of doors

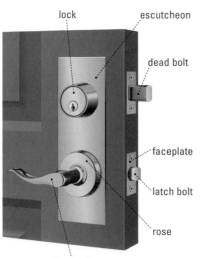

lock

escutcheon

dead bolt

faceplate

latch bolt

rose

doorknob

sliding door

conventional door

folding door

sliding folding door

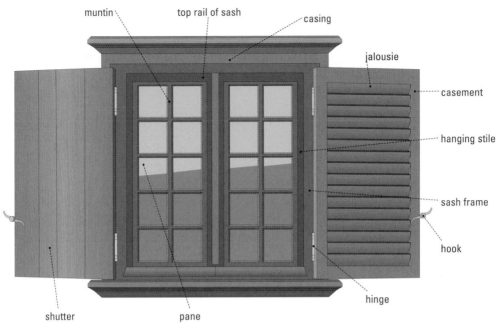

muntin
top rail of sash
casing
jalousie
casement
hanging stile
sash frame
hook
shutter
pane
hinge

HOUSE

examples of windows

French window

casement window

louvered window

horizontal pivoting window

sash window

vertical pivoting window

sliding window

sliding folding window

MAIN ROOMS

The rooms in a house may be situated on one level or spread over several floors. The number of rooms can vary greatly from one house to another, depending on the needs and budget of the residents. Most modern houses have a kitchen, dining room, living room, bathroom and at least one bedroom.

ELEVATION

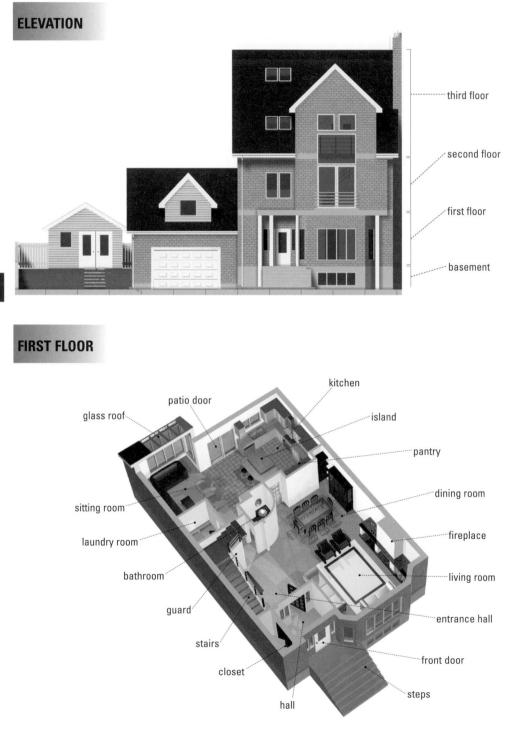

third floor

second floor

first floor

basement

FIRST FLOOR

kitchen

patio door

glass roof

island

pantry

sitting room

dining room

laundry room

fireplace

bathroom

living room

guard

entrance hall

stairs

closet

front door

steps

hall

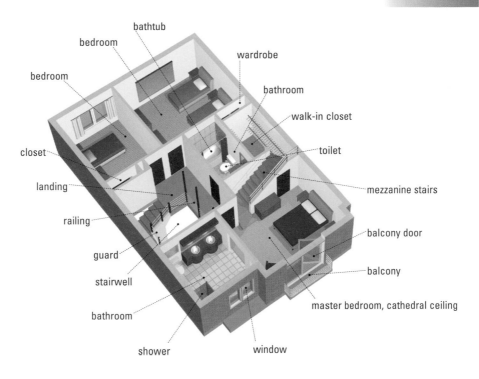

bathtub

bedroom

bedroom

wardrobe

bathroom

walk-in closet

closet

toilet

landing

railing

mezzanine stairs

guard

balcony door

stairwell

balcony

bathroom

master bedroom, cathedral ceiling

shower

window

HOUSE

THIRD FLOOR

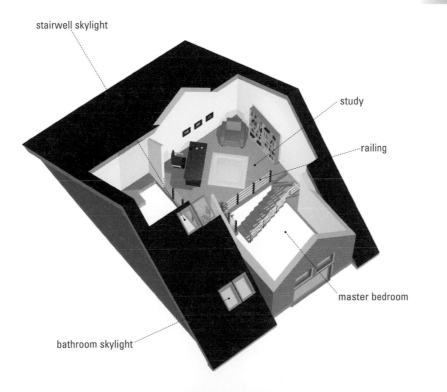

stairwell skylight

study

railing

master bedroom

bathroom skylight

HOUSE FURNITURE

The furniture in a house consists of the movable objects that its occupants use for sitting, lying down and displaying or storing objects. The type of furniture found in a home reflects the culture of the people living there, the way they live, and the period in history to which they belong. For example, desert nomads are never burdened by extra furniture. Meanwhile, many people in developing countries are too poor to own furniture.

SEATS, SIDE CHAIRS AND ARMCHAIRS

parts of a side chair

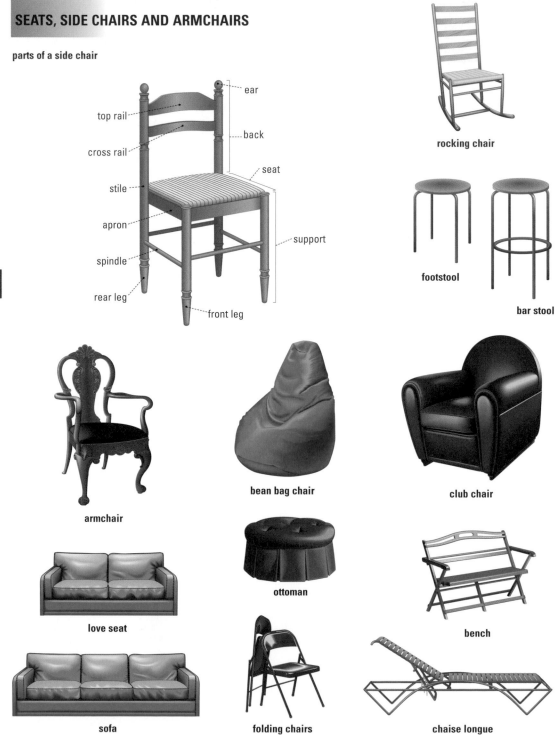

ear

top rail

back

cross rail

seat

stile

apron

support

spindle

rear leg

front leg

rocking chair

footstool

bar stool

armchair

bean bag chair

club chair

love seat

ottoman

bench

sofa

folding chairs

chaise longue

armoire

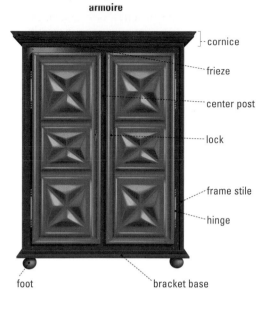

- cornice
- frieze
- center post
- lock
- frame stile
- hinge

foot

bracket base

dresser

chiffonier

changing table

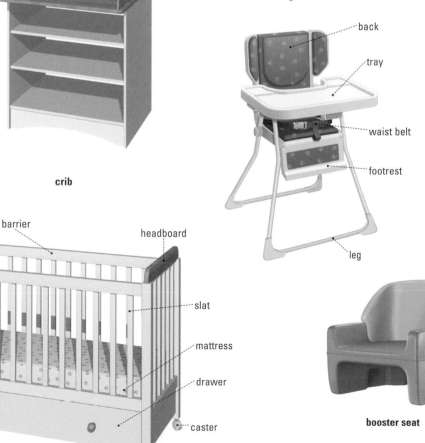

high chair

- back
- tray
- waist belt
- footrest

leg

crib

barrier

headboard

slat

mattress

drawer

caster

booster seat

BED

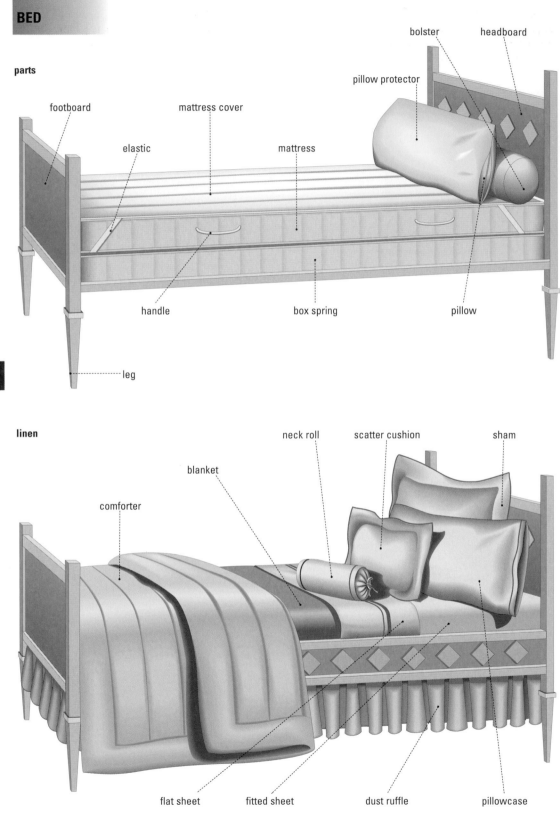

parts

footboard

elastic

mattress cover

mattress

bolster

headboard

pillow protector

handle

box spring

pillow

leg

linen

neck roll

scatter cushion

sham

blanket

comforter

flat sheet

fitted sheet

dust ruffle

pillowcase

Whether limited to a small corner or occupying a large room, the kitchen is the place where meals are prepared. The modern kitchen is equipped with a refrigerator, stove and an entire range of small electrical appliances and utensils. Cooks today have a variety of tools at their disposal to help them prepare and cook food quickly and efficiently.

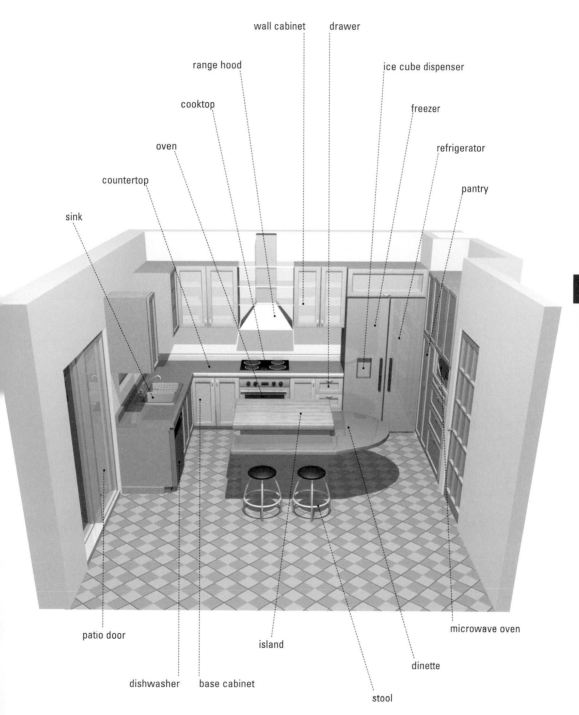

wall cabinet

drawer

range hood

ice cube dispenser

cooktop

freezer

oven

refrigerator

countertop

pantry

sink

patio door

microwave oven

island

dinette

dishwasher

base cabinet

stool

GLASSWARE

glass

burgundy glass

white wine glass

sparkling wine glass

champagne flute

decanter

small decanter

beer mug

DINNERWARE

cup

sugar bowl

demitasse

butter dish

creamer

coffee mug

ramekin

salt shaker

pepper shaker

gravy boat

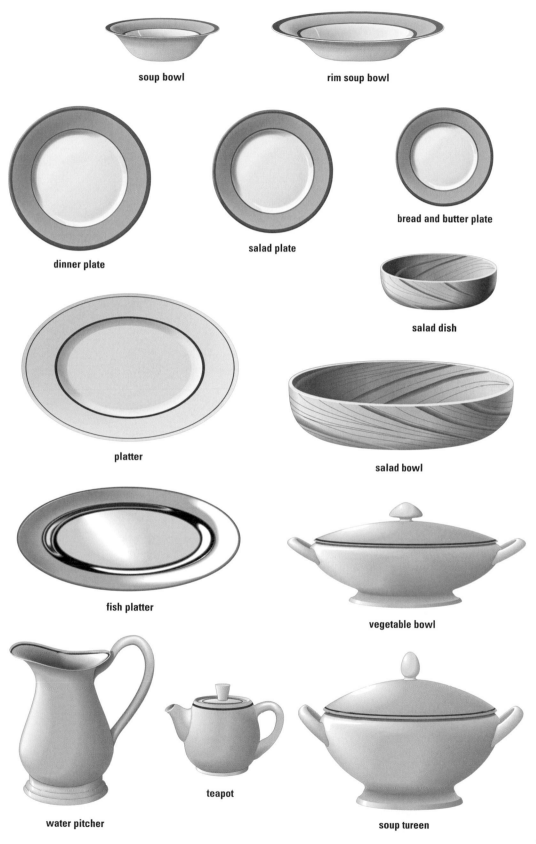

soup bowl

rim soup bowl

dinner plate

salad plate

bread and butter plate

salad dish

platter

salad bowl

fish platter

vegetable bowl

water pitcher

teapot

soup tureen

SILVERWARE

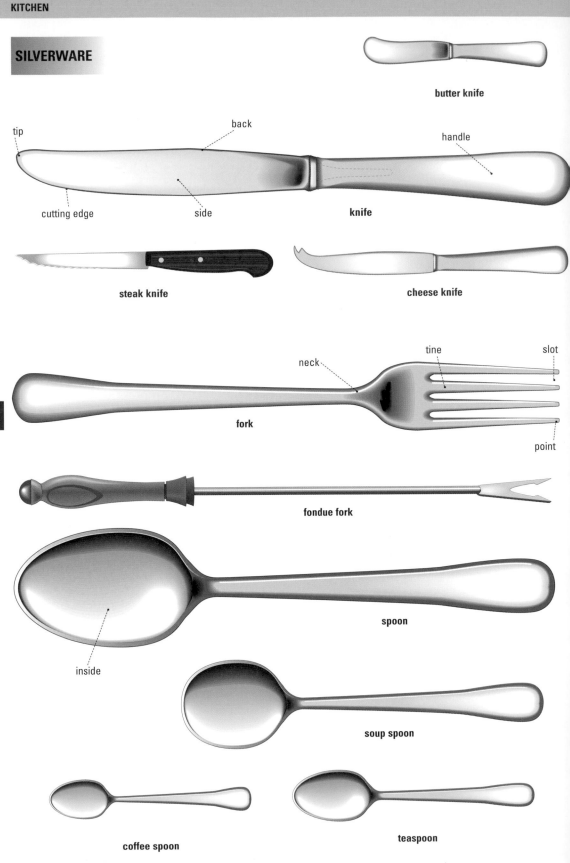

butter knife

back

tip

handle

cutting edge

side

knife

steak knife

cheese knife

neck

tine

slot

fork

point

fondue fork

spoon

inside

soup spoon

coffee spoon

teaspoon

HOUSE

kitchen scale

citrus juicer

HOUSE

salad spinner

colander

grater

apple corer

peeler

melon baller

vegetable brush

can opener

lever corkscrew

nutcracker

bottle opener

muffin pan

funnel

measuring cup

cookie cutters

measuring spoons

mixing bowls

whisk

egg beater

baster

rolling pin

potato masher

chef's knife

tongs

spatula

ladle

ice cream scoop

COOKING UTENSILS

stock pot

double boiler

saucepan

frying pan

sauté pan

lid

wok set

rack

wok

burner ring

roasting pans

fondue pot

stand

steamer basket

burner

fondue set

safety valve

pressure regulator

pressure cooker

HOUSE

DOMESTIC APPLIANCES

food processor

pusher

feed tube

lid

blade

bowl

speed selector

motor unit

spindle

blender

cap

container

cutting blade

motor unit

push button

motor unit

blending attachment

hand blender

electric knife

can opener

hand mixer

waffle iron

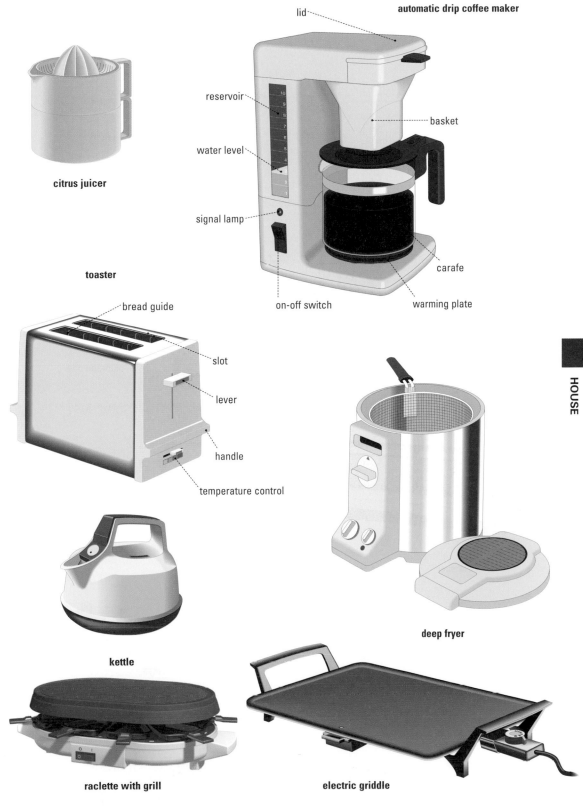

automatic drip coffee maker

lid

reservoir

water level

signal lamp

basket

carafe

on-off switch

warming plate

citrus juicer

toaster

bread guide

slot

lever

handle

temperature control

deep fryer

kettle

raclette with grill

electric griddle

refrigerator

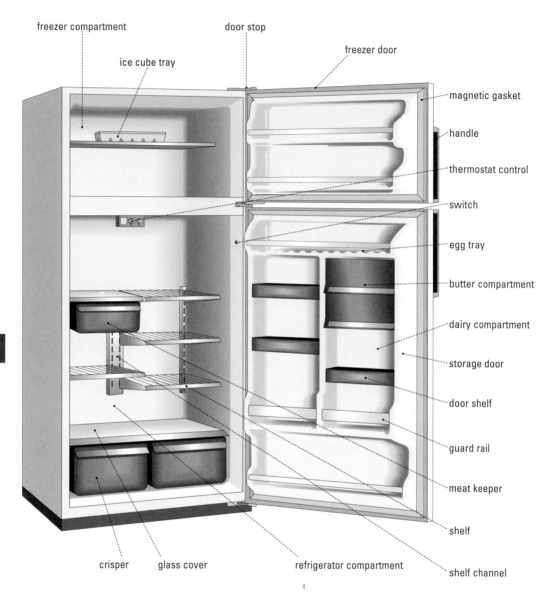

freezer compartment

ice cube tray

door stop

freezer door

magnetic gasket

handle

thermostat control

switch

egg tray

butter compartment

dairy compartment

storage door

door shelf

guard rail

meat keeper

shelf

crisper

glass cover

refrigerator compartment

shelf channel

HOUSE

microwave oven

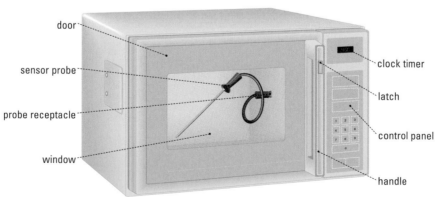

door

sensor probe

probe receptacle

window

clock timer

latch

control panel

handle

electric range

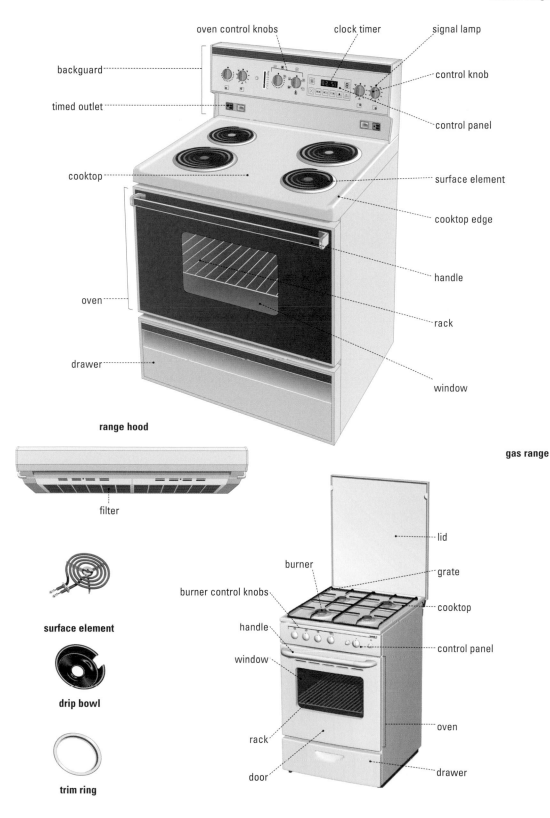

oven control knobs

clock timer

signal lamp

backguard

control knob

timed outlet

control panel

cooktop

surface element

cooktop edge

handle

oven

rack

drawer

window

range hood

filter

gas range

lid

burner

grate

burner control knobs

cooktop

handle

control panel

window

surface element

oven

drip bowl

rack

door

drawer

trim ring

Taking a bath is an activity as old as civilization. It was not until the 19th century, however, that the first bathroom with running water appeared. In modern houses, this room is often equipped with a toilet, sink, shower and bathtub. Small or large, simple or luxurious, the bathroom is above all a place dedicated to hygiene.

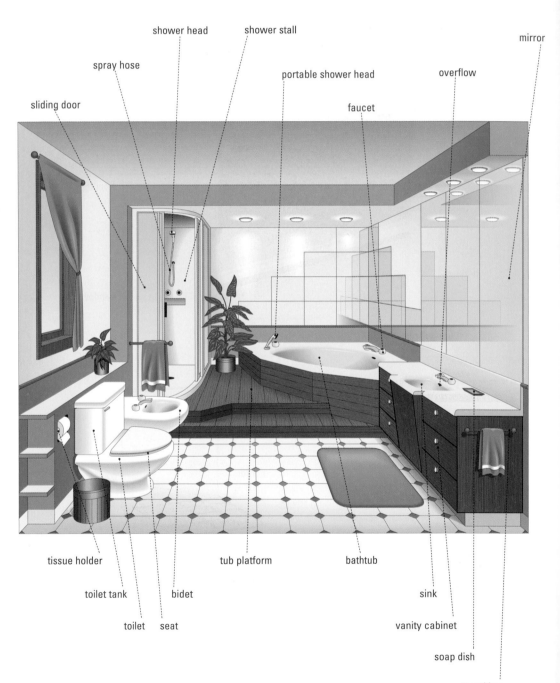

shower head

shower stall

mirror

spray hose

portable shower head

overflow

sliding door

faucet

tissue holder

tub platform

bathtub

toilet tank

bidet

sink

toilet   seat

vanity cabinet

soap dish

towel bar

Light and temperature conditions contribute to the comfort of a dwelling. Using different kinds of fixtures and lamps, lighting can be adapted to suit the purpose of any room. Heating, whether direct (as in the case of a fireplace) or indirect (as in a central system that sends heat to every room from a single point), is used to maintain a comfortable temperature.

LIGHTING

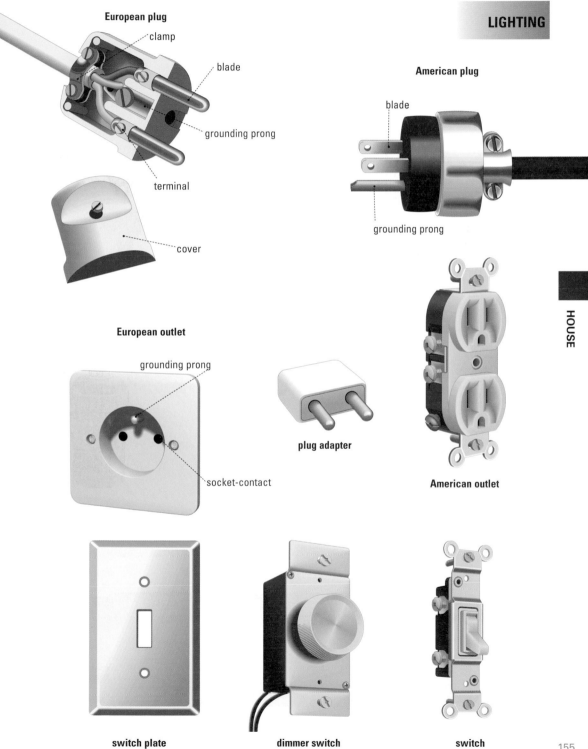

European plug

clamp

blade

grounding prong

terminal

cover

American plug

blade

grounding prong

European outlet

grounding prong

socket-contact

plug adapter

American outlet

switch plate

dimmer switch

switch

HOUSE

incandescent lightbulb

filament

inert gas

energy-saving bulb

bulb

fluorescent tube

tube retention clip

mounting plate

electronic ballast

housing

base

lead-in wire

base

bulb

bulb

screw base

bayonet base

lamp socket

fluorescent tube

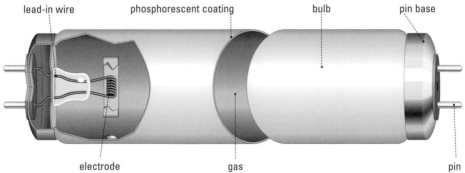

lead-in wire

phosphorescent coating

bulb

pin base

electrode

gas

pin

HOUSE

adjustable lamp

on-off switch

arm

shade

transformer

spot

track lighting

spring

hanging pendant

adjustable clamp

chandelier

ceiling fixture

clamp spotlight

desk lamp

shade

stand

base

floor lamp

post lantern

table lamp

HOUSE

HEATING

fire irons

fireplace

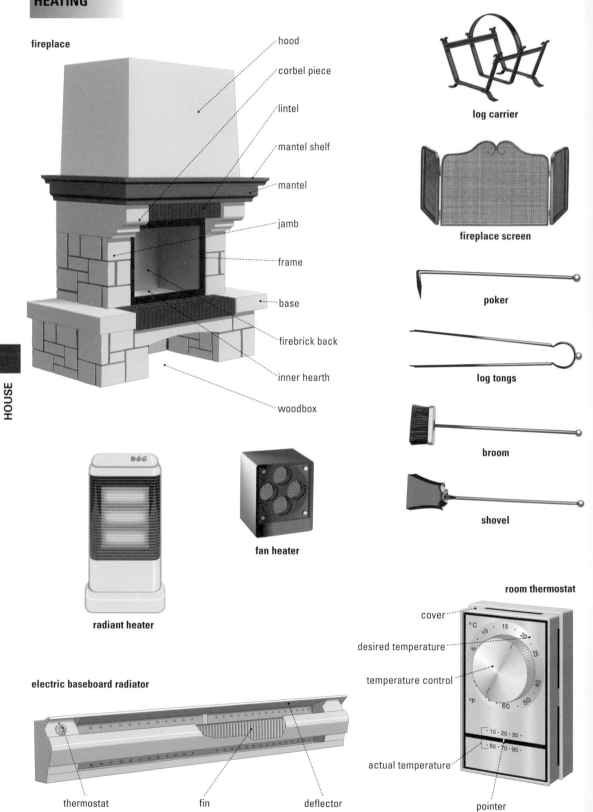

hood

corbel piece

lintel

mantel shelf

mantel

jamb

frame

base

firebrick back

inner hearth

woodbox

log carrier

fireplace screen

poker

log tongs

broom

shovel

fan heater

radiant heater

room thermostat

cover

desired temperature

temperature control

actual temperature

pointer

°C

°F

electric baseboard radiator

thermostat

fin

deflector

Until the invention of electricity, performing household tasks depended on human force. People swept, washed and dusted by hand. The earliest electrical appliances, the electric iron being the first, turned electricity into heat. With the invention of the motor, electricity could be turned into movement. This led to the development of a new generation of appliances like the clothes washer and dryer.

scouring pad

tea towel

pouring spout

handle

pail

brush

steam iron

mop

hand held vacuum cleaner

HOUSE

lid

handle

cylinder vacuum cleaner

upright vacuum cleaner

garbage can

dustpan

broom

HOUSE

washer

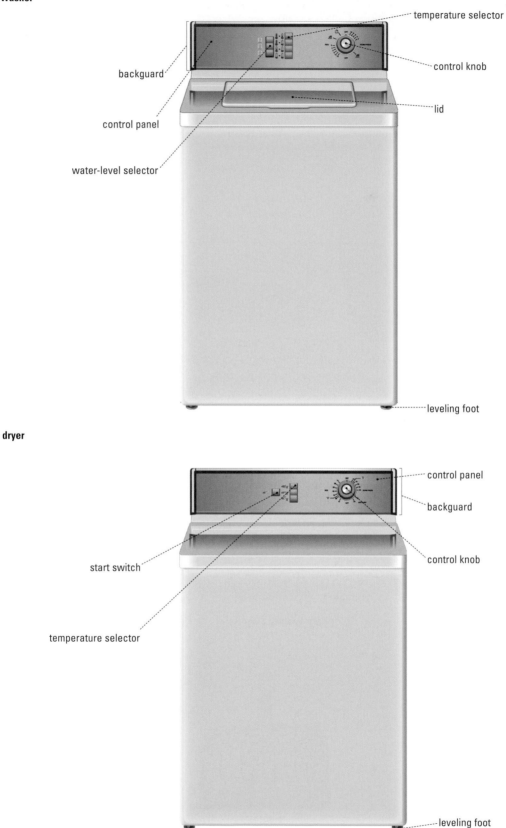

temperature selector

backguard

control knob

control panel

lid

water-level selector

leveling foot

dryer

control panel

backguard

start switch

control knob

temperature selector

leveling foot

Painting a room, changing a fuse or repairing a leaky faucet does not require the services of a professional. Any clever and inventive person can carry out these small manual tasks and become a devoted do-it-yourselfer. Even if the amateur handyperson can make do with whatever is at hand, selecting the right materials, using the correct method and having good tools makes the job easier.

CARPENTRY TOOLS

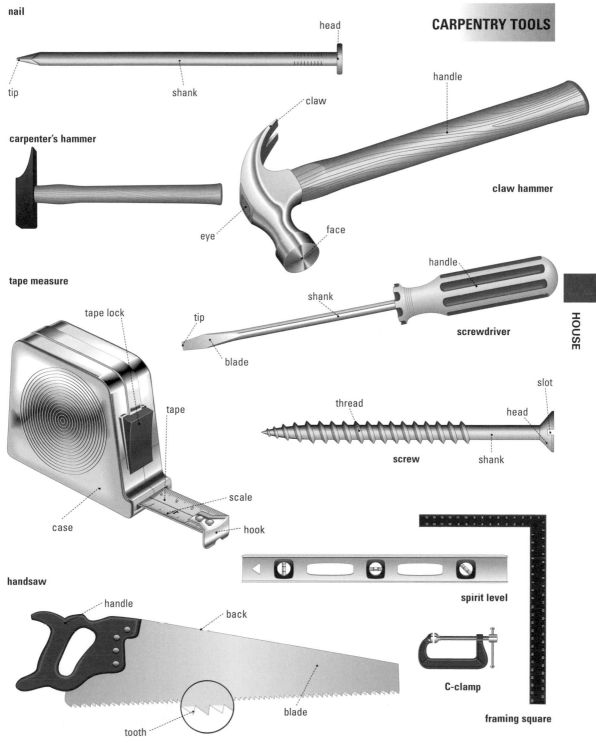

nail

head

tip

shank

carpenter's hammer

claw

handle

claw hammer

eye

face

tape measure

handle

shank

tip

blade

screwdriver

tape lock

thread

slot

head

tape

screw

shank

scale

case

hook

HOUSE

handsaw

handle

back

spirit level

C-clamp

blade

tooth

framing square

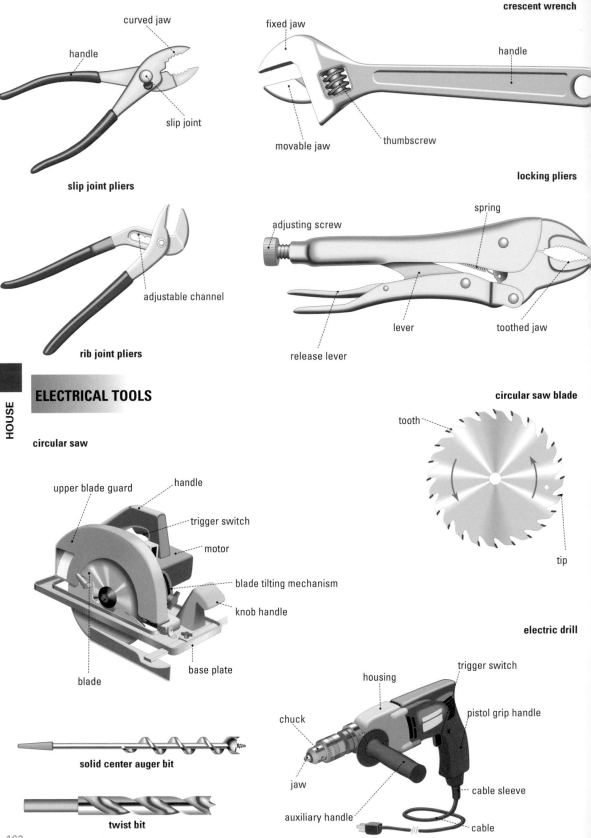

crescent wrench

curved jaw

handle

fixed jaw

handle

slip joint

movable jaw

thumbscrew

slip joint pliers

locking pliers

spring

adjusting screw

adjustable channel

lever

toothed jaw

rib joint pliers

release lever

ELECTRICAL TOOLS

circular saw blade

tooth

circular saw

upper blade guard

handle

trigger switch

motor

blade tilting mechanism

knob handle

tip

base plate

blade

electric drill

trigger switch

housing

pistol grip handle

chuck

solid center auger bit

jaw

twist bit

auxiliary handle

cable sleeve

cable

paint roller and tray

handle

roller frame

roller cover

handle

ferrule

bristles

brush

knurled bolt

blade

handle

scraper

extension ladder

rung

pulley

side rail

locking device

platform ladder

hoisting rope

antislip shoe

stepladder

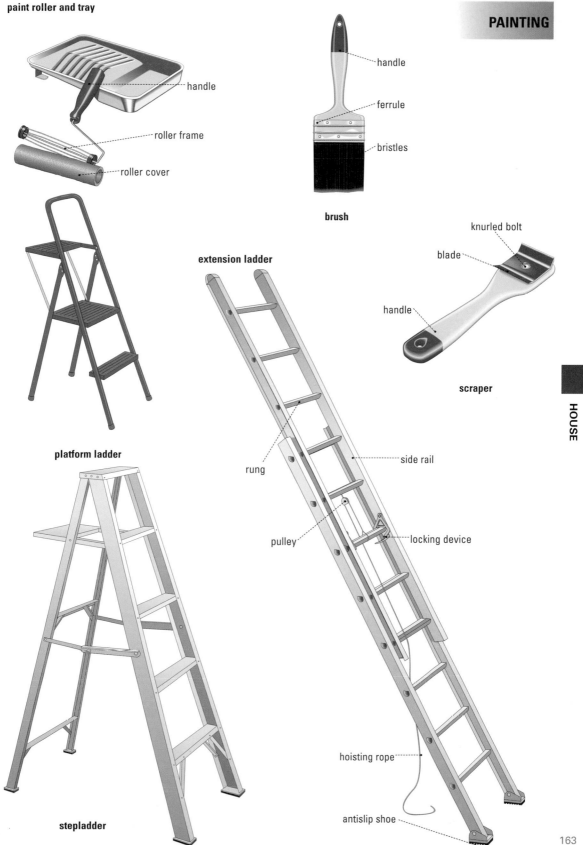

GARDENING

Whether cultivating an ornamental garden, growing a vegetable plot or arranging a modest flower box, gardening is an increasingly popular pastime. Gardens vary in appearance according to the gardener's tastes, the amount of space available and environmental conditions. A good knowledge of cultivated plants and a wise choice of tools help the gardener get the best out of his or her plot of land.

wheelbarrow

handle

tray

small hand cultivator

trowel

pruning shears

leg

wheel

weeder

hedge shears

sprayer

gardening gloves

shovel

lawn edger

spreader

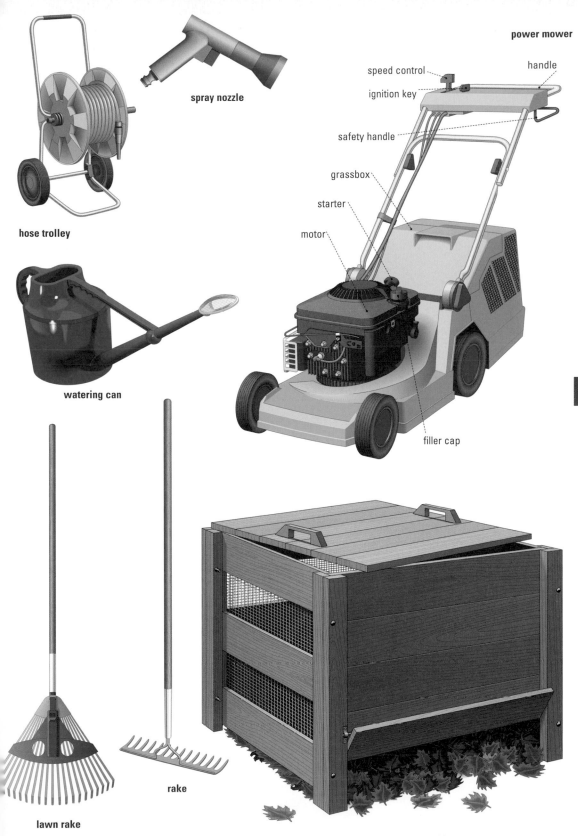

power mower

speed control

ignition key

handle

safety handle

grassbox

starter

motor

filler cap

spray nozzle

hose trolley

watering can

lawn rake

rake

compost bin

LABORATORY EQUIPMENT

Scientists working in laboratories use equipment specifically adapted for different types of experiments. Microbiologists use microscopes to observe the microorganisms that have developed in their Petri dishes. Chemists mix their materials in various kinds of measuring containers, like beakers, Erlenmeyer flasks and pipettes.

SCIENCE

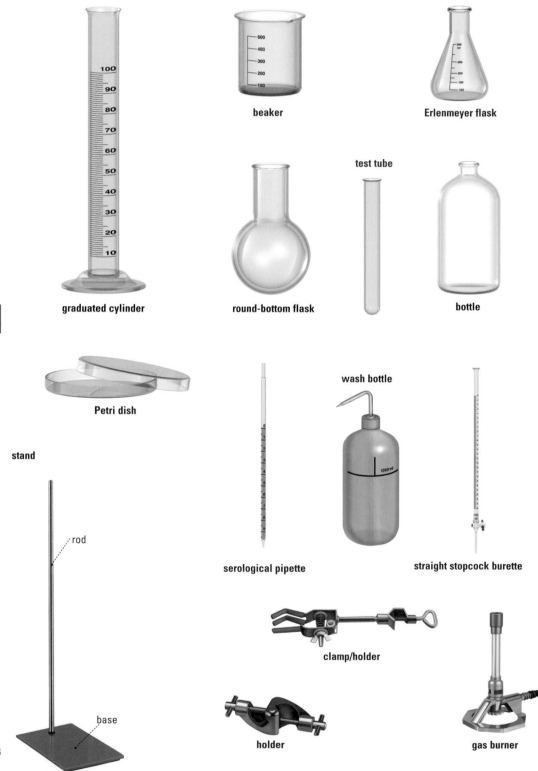

graduated cylinder

beaker

Erlenmeyer flask

round-bottom flask

test tube

bottle

Petri dish

stand

rod

base

serological pipette

wash bottle

straight stopcock burette

clamp/holder

holder

gas burner

MAGNIFYING GLASS AND MICROSCOPES

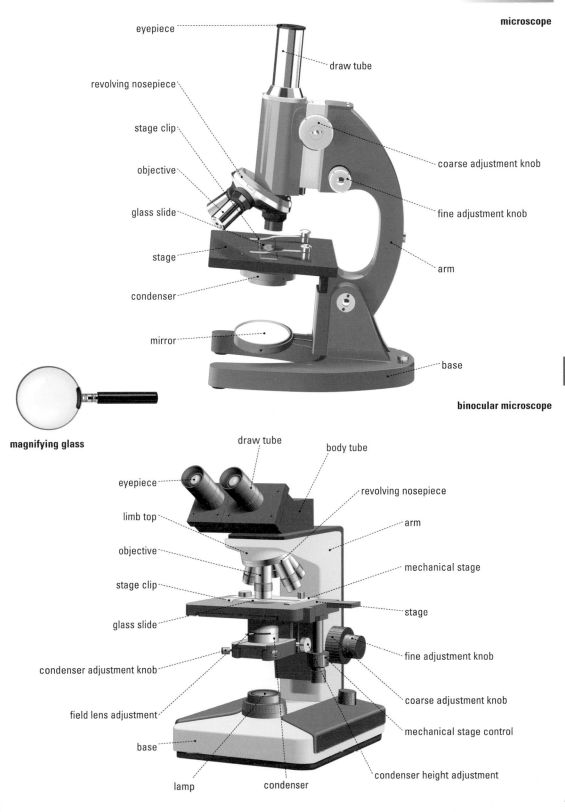

microscope

eyepiece

draw tube

revolving nosepiece

stage clip

objective

glass slide

stage

condenser

mirror

coarse adjustment knob

fine adjustment knob

arm

base

magnifying glass

binocular microscope

draw tube

body tube

eyepiece

revolving nosepiece

limb top

arm

objective

mechanical stage

stage clip

stage

glass slide

condenser adjustment knob

fine adjustment knob

coarse adjustment knob

field lens adjustment

mechanical stage control

base

condenser height adjustment

lamp

condenser

MEASURING DEVICES

From the beginning, people have invented different kinds of instruments to help them take measurements. The first instrument for measuring the passage of time, the sundial, goes back at least 3,000 years. In exact sciences like physics, chemistry and mathematics, precise measurements are extremely important. This need has resulted in the invention of a wide variety of measuring devices.

MEASUREMENT OF TIME

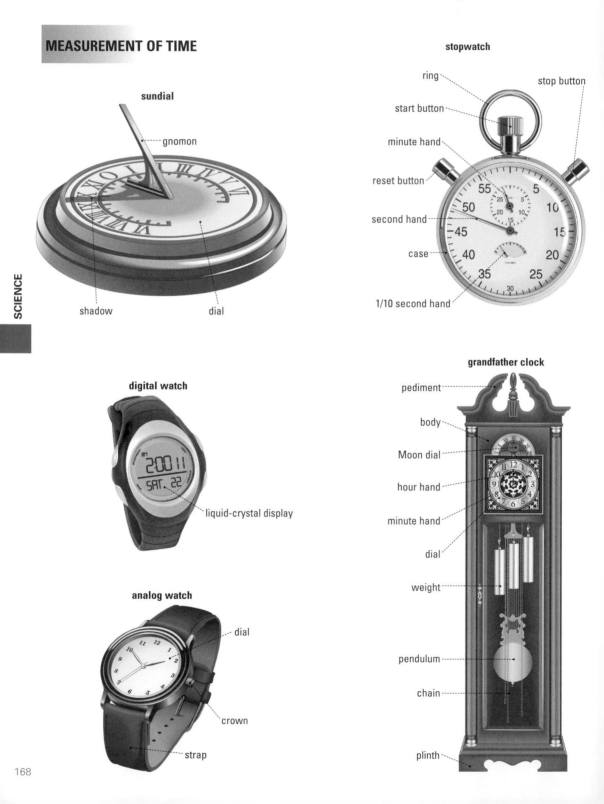

sundial

gnomon

shadow   dial

stopwatch

ring

stop button

start button

minute hand

reset button

second hand

case

55 5
50 25 5 10
20 10
45 15 15
40 20
35 25
30

1/10 second hand

digital watch

2:00 11
SAT. 22

liquid-crystal display

analog watch

dial

crown

strap

grandfather clock

pediment

body

Moon dial

hour hand

minute hand

dial

weight

pendulum

chain

plinth

mechanical watch

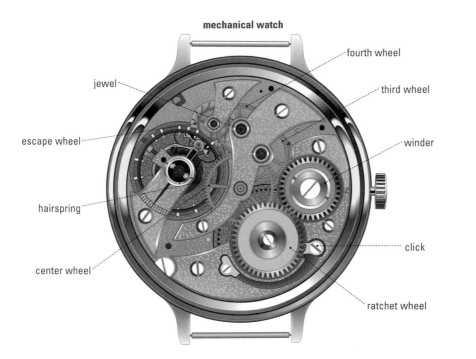

fourth wheel

jewel

third wheel

escape wheel

winder

hairspring

center wheel

click

ratchet wheel

MEASUREMENT OF TEMPERATURE

thermometer

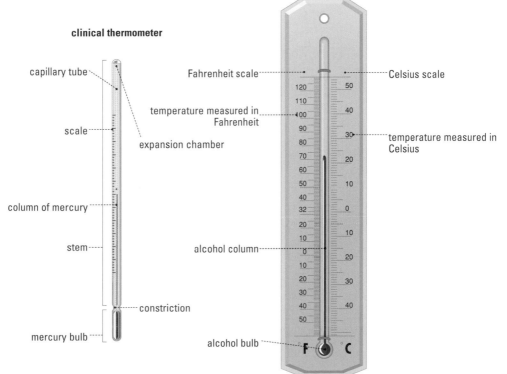

clinical thermometer

capillary tube

Fahrenheit scale

Celsius scale

temperature measured in Fahrenheit

scale

expansion chamber

temperature measured in Celsius

column of mercury

stem

alcohol column

constriction

mercury bulb

alcohol bulb

MEASUREMENT OF WEIGHT

steelyard

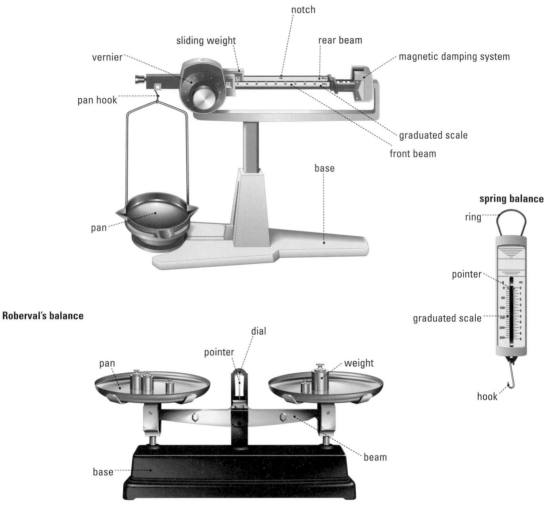

notch

sliding weight

vernier

rear beam

magnetic damping system

pan hook

graduated scale

front beam

pan

base

spring balance

ring

pointer

graduated scale

hook

Roberval's balance

dial

pointer

pan

weight

base

beam

SCIENCE

electronic scale

bathroom scale

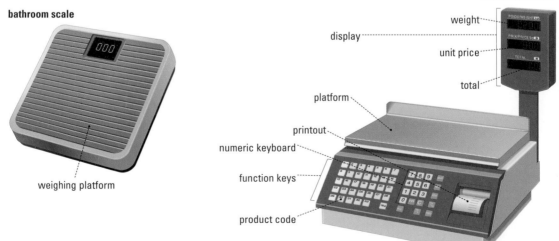

weight

display

unit price

total

platform

printout

numeric keyboard

function keys

weighing platform

product code

Geometry is a branch of mathematics that studies points, lines, surfaces such as circles or squares, and solids such as spheres and cubes. Geometry offers a variety of clever methods for measuring both two- and three-dimensional forms. By studying objects as they appear on flat planes as well as in space, geometry is at the heart of many disciplines, such as engineering and architecture.

GEOMETRICAL SHAPES

parts of a circle

examples of angles

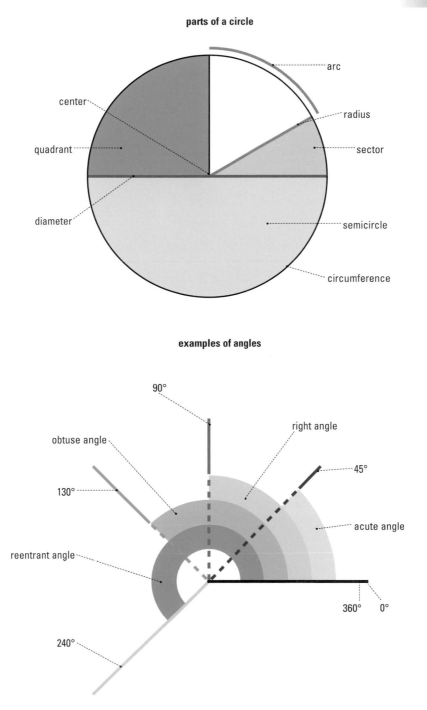

SCIENCE

SCIENCE

polygons

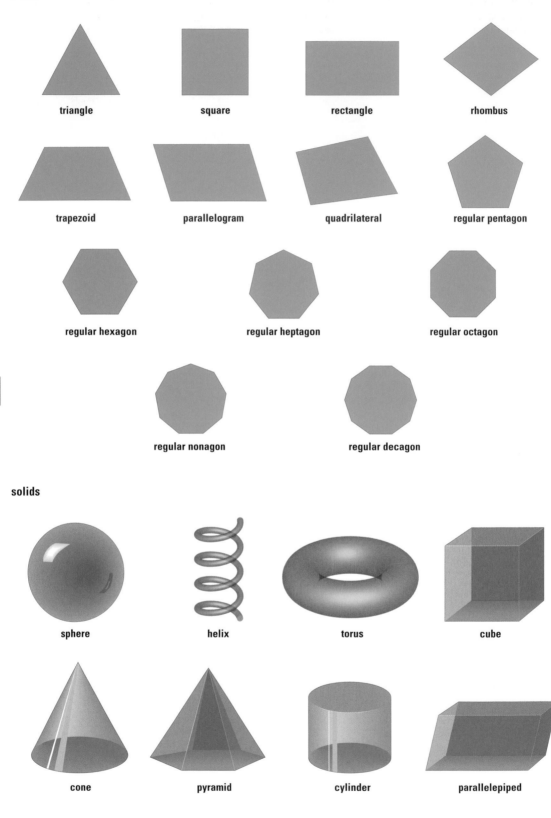

triangle

square

rectangle

rhombus

trapezoid

parallelogram

quadrilateral

regular pentagon

regular hexagon

regular heptagon

regular octagon

regular nonagon

regular decagon

solids

sphere

helix

torus

cube

cone

pyramid

cylinder

parallelepiped

Good or bad weather, our planet receives large amounts of energy from the Sun every day. Essential to life on Earth, solar energy can be captured by special cells and used to heat water and the insides of buildings. This never-ending and non-polluting source of energy can also be transformed into electricity with the help of solar cells.

SOLAR-CELL SYSTEM

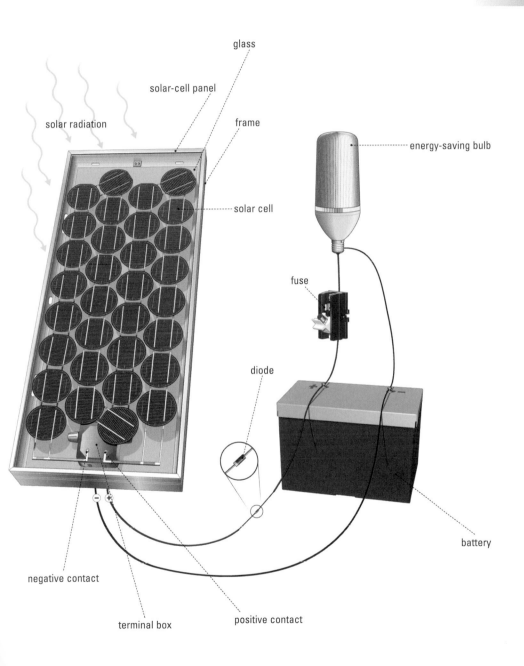

glass

solar-cell panel

solar radiation

frame

energy-saving bulb

solar cell

fuse

diode

negative contact

terminal box

positive contact

battery

ENERGY

HYDROELECTRICITY

Like everything in motion, running water possesses energy. Hydroelectric power stations transform water's energy into electricity. The water runs through several different types of dams, which collect it or build up its pressure. Arriving at the power station, the water is channeled into power turbines, which in turn drive machinery that produces an electrical current.

HYDROELECTRIC COMPLEX

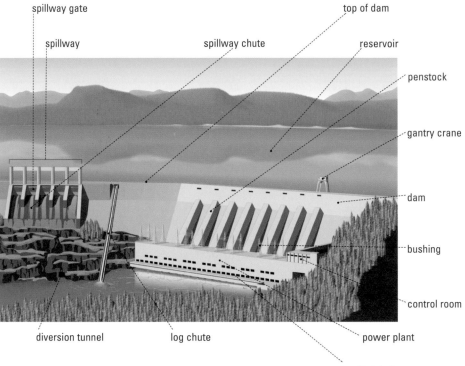

spillway gate

spillway

spillway chute

top of dam

reservoir

penstock

gantry crane

dam

bushing

control room

diversion tunnel

log chute

power plant

machine hall

examples of dams

embankment dam

gravity dam

arch dam

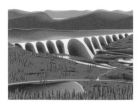

buttress dam

cross section of a hydroelectric power plant

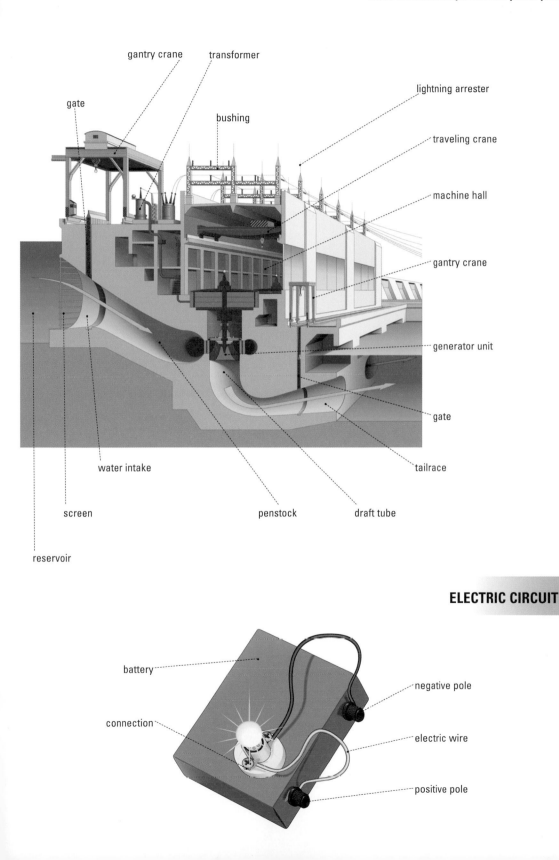

gantry crane

transformer

gate

bushing

lightning arrester

traveling crane

machine hall

gantry crane

generator unit

gate

tailrace

water intake

screen

penstock

draft tube

reservoir

ELECTRIC CIRCUIT

battery

connection

negative pole

electric wire

positive pole

ENERGY

STEPS IN PRODUCTION OF ELECTRICITY

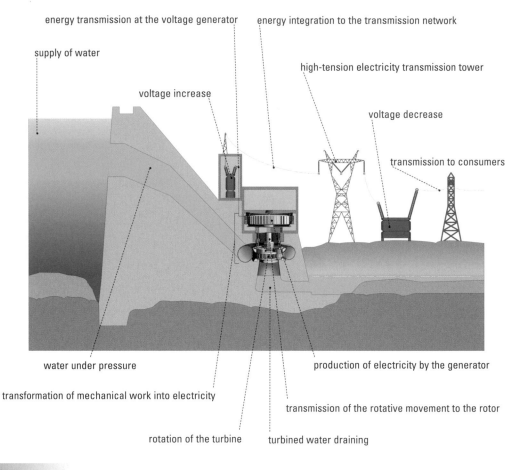

energy transmission at the voltage generator

energy integration to the transmission network

supply of water

high-tension electricity transmission tower

voltage increase

voltage decrease

transmission to consumers

water under pressure

production of electricity by the generator

transformation of mechanical work into electricity

transmission of the rotative movement to the rotor

rotation of the turbine

turbined water draining

ELECTRICITY TRANSMISSION

overhead connection

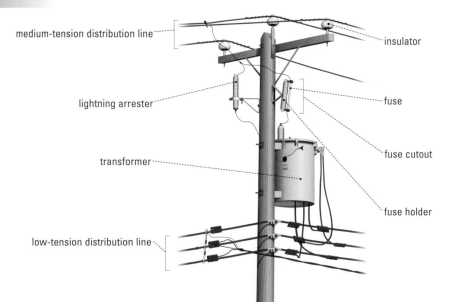

medium-tension distribution line

insulator

lightning arrester

fuse

transformer

fuse cutout

fuse holder

low-tension distribution line

Nuclear energy is produced by splitting apart the nucleus in certain atoms. The split nucleus of uranium, for example, releases an enormous amount of energy that can be transformed into electricity at a nuclear power station. These stations are equipped with safety devices to prevent dangerous radioactive substances from escaping into the environment.

NUCLEAR POWER PLANT

ENERGY

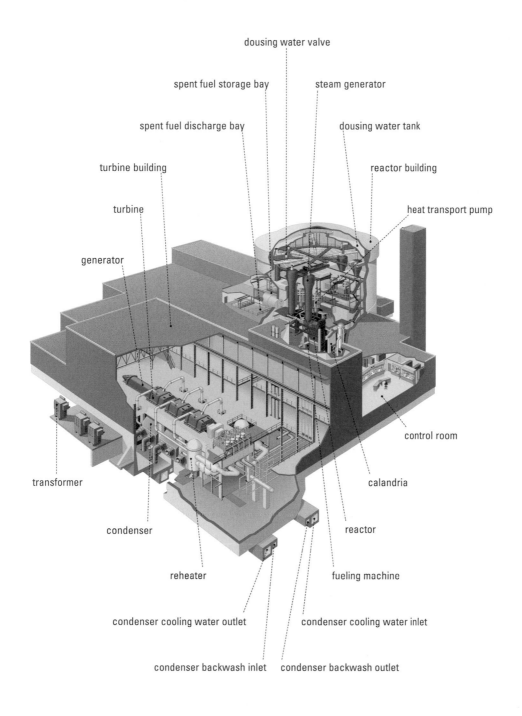

dousing water valve

spent fuel storage bay

steam generator

spent fuel discharge bay

dousing water tank

turbine building

reactor building

turbine

heat transport pump

generator

control room

transformer

calandria

condenser

reactor

reheater

fueling machine

condenser cooling water outlet

condenser cooling water inlet

condenser backwash inlet

condenser backwash outlet

PRODUCTION OF ELECTRICITY FROM NUCLEAR ENERGY

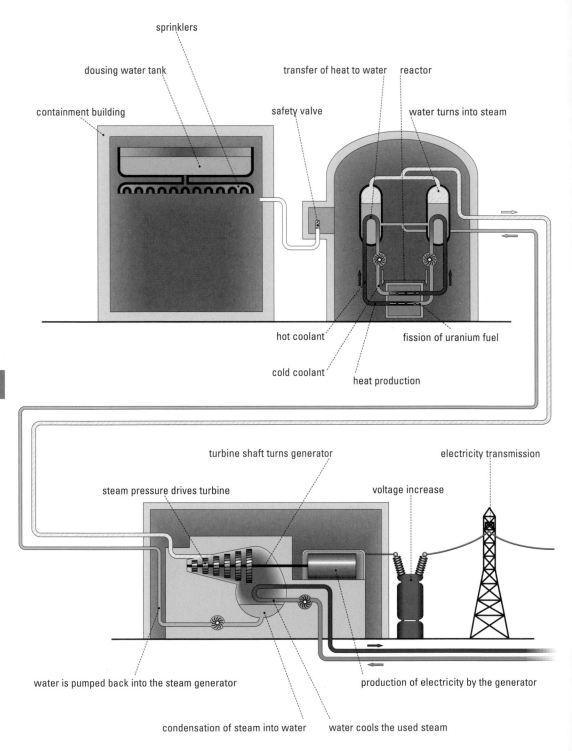

sprinklers

dousing water tank

transfer of heat to water   reactor

containment building

safety valve

water turns into steam

hot coolant

fission of uranium fuel

cold coolant

heat production

turbine shaft turns generator

electricity transmission

steam pressure drives turbine

voltage increase

water is pumped back into the steam generator

production of electricity by the generator

condensation of steam into water

water cools the used steam

Wind energy is also known as aeolian energy, after Aeolus, the Greek god of the winds. Long before motors were invented, wind was used to propel sailboats and to power windmills for grinding grain. For more than a century, this natural force has also been harnessed to help create electrical energy using turbines. Pushed by the wind, the blades of the turbine drive a generator that produces electricity.

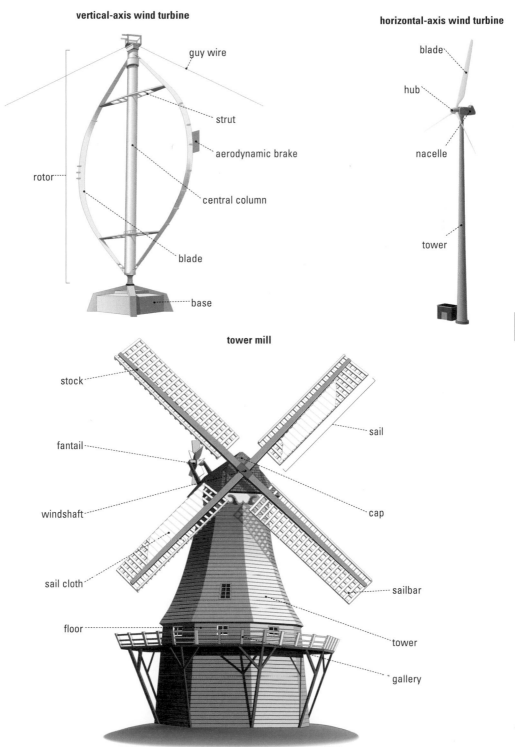

vertical-axis wind turbine

guy wire

strut

aerodynamic brake

rotor

central column

blade

base

horizontal-axis wind turbine

blade

hub

nacelle

tower

tower mill

stock

fantail

windshaft

sail cloth

floor

sail

cap

sailbar

tower

gallery

ENERGY

Oil, coal and natural gas originate in the residue of partially fossilized organisms that lived millions of years ago. These combustible fossils are found in limited quantities underground. Refining allows crude oil to be turned into more than 500 different consumer products. One of the most valuable, gasoline, is used to fuel engines, giving crude oil the nickname "black gold."

OIL

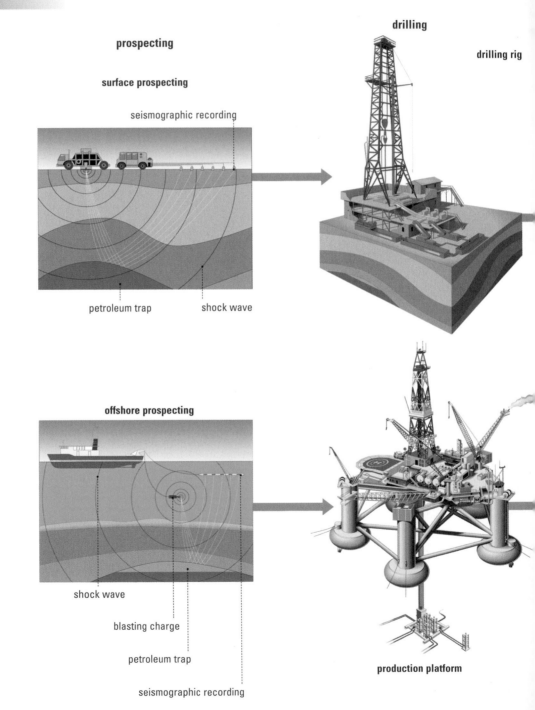

prospecting

surface prospecting

seismographic recording

petroleum trap

shock wave

drilling

drilling rig

offshore prospecting

shock wave

blasting charge

petroleum trap

seismographic recording

production platform

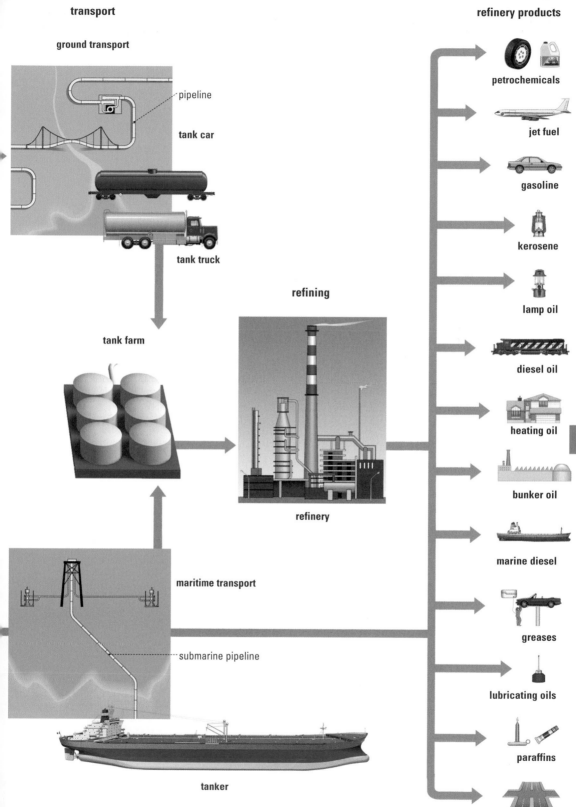

transport

ground transport

pipeline

tank car

tank truck

tank farm

refining

refinery

maritime transport

submarine pipeline

tanker

refinery products

petrochemicals

jet fuel

gasoline

kerosene

lamp oil

diesel oil

heating oil

bunker oil

marine diesel

greases

lubricating oils

paraffins

asphalt

ENERGY

By leading to the creation of the bicycle, which was followed by the motorcycle and the automobile, the invention of the wheel allowed people to travel farther and faster than they ever had before. The automobile has never stopped growing in popularity since its arrival in the 19th century. The millions of motor vehicles used today has led to an ever-growing system of roads, designed to handle the increased traffic.

ROAD SYSTEM

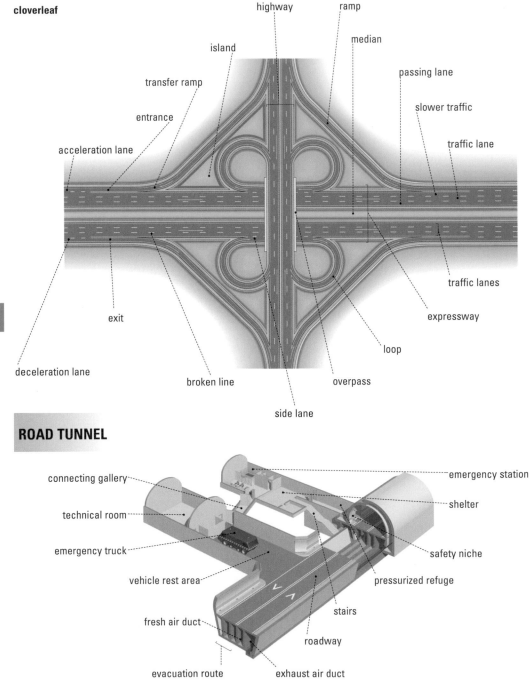

cloverleaf

highway

ramp

median

island

passing lane

transfer ramp

slower traffic

entrance

acceleration lane

traffic lane

exit

traffic lanes

expressway

deceleration lane

loop

broken line

overpass

side lane

ROAD TUNNEL

connecting gallery

emergency station

technical room

shelter

emergency truck

safety niche

vehicle rest area

pressurized refuge

fresh air duct

stairs

roadway

evacuation route

exhaust air duct

FIXED BRIDGES

suspension bridge

suspender

anchorage block

suspension cable

tower

approach ramp

abutment

foundation of tower

deck

center span

side span

beam bridge

arch bridge

cable-stayed bridge

cantilever bridge

MOVABLE BRIDGES

swing bridge

turntable

floating bridge

double-leaf bascule bridge

manrope

pontoon

AUTOMOBILE

body

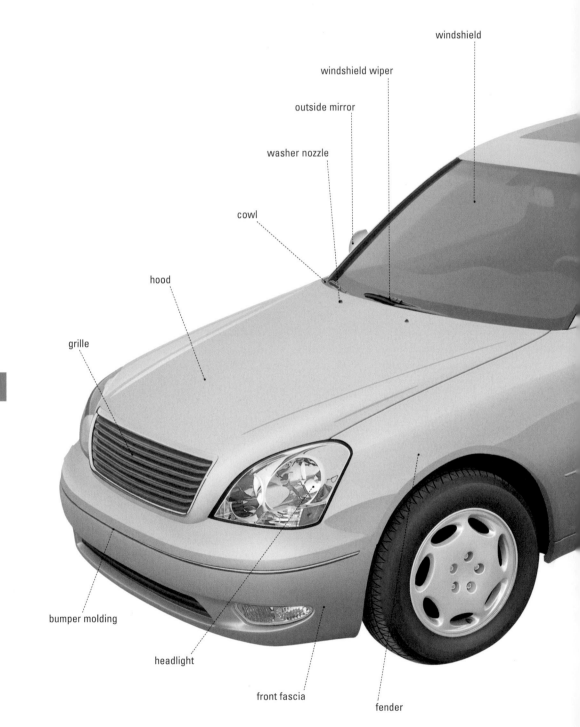

windshield

windshield wiper

outside mirror

washer nozzle

cowl

hood

grille

headlight

bumper molding

front fascia

fender

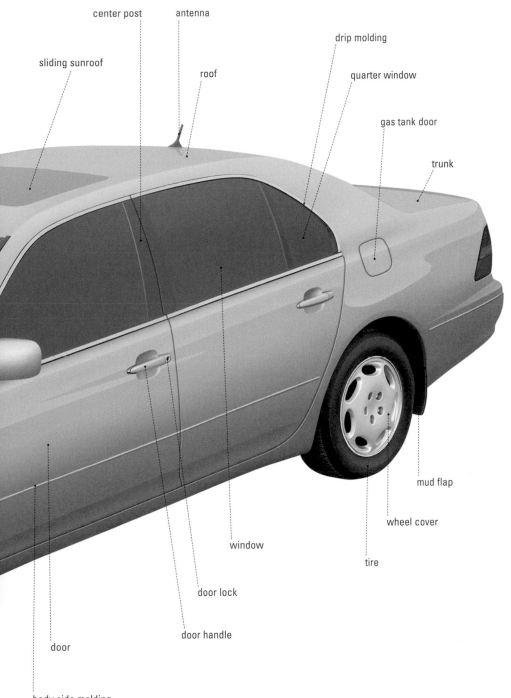

center post

antenna

drip molding

sliding sunroof

roof

quarter window

gas tank door

trunk

sliding sunroof

gas tank door

trunk

mud flap

wheel cover

window

tire

door lock

door handle

door

body side molding

examples of bodies

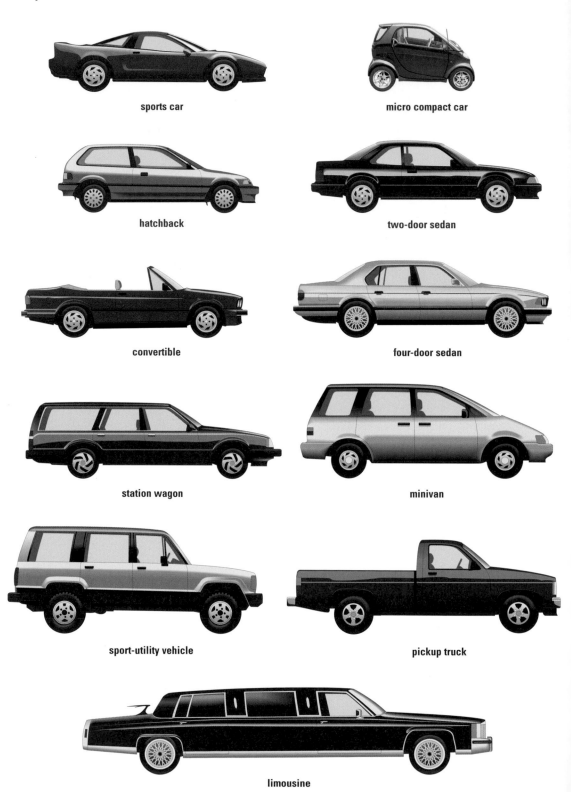

sports car

micro compact car

hatchback

two-door sedan

convertible

four-door sedan

station wagon

minivan

sport-utility vehicle

pickup truck

limousine

headlights

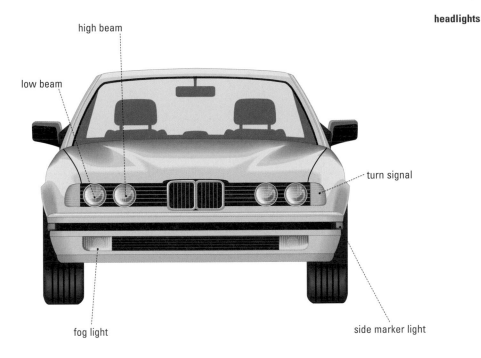

high beam

low beam

turn signal

fog light

side marker light

taillights

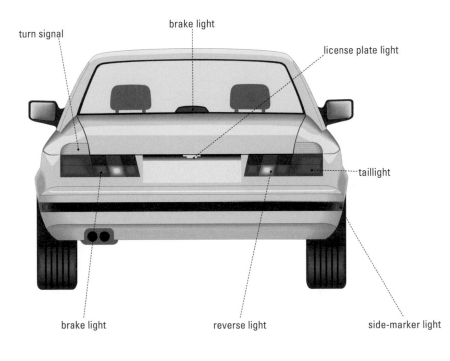

brake light

turn signal

license plate light

taillight

brake light

reverse light

side-marker light

dashboard

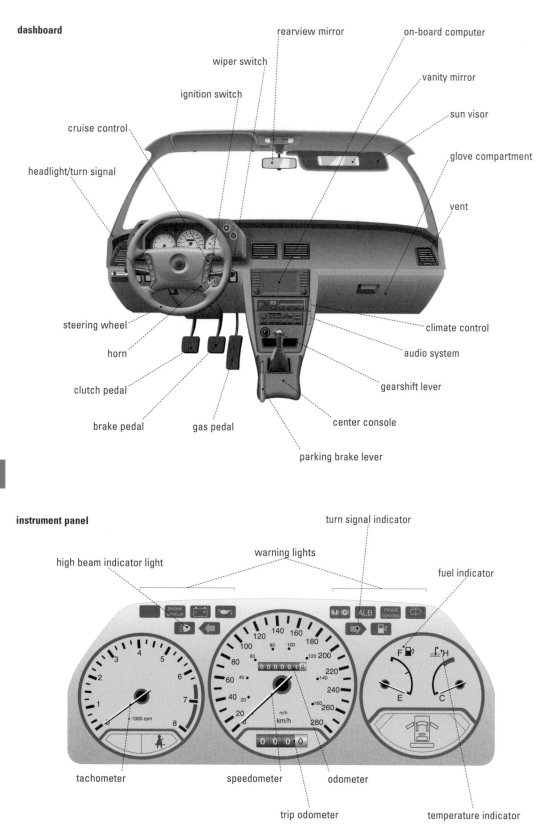

rearview mirror

on-board computer

wiper switch

vanity mirror

ignition switch

sun visor

cruise control

glove compartment

headlight/turn signal

vent

steering wheel

climate control

horn

audio system

clutch pedal

gearshift lever

brake pedal

gas pedal

center console

parking brake lever

instrument panel

turn signal indicator

warning lights

high beam indicator light

fuel indicator

tachometer

speedometer

odometer

temperature indicator

trip odometer

CARAVANS

roof

screen door

canopy

window

bunk

spare tire

stabilizer jack

body

tent trailer

luggage rack

air conditioner

ladder

motor home

trailer

BUSES

school bus

double-decker bus

city bus

minibus

coach

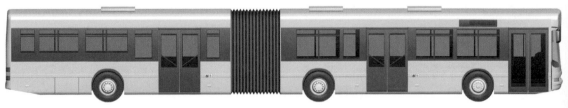

articulated bus

MOTORCYCLE

protective helmet

bubble

visor

chin protector

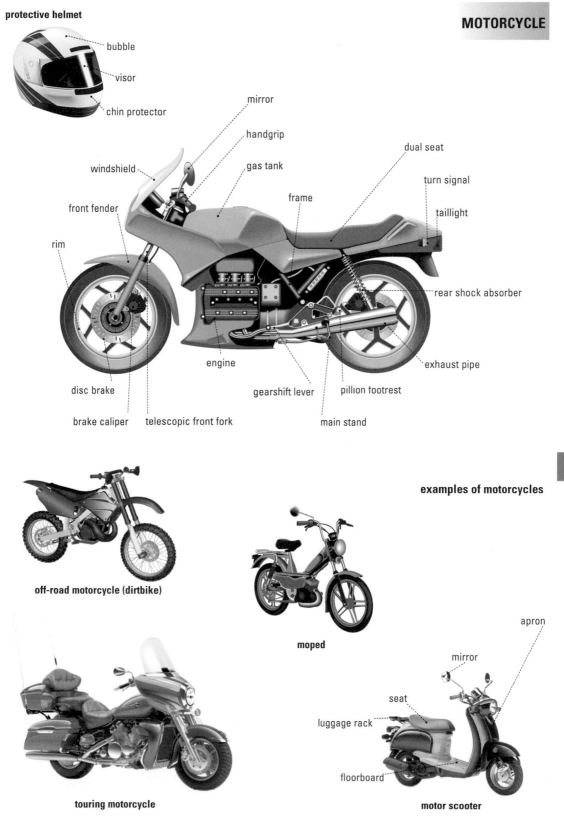

mirror

handgrip

dual seat

gas tank

turn signal

windshield

frame

taillight

front fender

rim

rear shock absorber

engine

exhaust pipe

disc brake

gearshift lever

pillion footrest

brake caliper

telescopic front fork

main stand

examples of motorcycles

off-road motorcycle (dirtbike)

moped

apron

mirror

seat

luggage rack

floorboard

touring motorcycle

motor scooter

191

TRUCKING

truck tractor

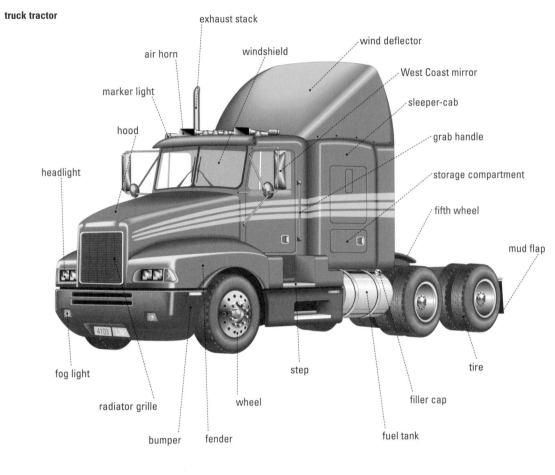

exhaust stack

air horn

windshield

wind deflector

West Coast mirror

marker light

sleeper-cab

hood

grab handle

headlight

storage compartment

fifth wheel

mud flap

fog light

tire

radiator grille

wheel

step

bumper

fender

filler cap

fuel tank

examples of trucks

cesspit emptier

dump truck

detachable body

truck tractor

semitrailer

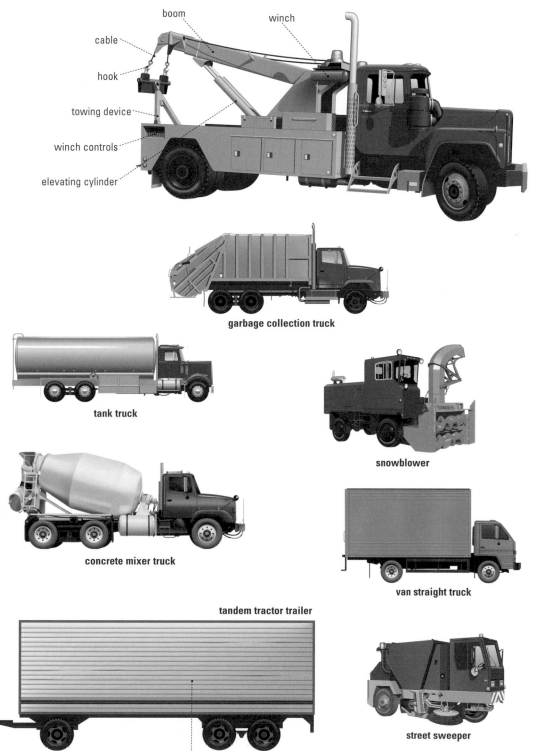

tow truck

boom

winch

cable

hook

towing device

winch controls

elevating cylinder

garbage collection truck

tank truck

snowblower

concrete mixer truck

van straight truck

tandem tractor trailer

street sweeper

truck trailer

BICYCLE

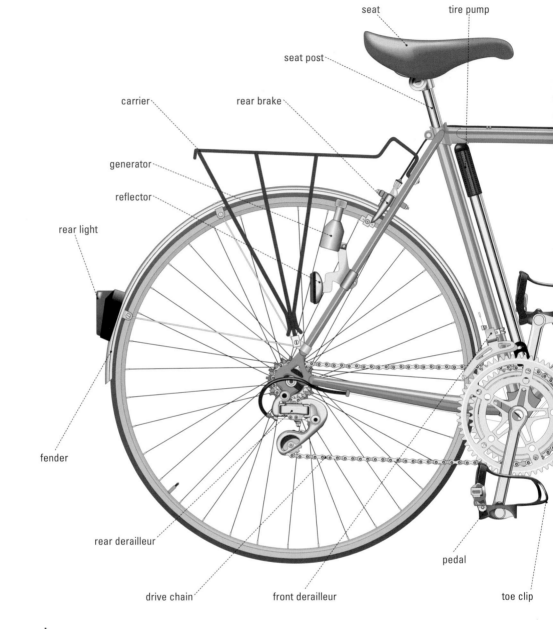

seat

tire pump

seat post

carrier

rear brake

generator

reflector

rear light

fender

rear derailleur

drive chain

front derailleur

pedal

toe clip

accessories

child carrier

protective helmet

lock

bicycle bag (pannier)

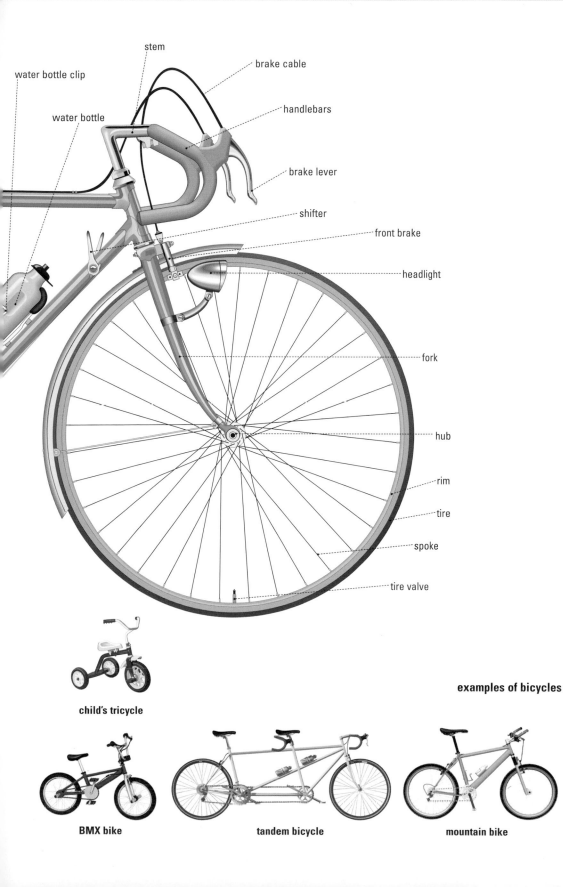

stem

brake cable

water bottle clip

handlebars

water bottle

brake lever

shifter

front brake

headlight

fork

hub

rim

tire

spoke

tire valve

child's tricycle

examples of bicycles

BMX bike

tandem bicycle

mountain bike

Railways were the most popular form of transportation in the 19th century. Even today, many travelers still prefer the train to the car or airplane. High-performance high-speed trains carry passengers at more than 180 mph (300 km/h) throughout Europe, America and Asia. In urban settings, however, rail transportation most often takes the form of subways and streetcars.

PASSENGER TRAIN

diesel-electric locomotive

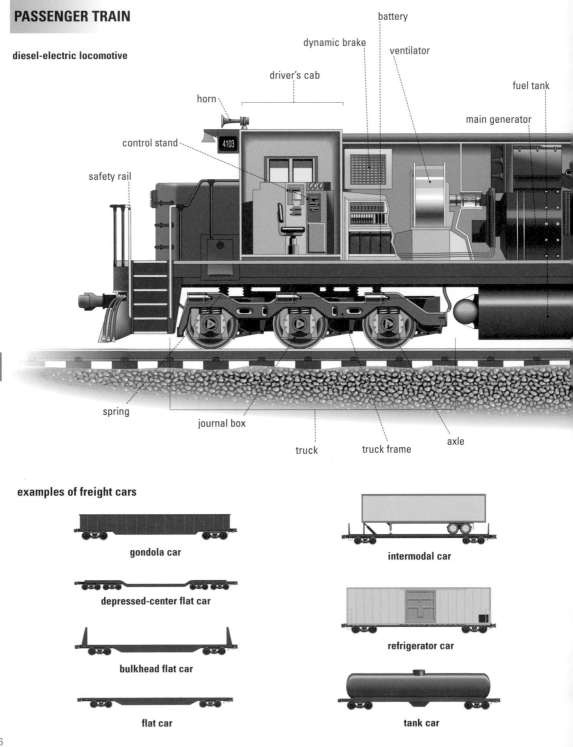

battery

dynamic brake

ventilator

driver's cab

fuel tank

horn

main generator

control stand

safety rail

4103

spring

journal box

truck

truck frame

axle

examples of freight cars

gondola car

intermodal car

depressed-center flat car

refrigerator car

bulkhead flat car

flat car

tank car

TRANSPORTATION AND HEAVY MACHINERY

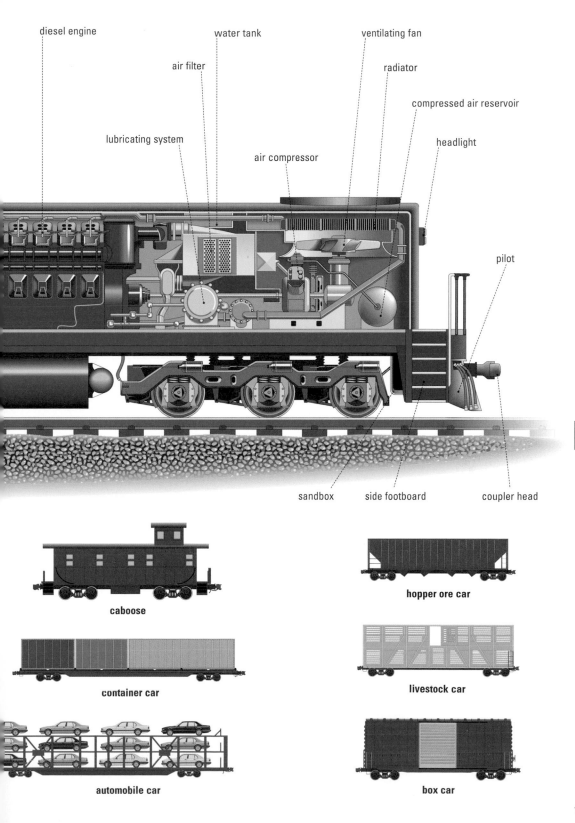

diesel engine

water tank

ventilating fan

air filter

radiator

compressed air reservoir

lubricating system

headlight

air compressor

pilot

sandbox

side footboard

coupler head

caboose

hopper ore car

container car

livestock car

automobile car

box car

high-speed train

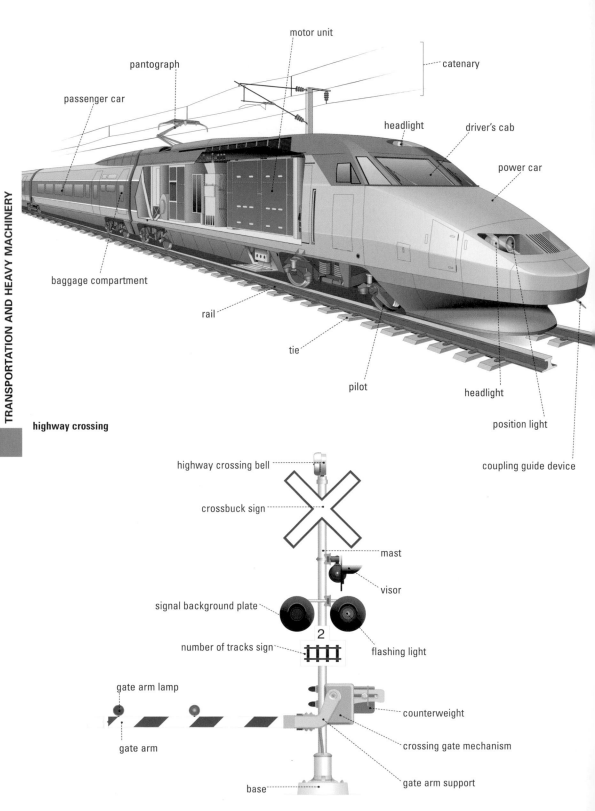

motor unit

pantograph

catenary

passenger car

headlight

driver's cab

power car

baggage compartment

rail

tie

pilot

headlight

position light

coupling guide device

highway crossing

highway crossing bell

crossbuck sign

mast

visor

signal background plate

flashing light

number of tracks sign

2

gate arm lamp

counterweight

gate arm

crossing gate mechanism

base

gate arm support

passenger car

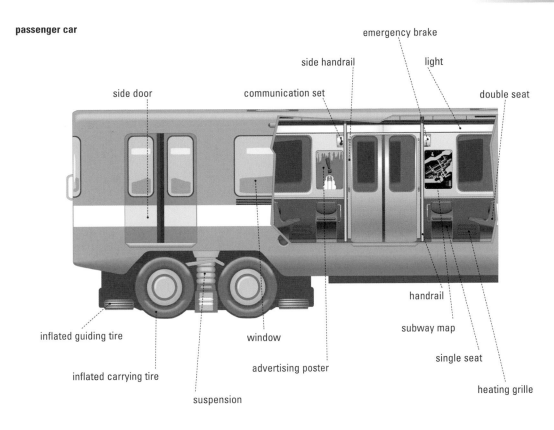

emergency brake

side handrail

light

side door

communication set

double seat

inflated guiding tire

window

handrail

inflated carrying tire

advertising poster

subway map

single seat

suspension

heating grille

subway train

motor car

trailer car

motor car

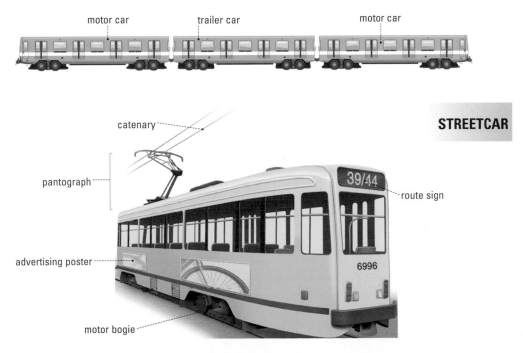

catenary

pantograph

route sign

advertising poster

motor bogie

MARITIME TRANSPORT

Next to the donkey and camel, boats are the oldest form of transportation. By the 14th century, the possibility of trade with unknown lands led to the development of large and efficient sailing ships. By the 19th century, the arrival of immense steamships freed sailors from a dependence on unreliable wind power. Today the world's sea-lanes are mainly used to transport merchandise at low cost.

HARBOR

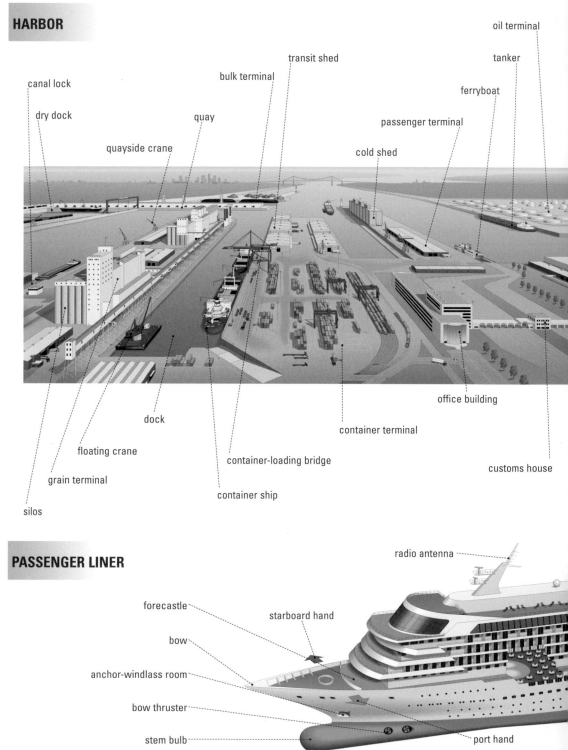

oil terminal

tanker

ferryboat

transit shed

bulk terminal

passenger terminal

canal lock

cold shed

dry dock

quay

quayside crane

office building

container terminal

dock

customs house

floating crane

container-loading bridge

grain terminal

container ship

silos

PASSENGER LINER

radio antenna

forecastle

starboard hand

bow

anchor-windlass room

bow thruster

stem bulb

port hand

FOUR-MASTED BARK

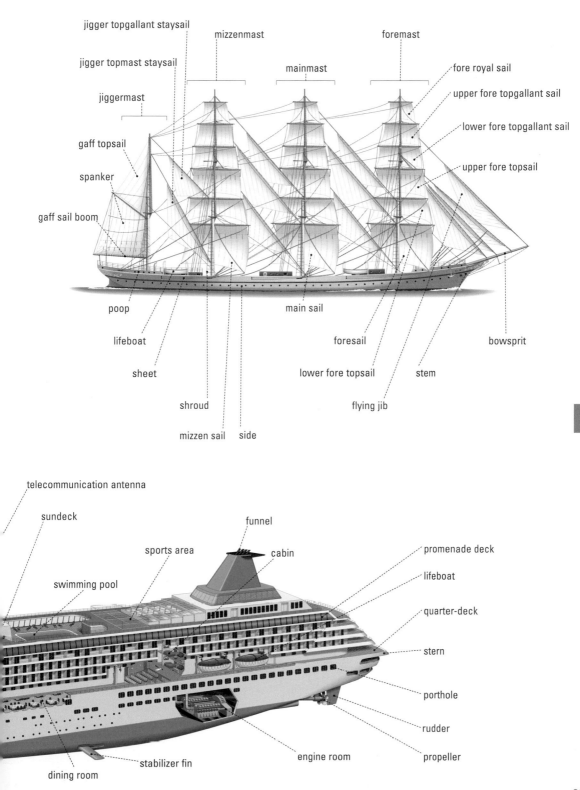

jigger topgallant staysail

jigger topmast staysail

jiggermast

gaff topsail

spanker

gaff sail boom

mizzenmast

mainmast

foremast

fore royal sail

upper fore topgallant sail

lower fore topgallant sail

upper fore topsail

poop

lifeboat

sheet

shroud

mizzen sail   side

main sail

foresail

lower fore topsail

flying jib

stem

bowsprit

telecommunication antenna

sundeck

sports area

swimming pool

funnel

cabin

promenade deck

lifeboat

quarter-deck

stern

porthole

rudder

dining room

stabilizer fin

engine room

propeller

EXAMPLES OF BOATS AND SHIPS

TRANSPORTATION AND HEAVY MACHINERY

speedboat

motor yacht

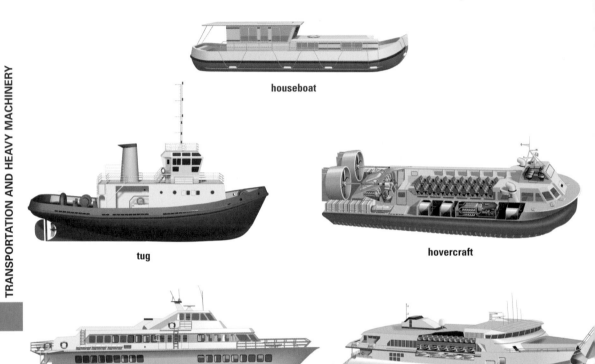

houseboat

tug

hovercraft

hydrofoil boat

catamaran ferryboat

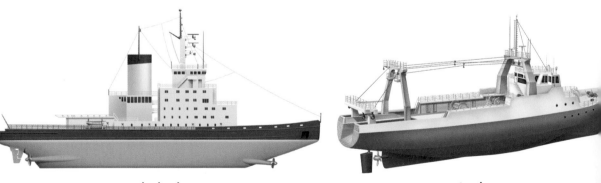

ice breaker

trawler

Before the invention of the helicopter and airplane, the train and boat were the only practical means of traveling long distances. In the 1950s, the jet airplane revolutionized air travel by offering flights that could transport passengers over long distances in a short amount of time. Helicopters are particularly useful in rescue operations because of their ability to take off and land in places inaccessible to airplanes.

HELICOPTER

TRANSPORTATION AND HEAVY MACHINERY

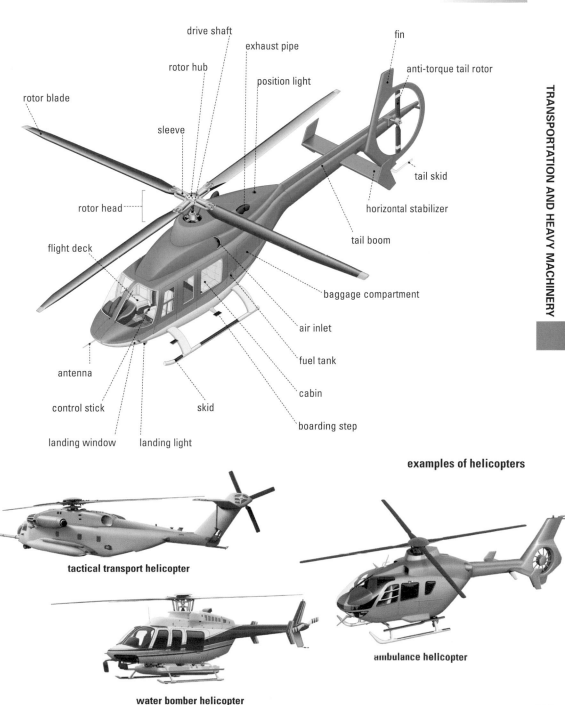

drive shaft

exhaust pipe

fin

rotor hub

anti-torque tail rotor

position light

rotor blade

sleeve

tail skid

rotor head

horizontal stabilizer

flight deck

tail boom

baggage compartment

air inlet

antenna

fuel tank

control stick

skid

cabin

landing window

landing light

boarding step

examples of helicopters

tactical transport helicopter

ambulance helicopter

water bomber helicopter

AIRPORT

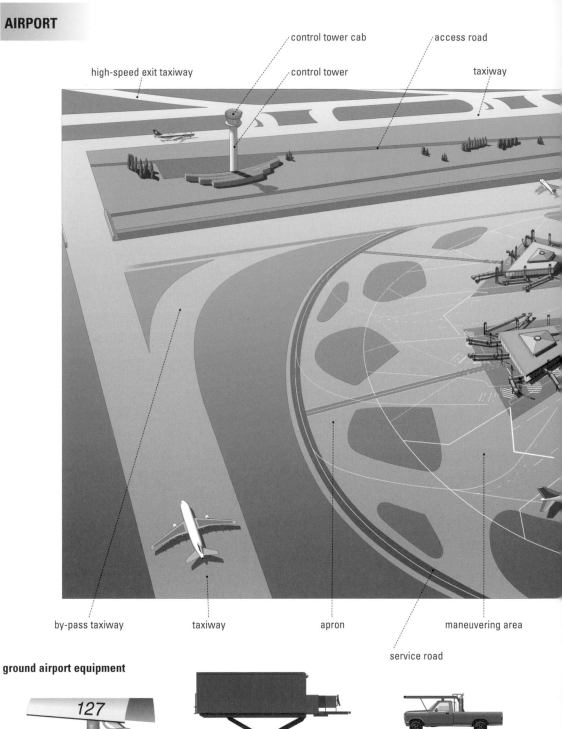

control tower cab

access road

high-speed exit taxiway

control tower

taxiway

by-pass taxiway

taxiway

apron

maneuvering area

service road

ground airport equipment

127

wheel chock

catering vehicle

aircraft maintenance truck

tow bar

passenger terminal

boarding walkway

maintenance hangar

parking area

radial passenger-loading area

telescopic corridor

service area

taxiway line

jet refueler

tow tractor

baggage conveyor

baggage trailer

tow tractor

container/pallet loader

AIRPLANES

examples of wing shapes

tapered wing

delta wing

variable geometry wing

straight wing

swept-back wing

long-range jet

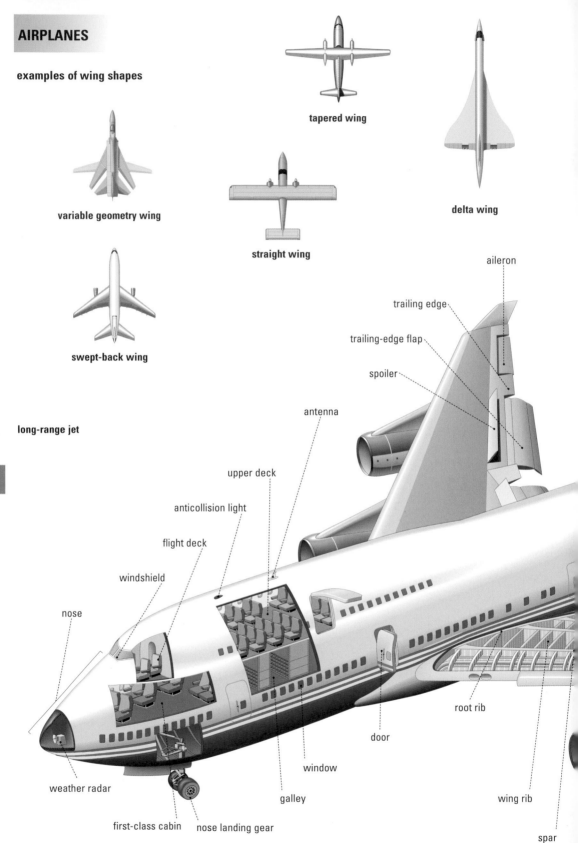

aileron

trailing edge

trailing-edge flap

spoiler

antenna

upper deck

anticollision light

flight deck

windshield

nose

root rib

door

weather radar

window

wing rib

first-class cabin

nose landing gear

galley

spar

examples of tail shapes

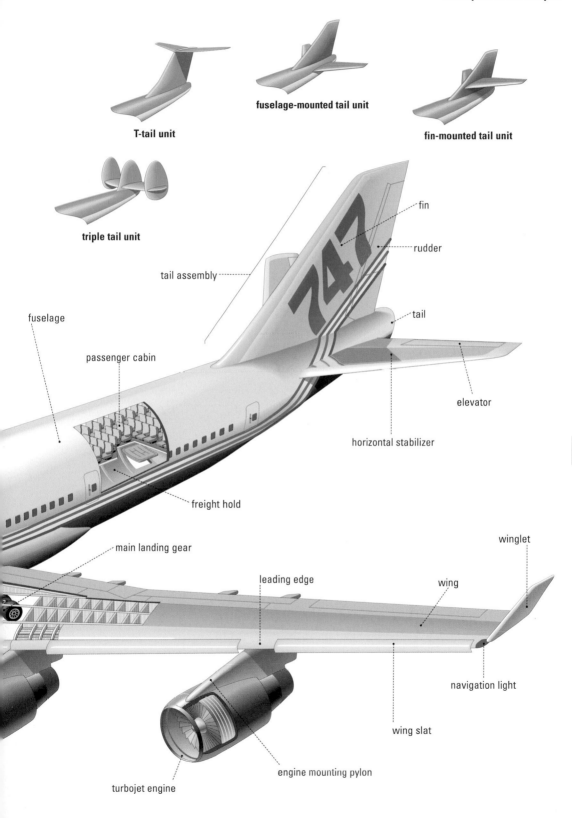

T-tail unit

fuselage-mounted tail unit

fin-mounted tail unit

triple tail unit

fin

rudder

tail assembly

tail

fuselage

elevator

passenger cabin

horizontal stabilizer

freight hold

main landing gear

winglet

leading edge

wing

navigation light

wing slat

engine mounting pylon

turbojet engine

examples of airplanes

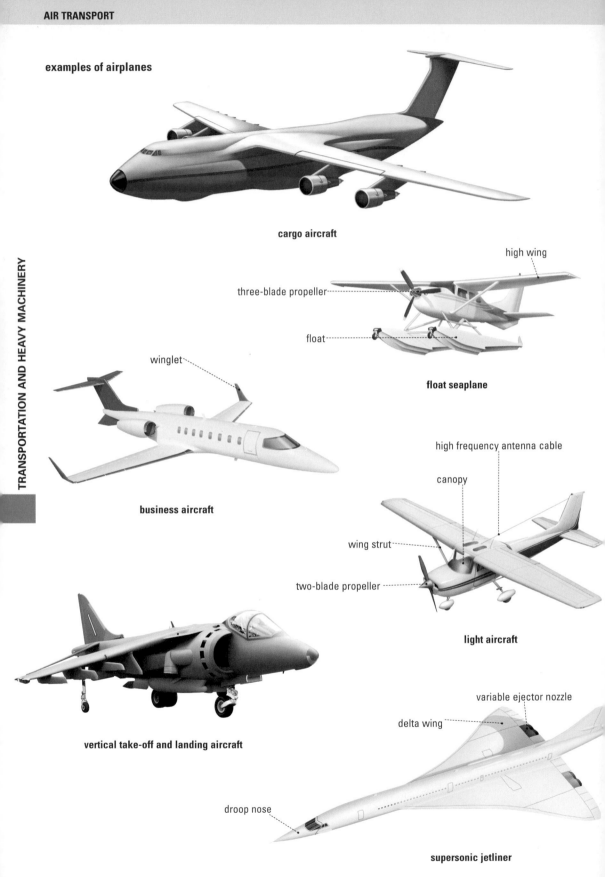

cargo aircraft

high wing

three-blade propeller

float

float seaplane

winglet

business aircraft

high frequency antenna cable

canopy

wing strut

two-blade propeller

light aircraft

vertical take-off and landing aircraft

variable ejector nozzle

delta wing

droop nose

supersonic jetliner

Heavy machinery is a separate category of motor vehicle. Although rarely driven on roads and highways, these vehicles dominate construction sites, quarries and mines. They are often equipped with caterpillar treads, which allow them to move effort- lessly over uneven terrain. Their heavy weight and powerful engines make it possible for them to dig deep into the ground or to move large loads of material from one spot to another.

wheel loader

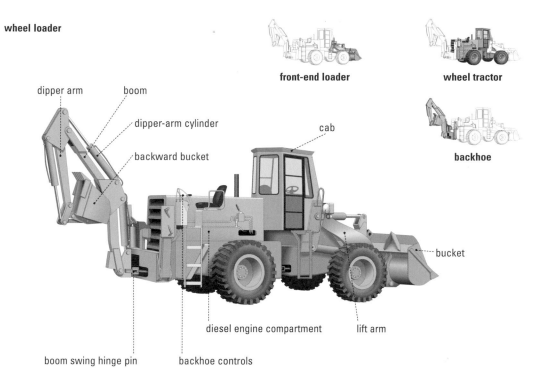

front-end loader

wheel tractor

backhoe

dipper arm

boom

dipper-arm cylinder

cab

backward bucket

bucket

diesel engine compartment

lift arm

boom swing hinge pin

backhoe controls

hydraulic shovel

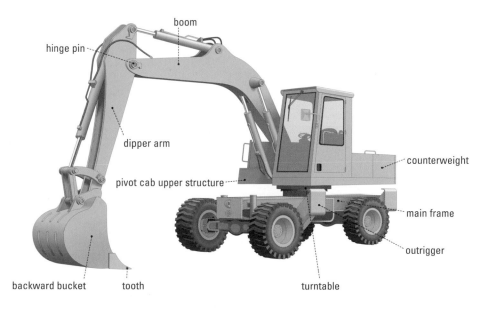

boom

hinge pin

dipper arm

counterweight

pivot cab upper structure

main frame

outrigger

backward bucket

tooth

turntable

bulldozer

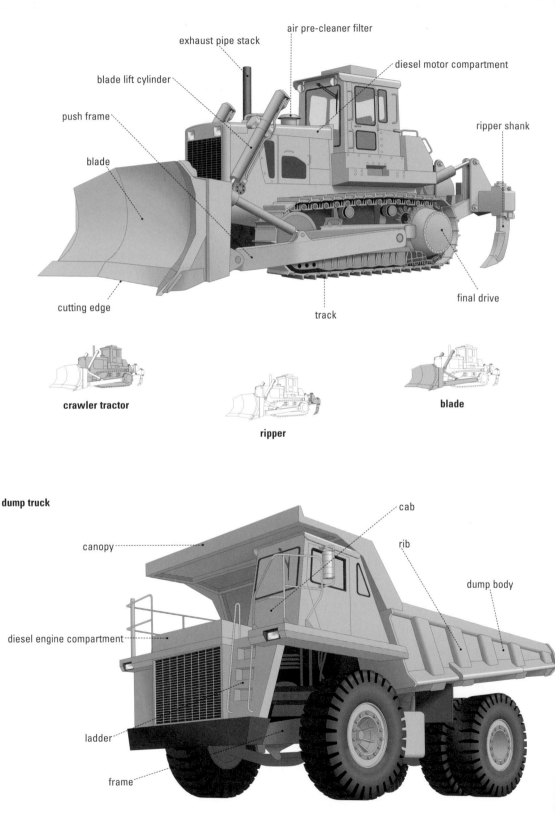

exhaust pipe stack

air pre-cleaner filter

diesel motor compartment

blade lift cylinder

push frame

ripper shank

blade

cutting edge

final drive

track

crawler tractor

ripper

blade

dump truck

cab

canopy

rib

dump body

diesel engine compartment

ladder

frame

Today the term "fine arts" is reserved for graphic and visual arts. Since the beginning of civilization, people have translated their feelings and perceptions of the world into art, for example, by painting or sculpting. Artists have a wide range of materials and techniques to choose from, and their choices give their work a highly personal style.

PAINTING AND DRAWING

color circle

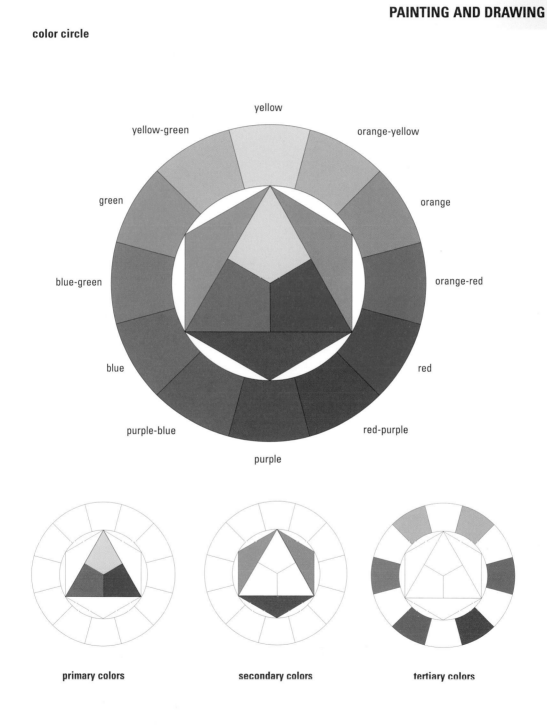

primary colors

secondary colors

tertiary colors

drawing supplies

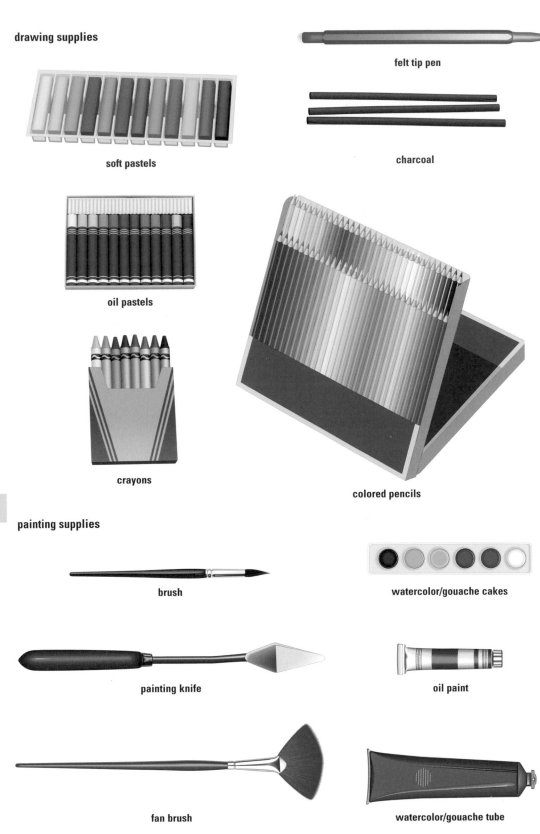

soft pastels

felt tip pen

charcoal

oil pastels

colored pencils

crayons

painting supplies

brush

watercolor/gouache cakes

painting knife

oil paint

fan brush

watercolor/gouache tube

ARTS

WOOD CARVING

steps

examples of tools

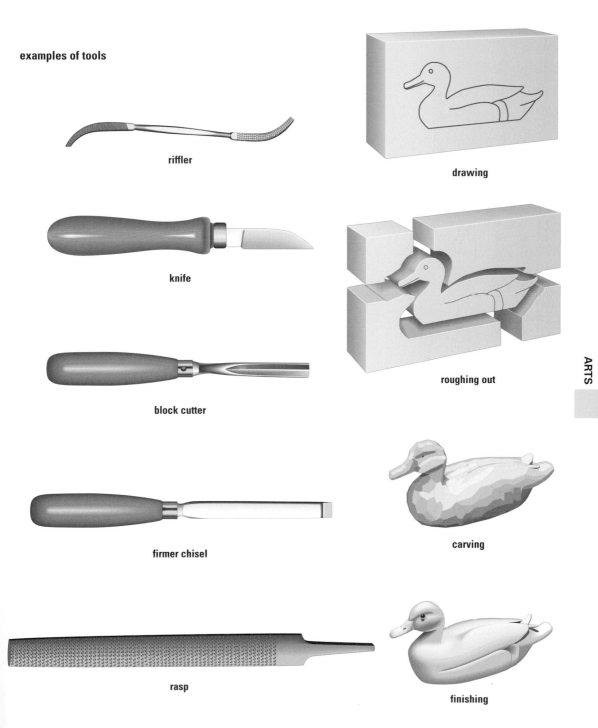

riffler

drawing

knife

roughing out

block cutter

firmer chisel

carving

rasp

finishing

CRAFTS

Sewing and knitting are ancient crafts. Until quite recently, these types of activities were generally performed by women. Back in the days when all clothing was made by hand, sewing and knitting served an entirely practical purpose. In modern society, however, these handicrafts are mainly hobbies rather than necessities.

SEWING AND KNITTING

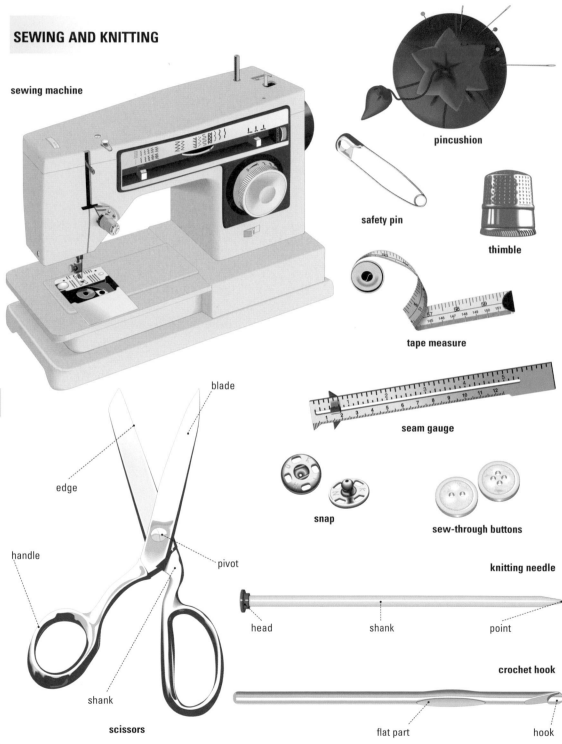

sewing machine

pincushion

safety pin

thimble

tape measure

seam gauge

blade

edge

snap

sew-through buttons

handle

pivot

knitting needle

head

shank

point

shank

crochet hook

scissors

flat part

hook

Around the world, people construct their shelters from readily available materials. That is why traditional housing can be made from sheet metal, mud, stones, branches, straw, grass or even snow.

Although many houses built locally are of traditional design, modern buildings often resemble one another, whether they are constructed in the East or the West.

TRADITIONAL HOUSES

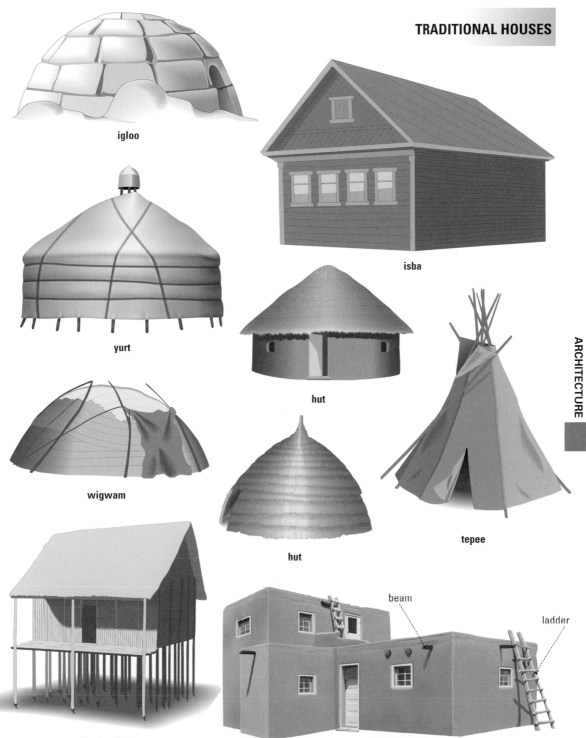

igloo

isba

yurt

hut

wigwam

hut

tepee

pile dwelling

beam

ladder

adobe house

ARCHITECTURE

CITY HOUSES

semidetached house

one-storey house

two-storey house

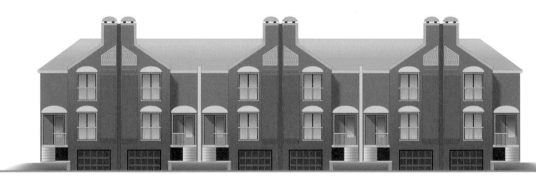

town houses

high-rise apartment building

condominiums

The history of the world can be charted by comparing different styles of architecture and admiring the many masterpieces that mark their respective eras. Whether practical, like a castle's keep, or symbolic, like a cathedral's bell tower that rises to the heavens, every element in a work of architecture takes into account the intended function of the building.

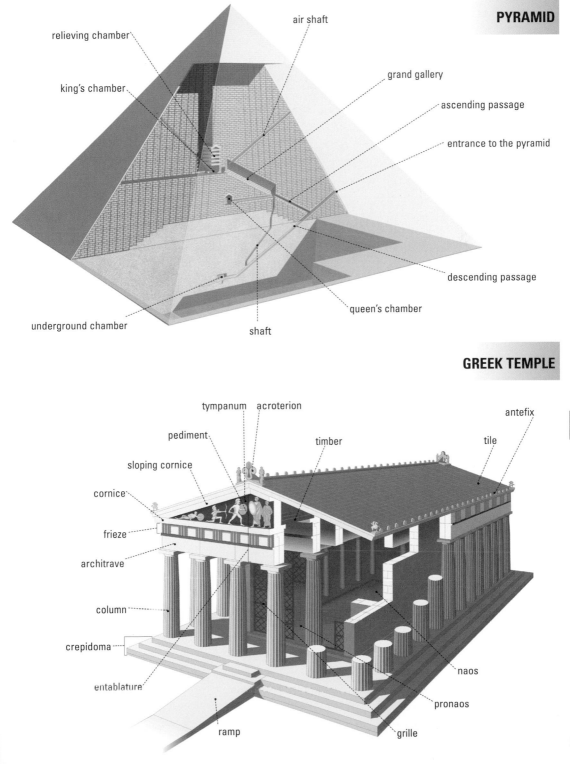

PYRAMID

relieving chamber

air shaft

king's chamber

grand gallery

ascending passage

entrance to the pyramid

descending passage

queen's chamber

underground chamber

shaft

GREEK TEMPLE

tympanum   acroterion

antefix

pediment

timber

tile

sloping cornice

cornice

frieze

architrave

column

crepidoma

naos

entablature

pronaos

ramp

grille

ROMAN HOUSE

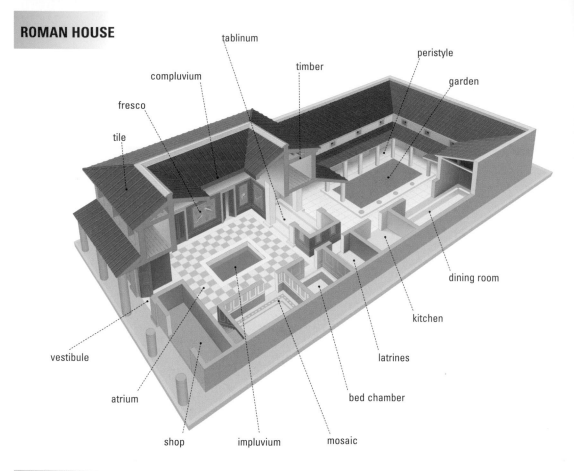

tablinum

compluvium

timber

peristyle

garden

fresco

tile

dining room

kitchen

vestibule

latrines

atrium

bed chamber

shop

impluvium

mosaic

ROMAN AMPHITHEATER

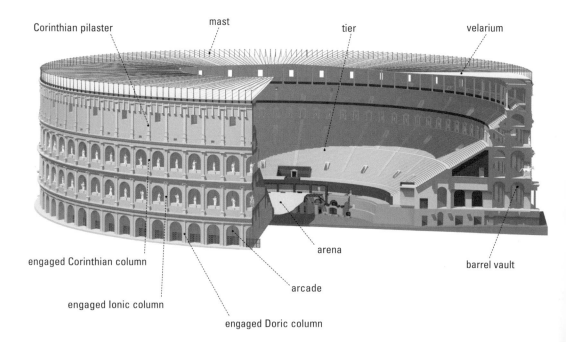

Corinthian pilaster

mast

tier

velarium

engaged Corinthian column

arena

barrel vault

engaged Ionic column

arcade

engaged Doric column

MOSQUE

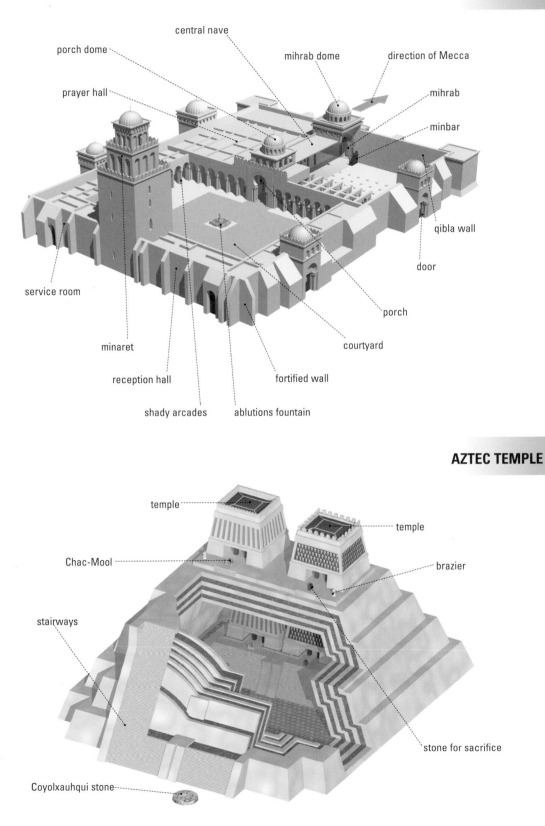

porch dome

central nave

mihrab dome

direction of Mecca

prayer hall

mihrab

minbar

service room

qibla wall

door

minaret

porch

reception hall

courtyard

shady arcades

fortified wall

ablutions fountain

AZTEC TEMPLE

temple

temple

Chac-Mool

brazier

stairways

stone for sacrifice

Coyolxauhqui stone

CASTLE

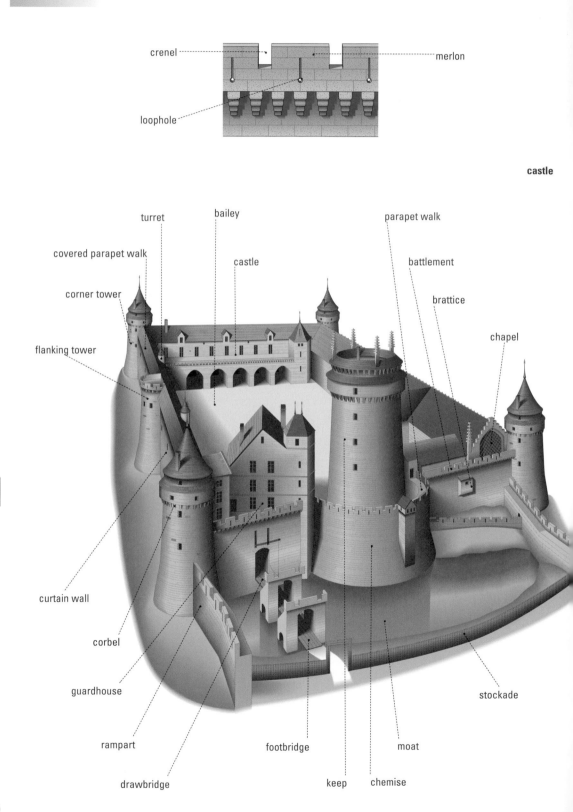

machicolation

crenel

merlon

loophole

castle

turret

bailey

parapet walk

covered parapet walk

castle

battlement

corner tower

brattice

chapel

flanking tower

ARCHITECTURE

curtain wall

corbel

guardhouse

stockade

rampart

footbridge

moat

drawbridge

keep

chemise

façade

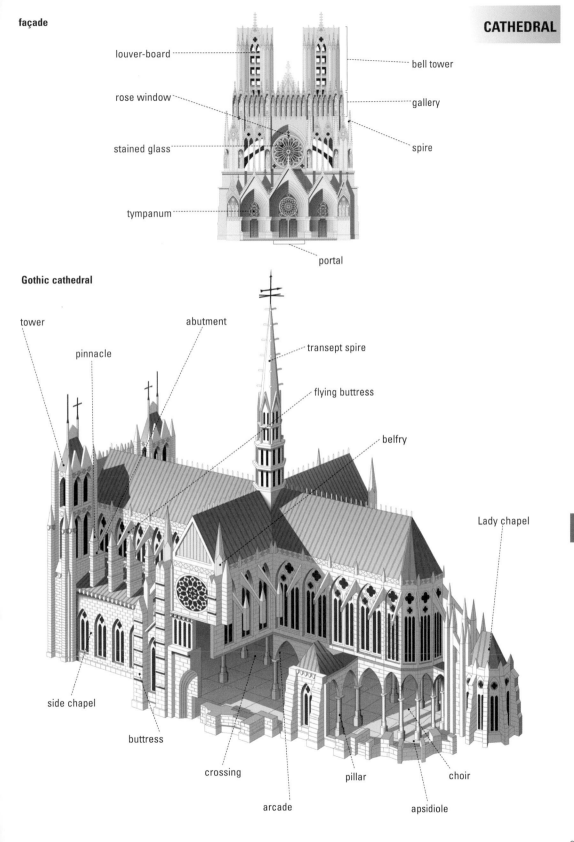

louver-board

rose window

stained glass

tympanum

bell tower

gallery

spire

portal

Gothic cathedral

tower

pinnacle

abutment

transept spire

flying buttress

belfry

Lady chapel

side chapel

buttress

crossing

arcade

pillar

apsidiole

choir

MUSICAL NOTATION

Musical notation allows the many elements needed to perform a piece of music to be written down on a staff of five lines. With hundreds of different symbols to represent sounds, their pitch and their duration, musical notation is a precious tool. Its universal language gives musicians of every culture access to the same vast musical library.

staff

space line ledger line

clefs

treble clef bass clef C clef

time signatures

three-four time bar line

two-two time four-four time repeat mark

intervals

unison third fifth seventh

second fourth sixth octave

scale

C D E F G A B C

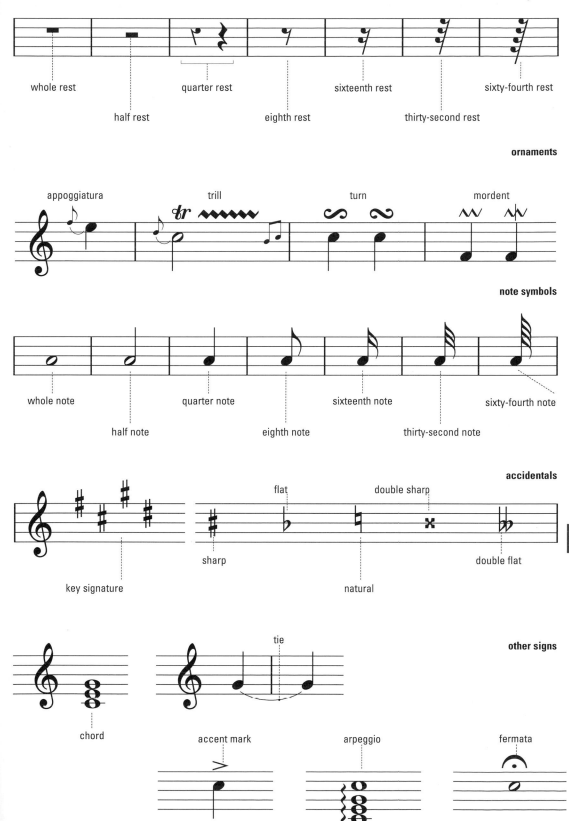

MUSICAL INSTRUMENTS

In every civilization, people have found ways to make music with many different kinds of objects. Today, there are thousands of musical instruments, from traditional to electronic, adapted for every style of music. Instruments can be classified in three basic categories: wind, string and percussion. They can also be grouped according to other criteria, for example, instruments with keyboards.

TRADITIONAL MUSICAL INSTRUMENTS

accordion

bass keyboard

treble register

button

treble keyboard

bass register

key

bellows

grille

bagpipes

harmonica

drone pipe

blow pipe

panpipe

windbag

banjo

chanter

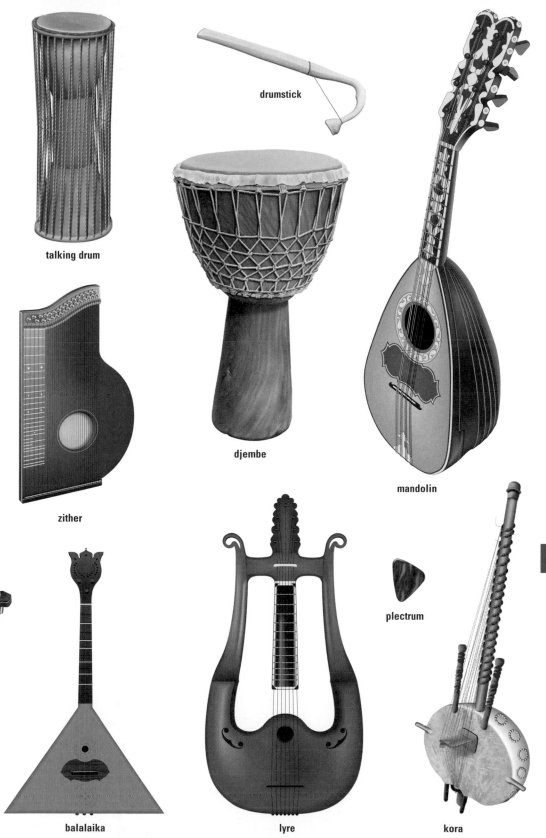

talking drum

drumstick

djembe

mandolin

zither

plectrum

balalaika

lyre

kora

KEYBOARD INSTRUMENTS

upright piano

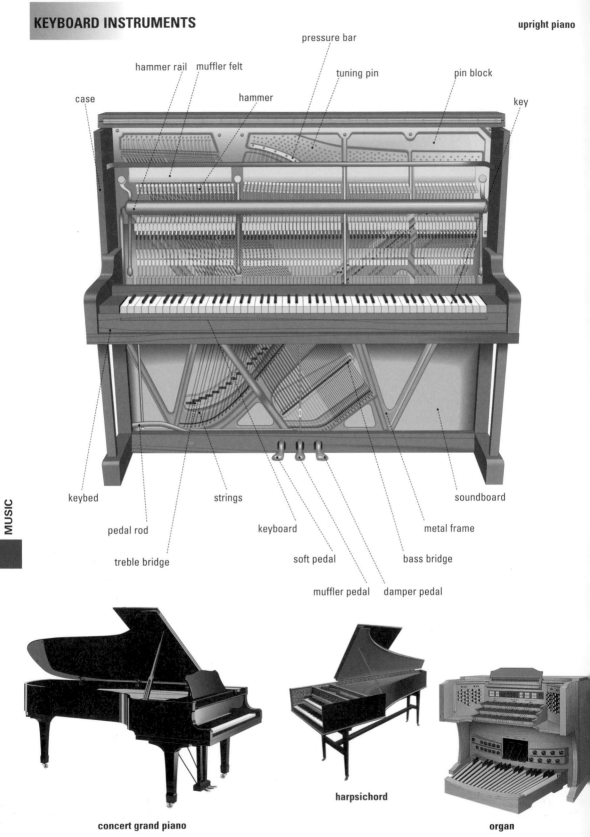

pressure bar

hammer rail muffler felt

tuning pin

pin block

case

hammer

key

keybed

strings

soundboard

pedal rod

keyboard

metal frame

treble bridge

soft pedal

bass bridge

muffler pedal damper pedal

concert grand piano

harpsichord

organ

STRINGED INSTRUMENTS

violin

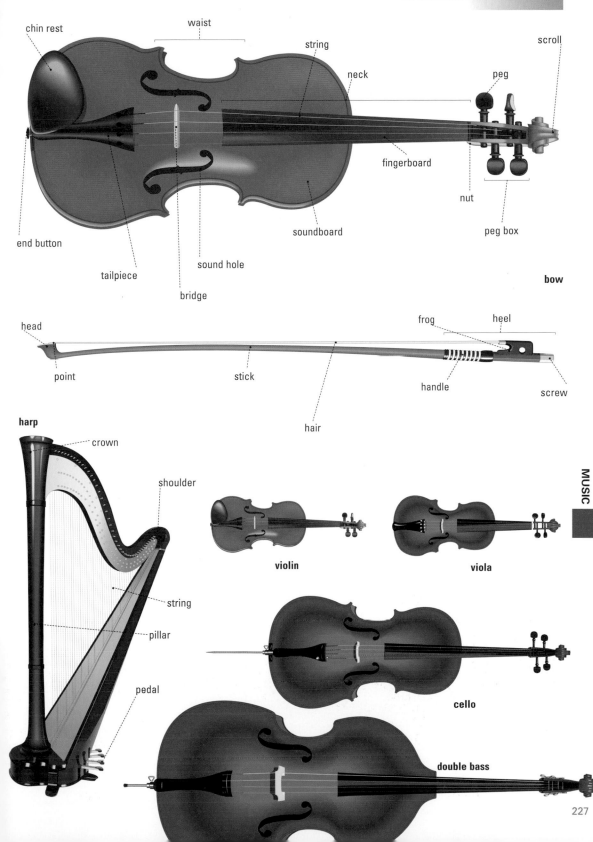

chin rest

waist

string

neck

scroll

peg

fingerboard

nut

peg box

end button

soundboard

tailpiece

sound hole

bridge

bow

head

frog

heel

point

stick

handle

screw

hair

harp

crown

shoulder

string

pillar

pedal

violin

viola

cello

double bass

MUSIC

227

electric guitar

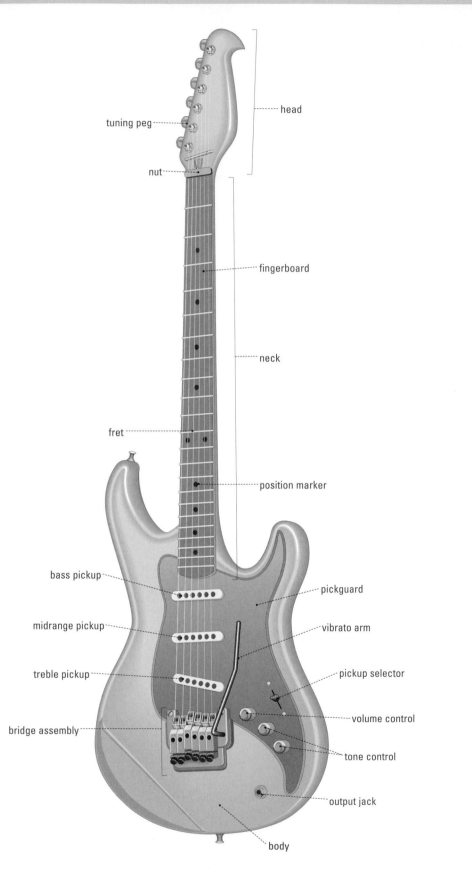

tuning peg

head

nut

fingerboard

neck

fret

position marker

bass pickup

pickguard

midrange pickup

vibrato arm

treble pickup

pickup selector

bridge assembly

volume control

tone control

output jack

body

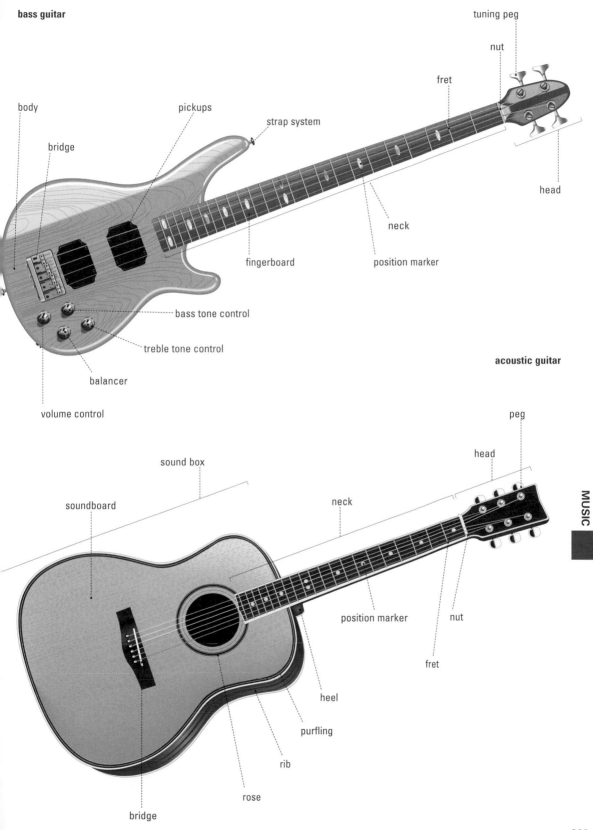

bass guitar

body

pickups

bridge

strap system

tuning peg

nut

fret

head

neck

fingerboard

position marker

bass tone control

treble tone control

balancer

volume control

acoustic guitar

peg

head

sound box

soundboard

neck

position marker

nut

fret

heel

purfling

rib

rose

bridge

MUSIC

WIND INSTRUMENTS

trumpet

key

little finger hook

bell

mouthpipe

ring

mouthpiece receiver

mouthpiece

first valve slide

tuning slide

third valve slide

spit valve

thumb hook

valve

valve casing

second valve slide

cornet

bugle

mute

trombone

French horn

saxhorn

tuba

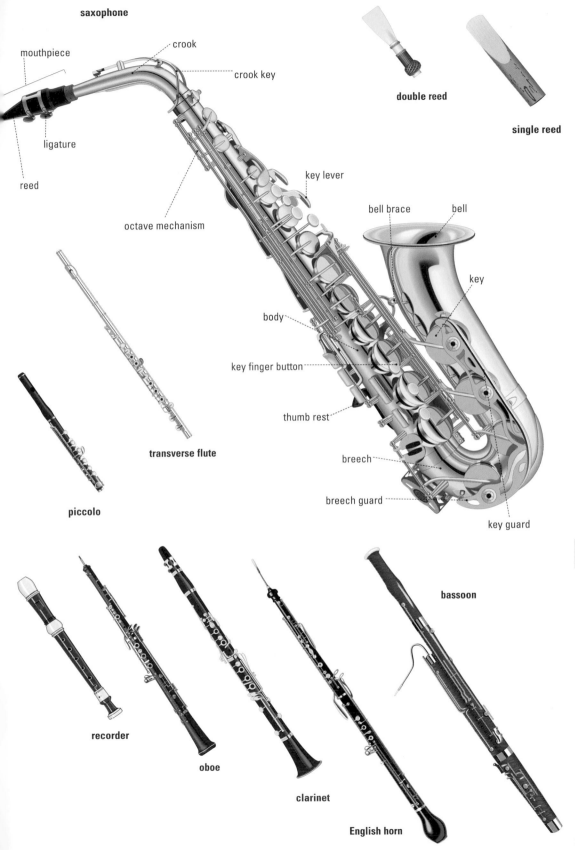

saxophone

mouthpiece

crook

crook key

ligature

reed

octave mechanism

key lever

double reed

single reed

bell brace

bell

key

body

key finger button

thumb rest

breech

breech guard

key guard

transverse flute

piccolo

bassoon

recorder

oboe

clarinet

English horn

PERCUSSION INSTRUMENTS

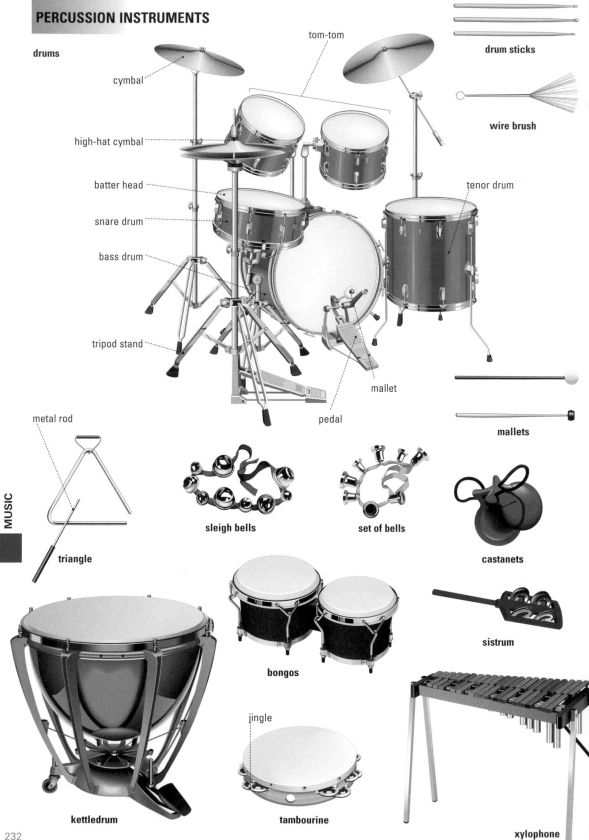

drum sticks

tom-tom

drums

cymbal

wire brush

high-hat cymbal

tenor drum

batter head

snare drum

bass drum

mallet

tripod stand

pedal

mallets

metal rod

triangle

sleigh bells

set of bells

castanets

bongos

sistrum

kettledrum

jingle

tambourine

xylophone

ELECTRONIC INSTRUMENTS

synthesizer

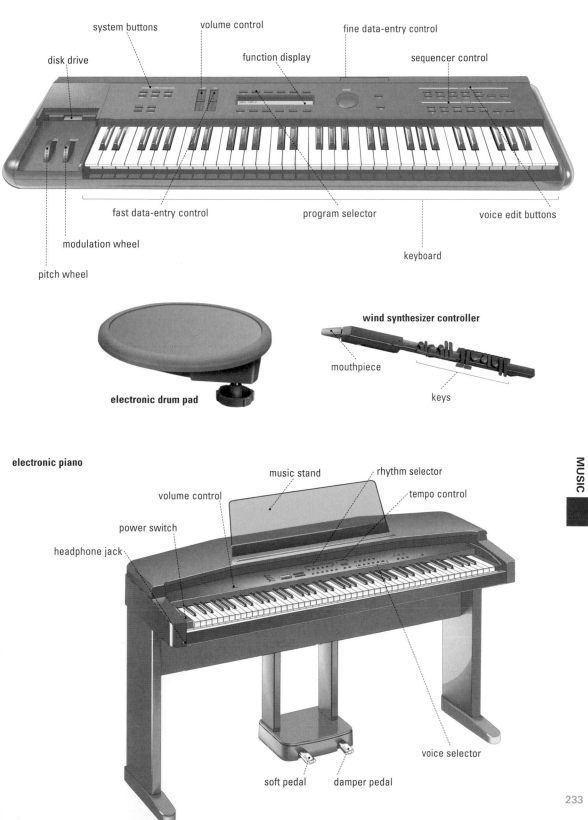

system buttons

volume control

fine data-entry control

disk drive

function display

sequencer control

fast data-entry control

program selector

voice edit buttons

modulation wheel

keyboard

pitch wheel

electronic drum pad

wind synthesizer controller

mouthpiece

keys

electronic piano

music stand

rhythm selector

volume control

tempo control

power switch

headphone jack

voice selector

soft pedal

damper pedal

An orchestra is a variety of musicians who form a musical group, called an ensemble. There are different types of ensembles, depending on the number and kind of instruments being brought together. The symphony orchestra, with 100 to 150 instruments distributed in four sections—strings, woodwinds, brass, and percussion—is the biggest kind of orchestra. The musicians play under the direction of a conductor.

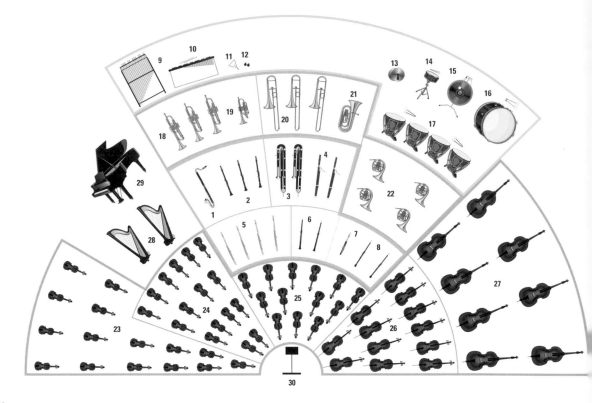

woodwind section	percussion section	brass section	string section
1 bass clarinet	**9** tubular bells	**18** trumpets	**23** first violins
2 clarinets	**10** xylophone	**19** cornet	**24** second violins
3 contrabassoons	**11** triangle	**20** trombones	**25** violas
4 bassoons	**12** castanets	**21** tuba	**26** cellos
5 flutes	**13** cymbals	**22** French horns	**27** double basses
6 oboes	**14** snare drum		
7 piccolo	**15** gong	**28** harps	
8 English horns	**16** bass drum	**29** piano	
	17 timpani	**30** conductor's podium	

When a photograph is taken, an image is produced on the light-sensitive film inside the camera. After it has been exposed to the light, the film is developed and a negative is obtained. When the negative is projected onto white photographic paper, the image that was photographed appears. There are many different types of cameras available today, the latest being digital.

single-lens reflex (SLR) camera

film rewind knob

accessory shoe

control panel

hot-shoe contact

command control dial

film advance mode

film speed

exposure mode

lens cap

remote control terminal

zoom lens

focus mode selector

camera body

shutter release button

objective lens

photographic accessories

electronic flash

flashtube

compact flash memory card

still video film disk

photoelectric cell

mounting foot

cartridge film

film disk

examples of still cameras

pocket camera

Polaroid® camera

disk camera

rangefinder

underwater camera

digital camera

disposable camera

view camera

Radio makes it possible to transmit, in real time, important events that happen over great distances. During a radio broadcast, the voice of the announcer is transformed into electronic signals with the help of a microphone. These signals are then converted into radio waves by the radio station. When a radio set or a receiver picks up these waves, they are changed back into sounds.

radio (studio and control room)

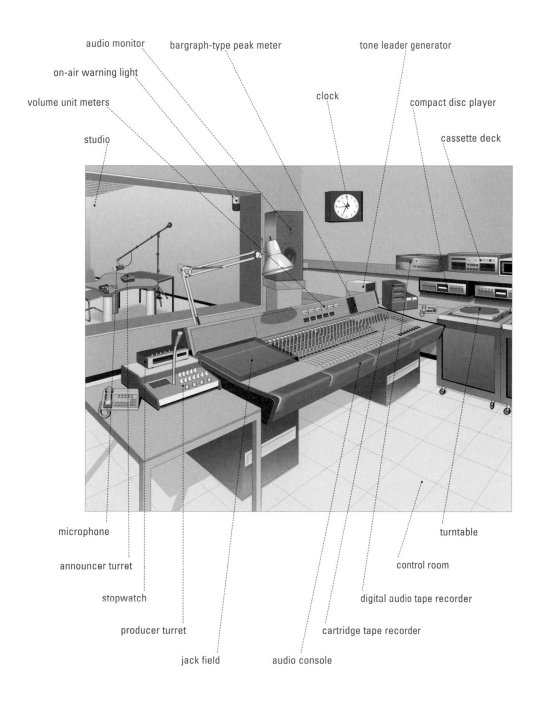

audio monitor

bargraph-type peak meter

tone leader generator

on-air warning light

clock

compact disc player

volume unit meters

cassette deck

studio

microphone

turntable

announcer turret

control room

stopwatch

digital audio tape recorder

producer turret

cartridge tape recorder

jack field

audio console

COMMUNICATIONS

TELEVISION

The video cameras and microphones in a television studio transform images and sounds into electronic signals. These signals are converted into radio waves by the television station, which then broadcasts them. Television programs are sent to television sets by satellite, by underground cable or directly to the television's antenna. The television set can also receive signals from a video cassette player or DVD player.

studio floor

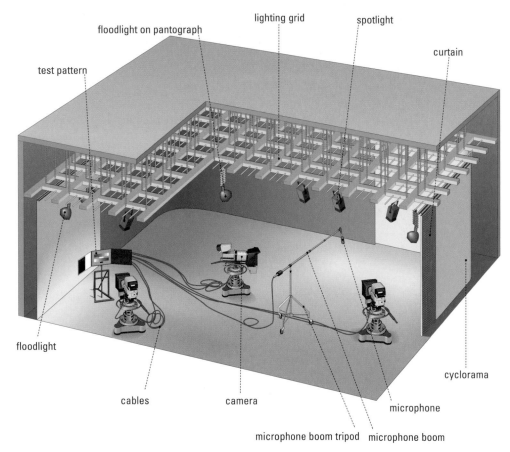

test pattern

floodlight on pantograph

lighting grid

spotlight

curtain

floodlight

cables

camera

cyclorama

microphone

microphone boom tripod

microphone boom

COMMUNICATIONS

camera

camera viewfinder

zoom lens

TelePrompTer

camera pedestal

dish antenna

dish

feedhorn

pole

238

television set

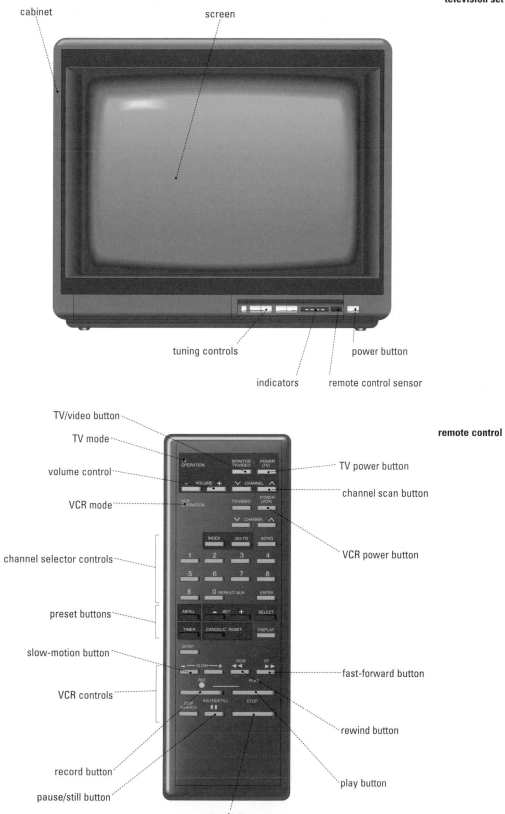

cabinet

screen

tuning controls

power button

indicators

remote control sensor

remote control

TV/video button

TV mode

volume control

VCR mode

TV power button

channel scan button

VCR power button

channel selector controls

preset buttons

slow-motion button

VCR controls

fast-forward button

rewind button

record button

play button

pause/still button

stop button

videocassette recorder (VCR)

videocassette

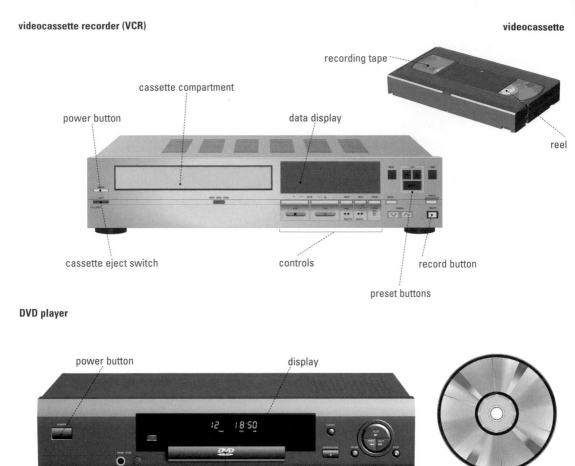

recording tape

cassette compartment

power button

data display

reel

cassette eject switch

controls

record button

preset buttons

DVD player

power button

display

disc tray

digital versatile disc (DVD)

analog camcorder

eyecup

edit search button

power/functions switch

electronic viewfinder

videotape operation controls

zoom lens

display panel

nightshot switch

microphone

focus selector

near/far dial

Technological advances in the recording and reproduction of music in the last century have steadily improved sound quality. Music lovers now have a wide range of musical equipment to choose from.

Cassettes and compact discs can be played on individual components or on complete mini stereo sound systems. Some homes even have a record player for listening to old vinyl records.

system components

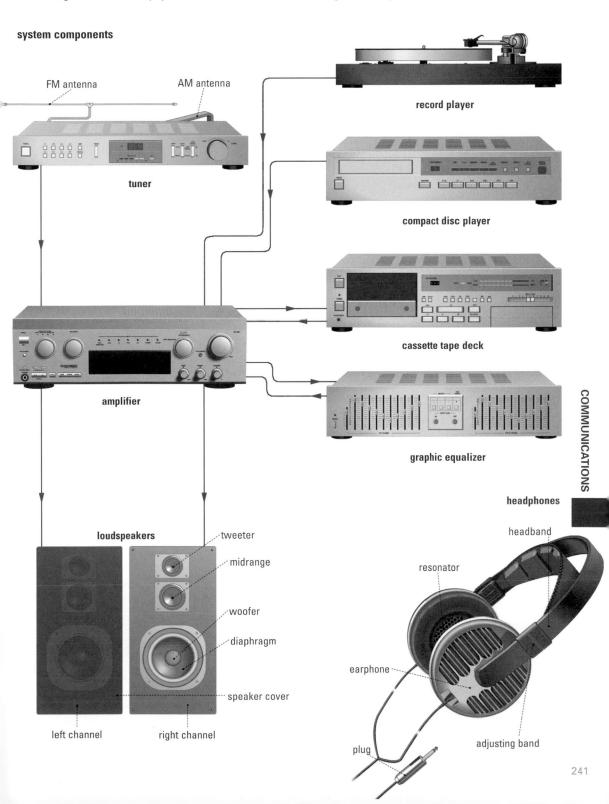

record player

FM antenna

AM antenna

tuner

compact disc player

cassette tape deck

amplifier

graphic equalizer

COMMUNICATIONS

headphones

headband

loudspeakers

tweeter

midrange

resonator

woofer

diaphragm

earphone

speaker cover

left channel

right channel

plug

adjusting band

With the miniaturization of electronic components, people can easily listen to their favorite music while taking a stroll. Some devices, such as the portable CD player, have only one specific function, while others resemble miniature sound systems. The portable CD-radio-cassette recorder allows you to listen to music that is has been recorded on a cassette or compact disc, as well as music that is being broadcast by a radio station.

portable CD/radio/cassette recorder

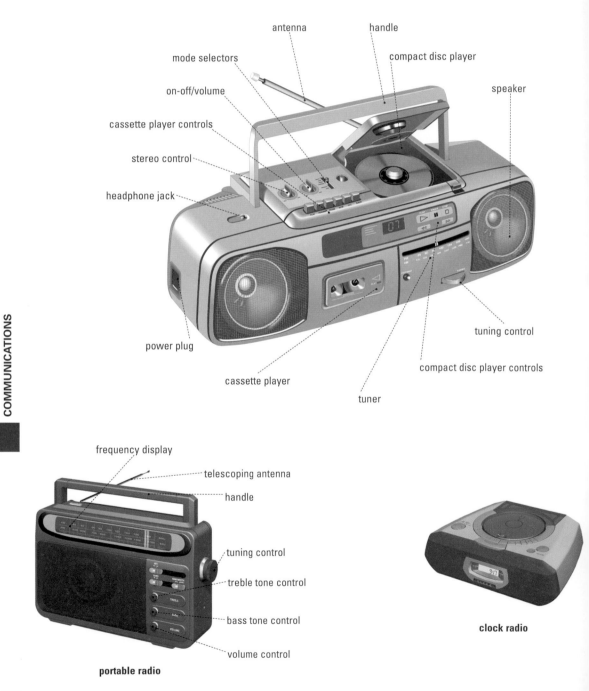

antenna

handle

mode selectors

compact disc player

on-off/volume

speaker

cassette player controls

stereo control

headphone jack

power plug

tuning control

cassette player

compact disc player controls

tuner

frequency display

telescoping antenna

handle

tuning control

treble tone control

bass tone control

volume control

clock radio

portable radio

compact disc

portable compact disc player

technical identification band

pressed area

display

earphones

reading start

cassette

take-up reel

housing

recording tape

guide roller

tape-guide

playing window

portable digital audio player

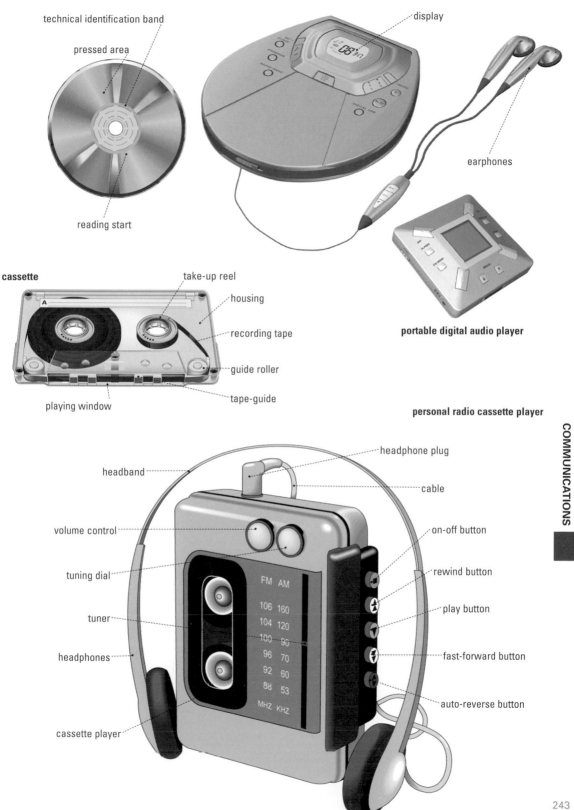

personal radio cassette player

headphone plug

headband

cable

volume control

on-off button

tuning dial

rewind button

FM AM

106 160
104 120
100 90
96 70
92 60
88 53

MHZ KHZ

tuner

play button

fast-forward button

headphones

auto-reverse button

cassette player

Whether portable, fixed or wireless, the telephone, along with television and radio, remains one of the most important forms of telecommunications. Two people separated by thousands of miles can have a conversation, communicate in writing over the Internet, or fax each other written documents. This exchange of information is happening at a faster and faster pace due, in particular, to the number of communication satellites.

telephone set

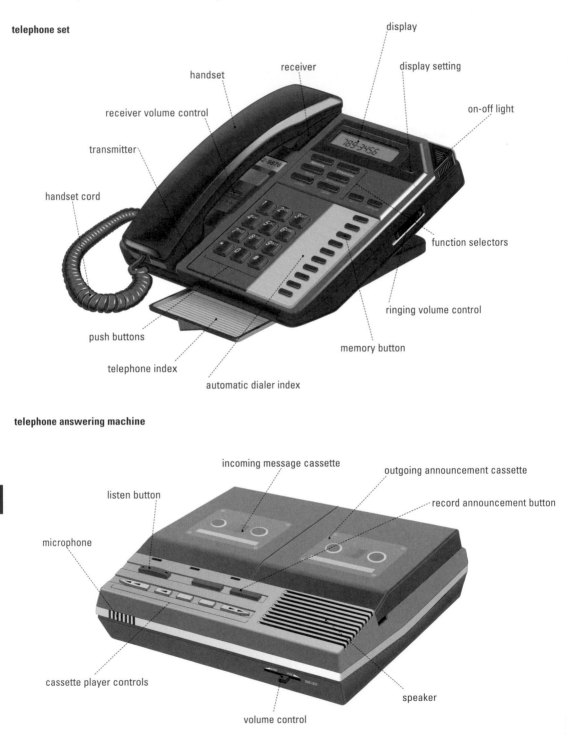

display

receiver

display setting

handset

on-off light

receiver volume control

transmitter

function selectors

handset cord

ringing volume control

push buttons

memory button

telephone index

automatic dialer index

telephone answering machine

incoming message cassette

outgoing announcement cassette

listen button

record announcement button

microphone

cassette player controls

speaker

volume control

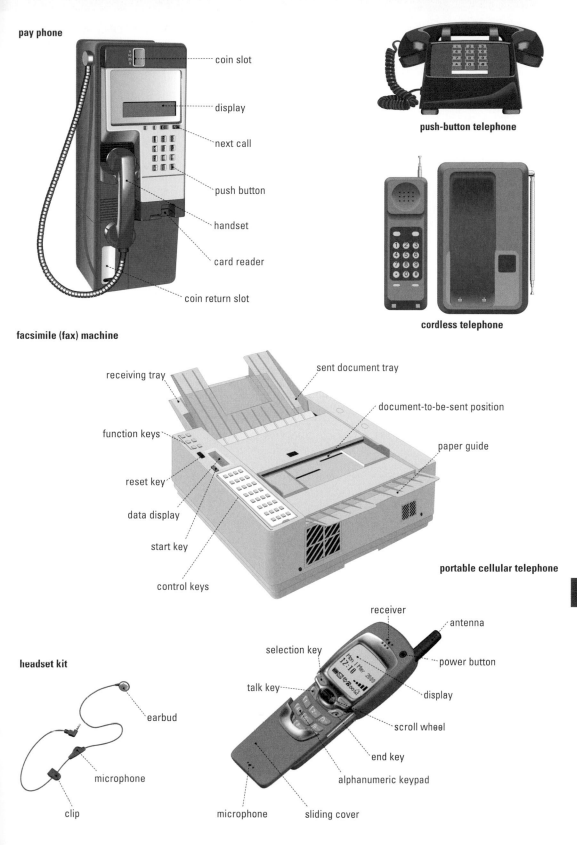

pay phone

coin slot

display

next call

push button

handset

card reader

coin return slot

push-button telephone

cordless telephone

facsimile (fax) machine

receiving tray

sent document tray

document-to-be-sent position

function keys

paper guide

reset key

data display

start key

control keys

portable cellular telephone

receiver

antenna

selection key

power button

headset kit

talk key

display

earbud

scroll wheel

microphone

end key

clip

alphanumeric keypad

microphone

sliding cover

A computer is an electronic appliance capable of transforming, storing and sending coded information at amazing speeds. The personal computer has several main elements. They are housed in a central case surrounded by different devices, including a mouse, keyboard, monitor and printer. Whether they are visible or hidden, computers can now be found everywhere.

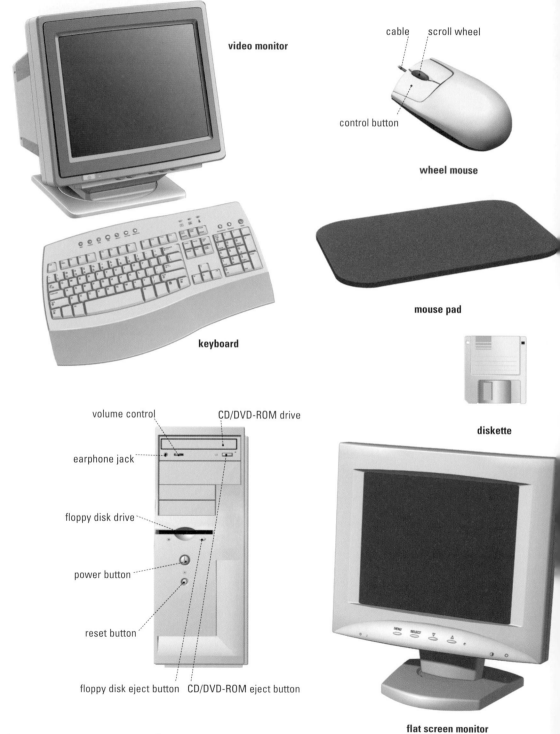

video monitor

cable   scroll wheel

control button

wheel mouse

mouse pad

keyboard

diskette

volume control   CD/DVD-ROM drive

earphone jack

floppy disk drive

power button

reset button

floppy disk eject button   CD/DVD-ROM eject button

tower case

flat screen monitor

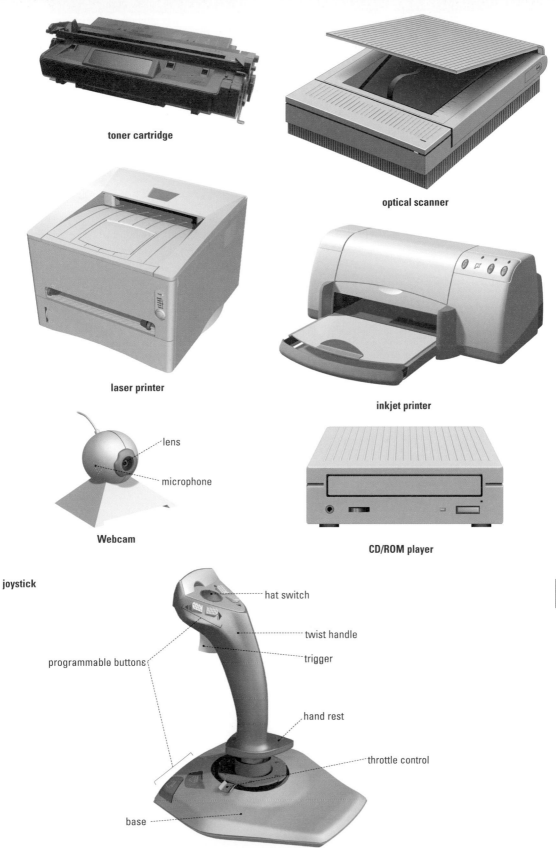

toner cartridge

optical scanner

laser printer

inkjet printer

lens

microphone

Webcam

CD/ROM player

joystick

hat switch

twist handle

trigger

programmable buttons

hand rest

throttle control

base

INTERNET

The Internet is an enormous system of international communication. It is made up of a series of computer networks, which are connected by telephone and cable lines that communicate in a common computer language. Developed in 1991 in the United States, the World Wide Web (WWW) has allowed millions of computers and computer users around the world to link up, making communication and the exchange of information easier.

uniform resource locator (URL)

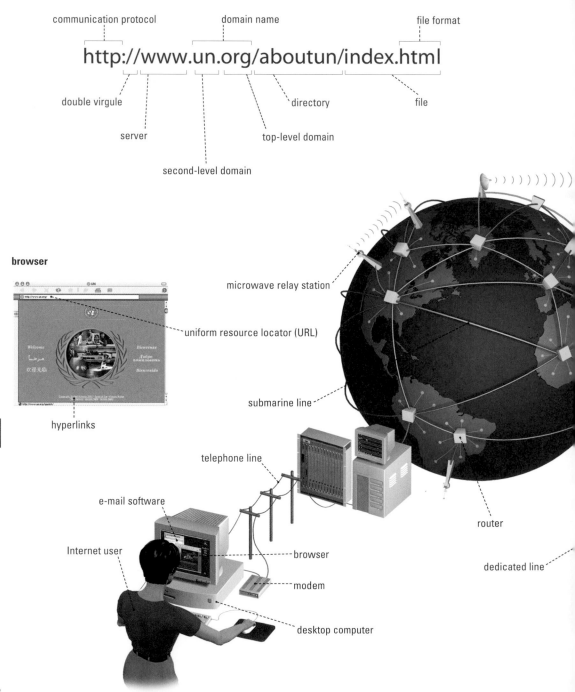

communication protocol

domain name

file format

http://www.un.org/aboutun/index.html

double virgule

server

second-level domain

top-level domain

directory

file

browser

uniform resource locator (URL)

hyperlinks

microwave relay station

submarine line

telephone line

e-mail software

Internet user

browser

router

dedicated line

modem

desktop computer

Internet uses

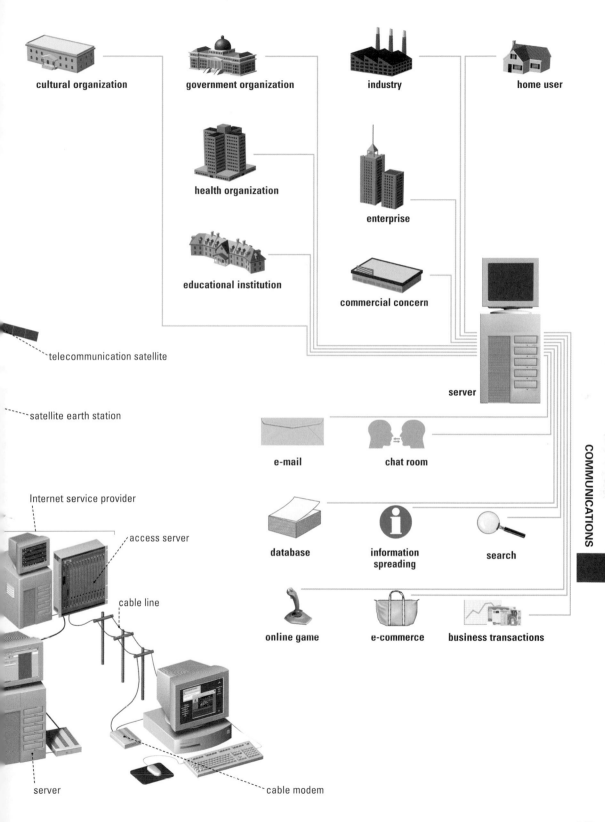

cultural organization

government organization

industry

home user

health organization

enterprise

educational institution

commercial concern

telecommunication satellite

satellite earth station

server

e-mail

chat room

Internet service provider

access server

database

information
spreading

search

cable line

online game

e-commerce

business transactions

server

cable modem

DOWNTOWN

Cities are built-up areas that bring together a large number of people. Most people live in residential neighborhoods and work in large office buildings downtown or in industrial zones on the city's outskirts. The heart of a typical city includes a business district and establishments that offer a variety of goods and services. These establishments may include a city hall, universities and museums, to name a few.

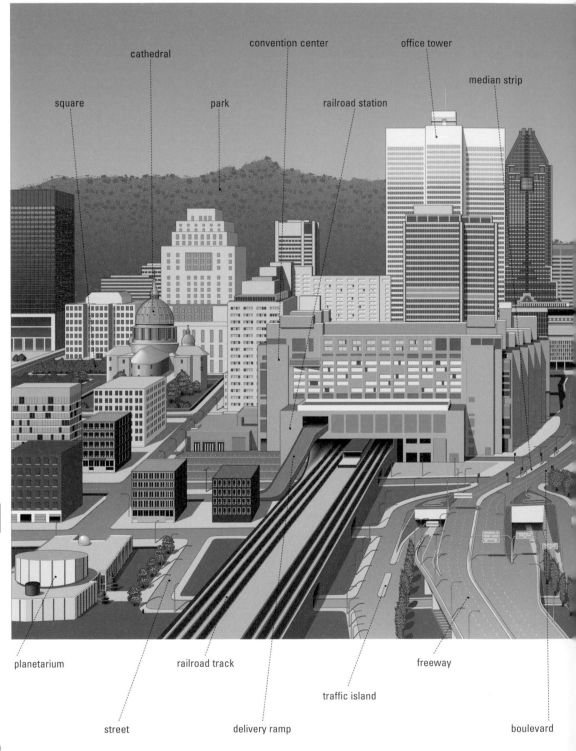

cathedral

convention center

office tower

median strip

square

park

railroad station

planetarium

railroad track

freeway

traffic island

street

delivery ramp

boulevard

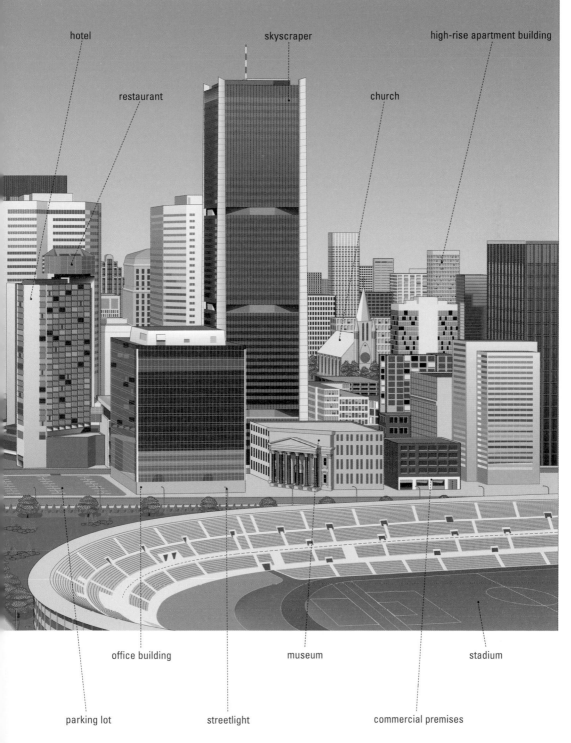

hotel

skyscraper

high-rise apartment building

restaurant

church

SOCIETY

office building

museum

stadium

parking lot

streetlight

commercial premises

TERMINAL AND STATIONS

In every city, there are areas specially reserved for the arrival and departure of vehicles such as trains, airplanes and subways. While airports are always built outside of large city centers, subway stations are usually located in urban areas. Stations where trains pick up and drop off passengers can be found in every kind of setting.

PASSENGER TERMINAL

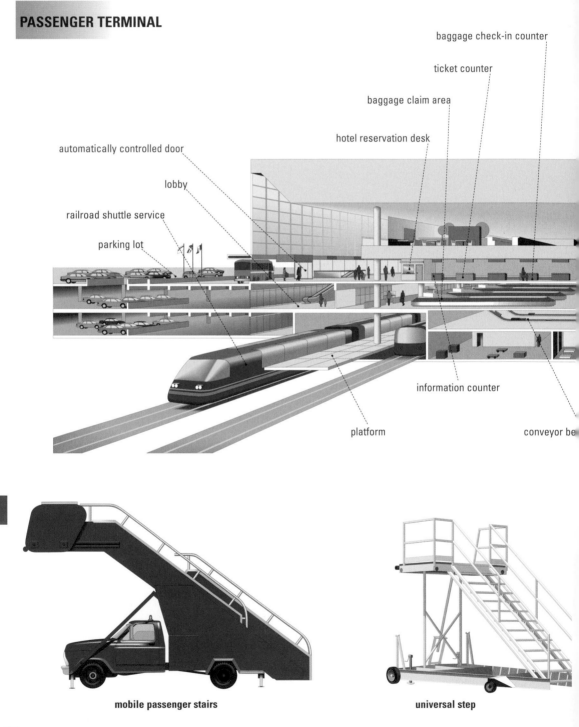

baggage check-in counter

ticket counter

baggage claim area

hotel reservation desk

automatically controlled door

lobby

railroad shuttle service

parking lot

information counter

platform

conveyor be

mobile passenger stairs

universal step

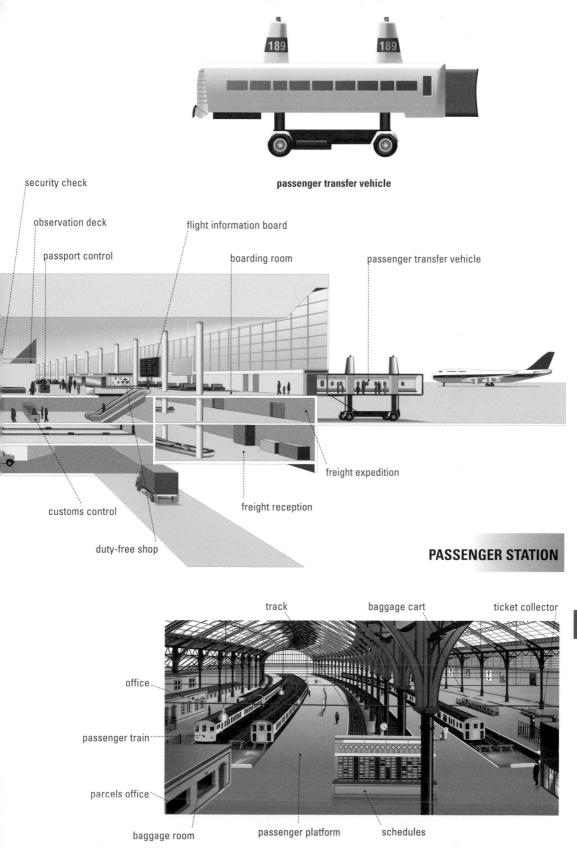

passenger transfer vehicle

security check

observation deck

passport control

flight information board

boarding room

passenger transfer vehicle

freight expedition

freight reception

customs control

duty-free shop

PASSENGER STATION

SOCIETY

track

baggage cart

ticket collector

office

passenger train

parcels office

baggage room

passenger platform

schedules

SUBWAY STATION

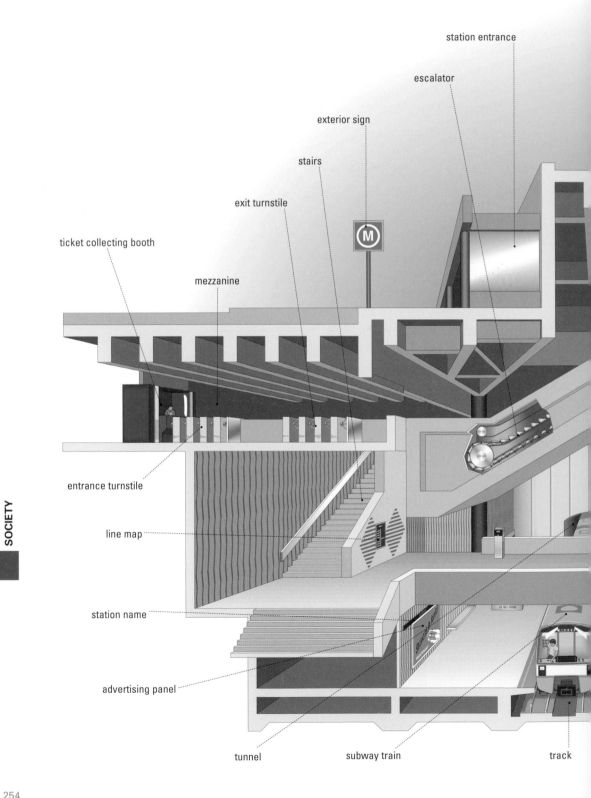

station entrance

escalator

exterior sign

stairs

exit turnstile

ticket collecting booth

mezzanine

M

entrance turnstile

line map

station name

advertising panel

tunnel

subway train

track

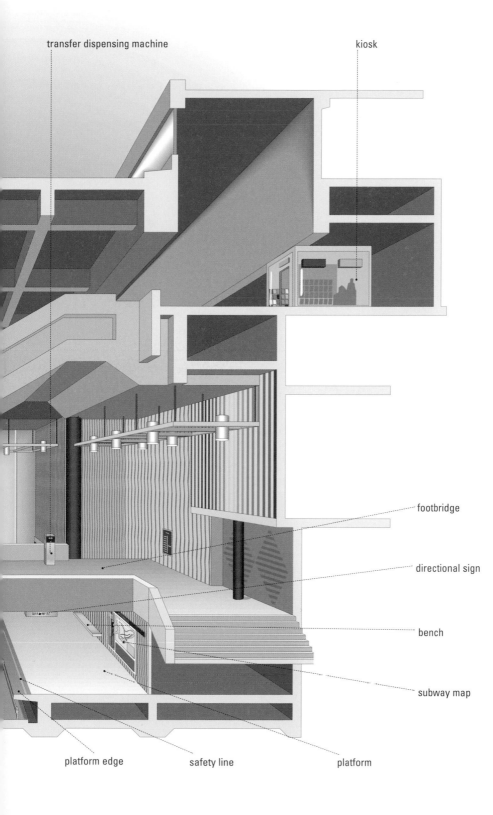

transfer dispensing machine

kiosk

footbridge

directional sign

bench

subway map

platform edge

safety line

platform

Every city has a large number of commercial establishments that offer a wide range of goods and services to the public. Supermarkets, shopping malls, restaurants and gas stations are just a few of the businesses that operate in a typical city. In these establishments, you can buy all kinds of consumer goods, including food, clothing, prepared meals and gas.

SUPERMARKET

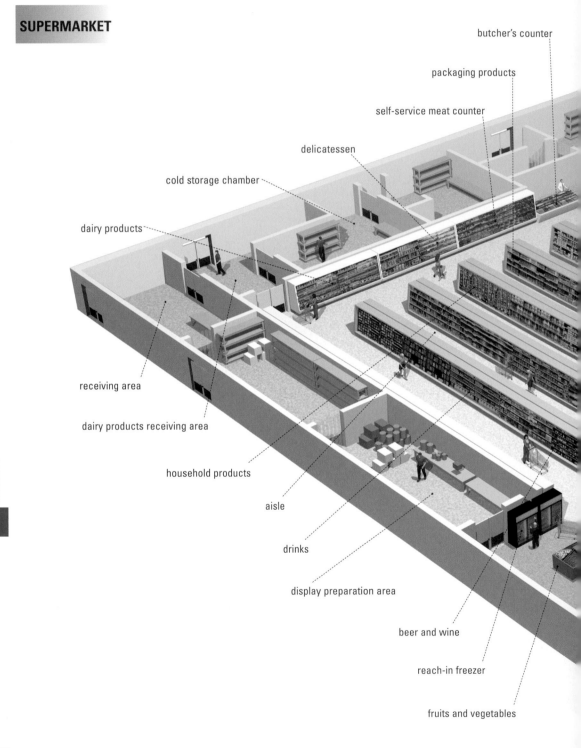

butcher's counter

packaging products

self-service meat counter

delicatessen

cold storage chamber

dairy products

receiving area

dairy products receiving area

household products

aisle

drinks

display preparation area

beer and wine

reach-in freezer

fruits and vegetables

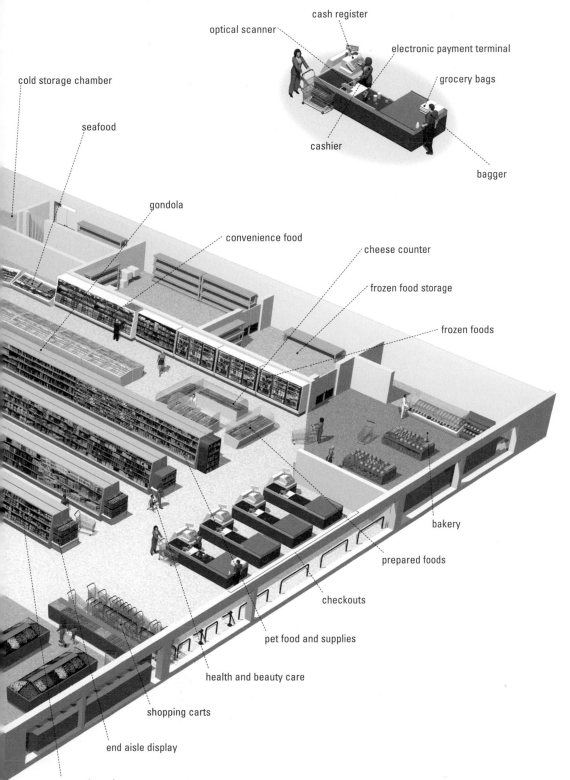

checkout

cash register

optical scanner

electronic payment terminal

grocery bags

cold storage chamber

seafood

cashier

bagger

gondola

convenience food

cheese counter

frozen food storage

frozen foods

bakery

prepared foods

checkouts

pet food and supplies

health and beauty care

shopping carts

end aisle display

canned goods

SOCIETY

SHOPPING CENTER

bookstore

clothing store

electronics store

restaurant

jewelry store

leather goods shop

pet shop

gift store

do-it-yourself shop

toy store

bowling alley

bar

lingerie shop

perfume shop

pharmacy

hairdressing salon

photographer

music store

travel agency

smoke shop

movie theater

walkway

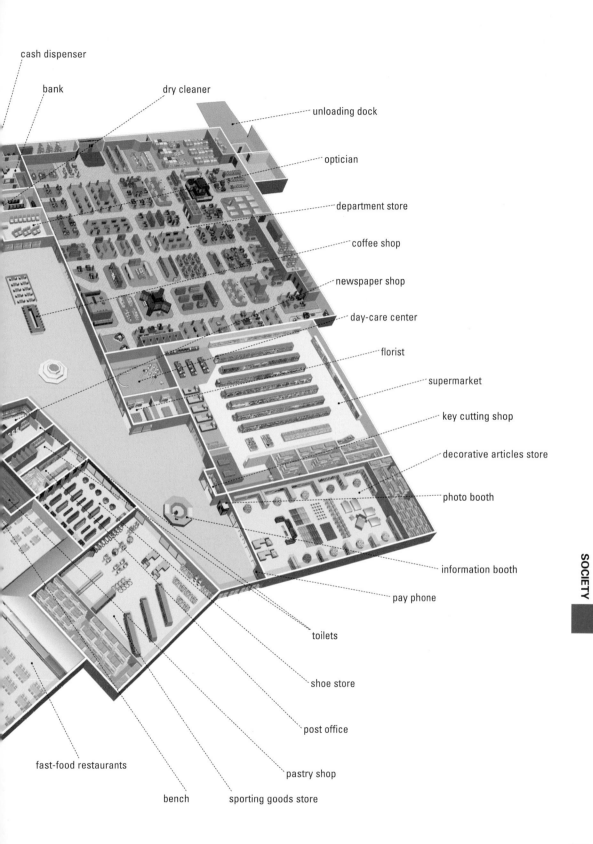

cash dispenser

bank

dry cleaner

unloading dock

optician

department store

coffee shop

newspaper shop

day-care center

florist

supermarket

key cutting shop

decorative articles store

photo booth

information booth

pay phone

toilets

shoe store

post office

fast-food restaurants

bench

sporting goods store

pastry shop

RESTAURANT

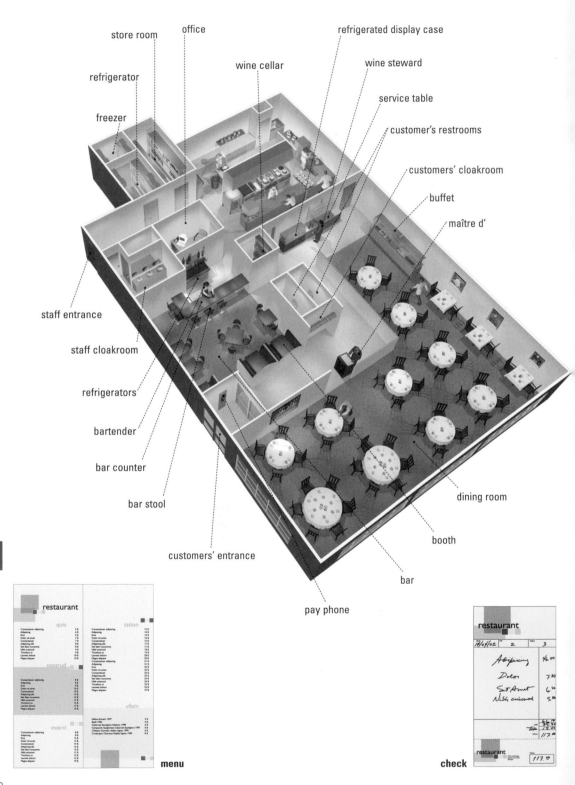

store room

office

refrigerated display case

wine cellar

wine steward

refrigerator

service table

freezer

customer's restrooms

customers' cloakroom

buffet

maître d'

staff entrance

staff cloakroom

refrigerators

bartender

bar counter

bar stool

customers' entrance

pay phone

dining room

booth

bar

menu

check

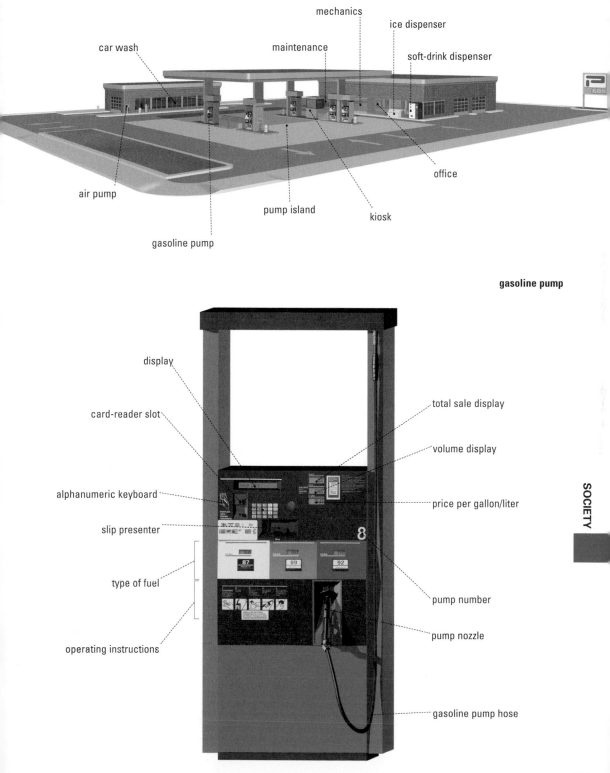

mechanics

ice dispenser

car wash

maintenance

soft-drink dispenser

office

air pump

pump island

kiosk

gasoline pump

gasoline pump

display

total sale display

card-reader slot

volume display

price per gallon/liter

alphanumeric keyboard

slip presenter

87

89

92

type of fuel

pump number

pump nozzle

operating instructions

gasoline pump hose

In addition to fighting fires and rescuing victims, firefighters look after the public's safety in several ways. Firefighters are among the first to rush to the scene of a road accident or the site of a flood. The police are also responsible for people's safety. Besides maintaining order and investigating crimes, law enforcement officers discourage criminal activity by patrolling and surveying public areas.

FIRE PREVENTION

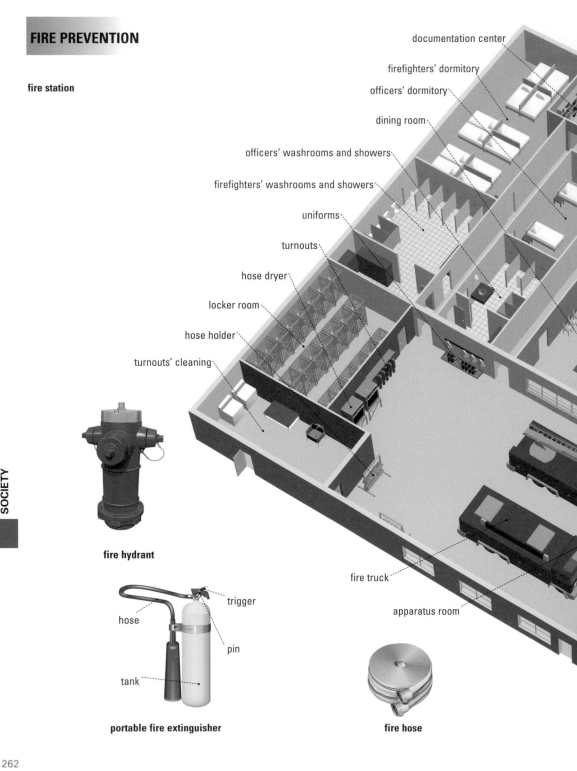

fire station

documentation center

firefighters' dormitory

officers' dormitory

dining room

officers' washrooms and showers

firefighters' washrooms and showers

uniforms

turnouts

hose dryer

locker room

hose holder

turnouts' cleaning

fire hydrant

portable fire extinguisher

trigger

hose

pin

tank

fire truck

apparatus room

fire hose

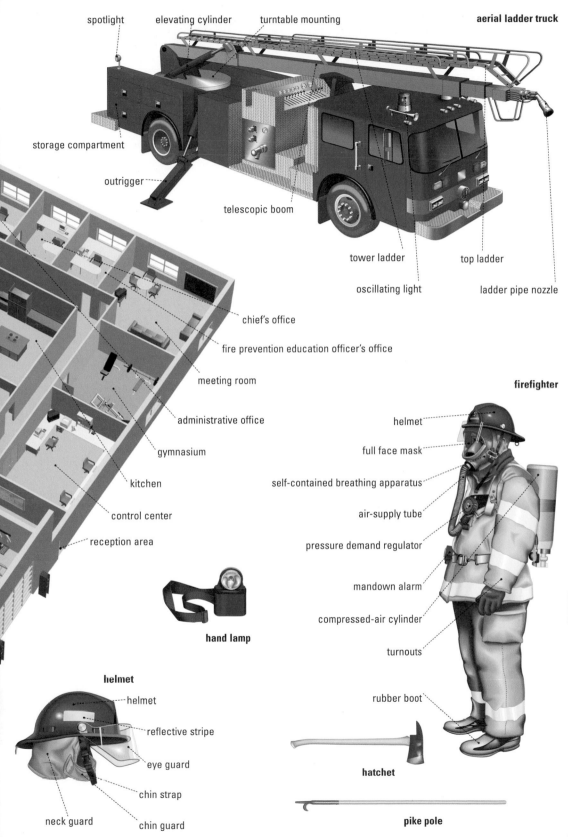

spotlight

elevating cylinder

turntable mounting

aerial ladder truck

storage compartment

outrigger

telescopic boom

tower ladder

top ladder

oscillating light

ladder pipe nozzle

chief's office

fire prevention education officer's office

meeting room

firefighter

helmet

full face mask

self-contained breathing apparatus

air-supply tube

administrative office

gymnasium

pressure demand regulator

kitchen

control center

mandown alarm

reception area

compressed-air cylinder

turnouts

hand lamp

rubber boot

SOCIETY

helmet

helmet

reflective stripe

eye guard

chin strap

hatchet

neck guard

chin guard

pike pole

263

CRIME PREVENTION

police station

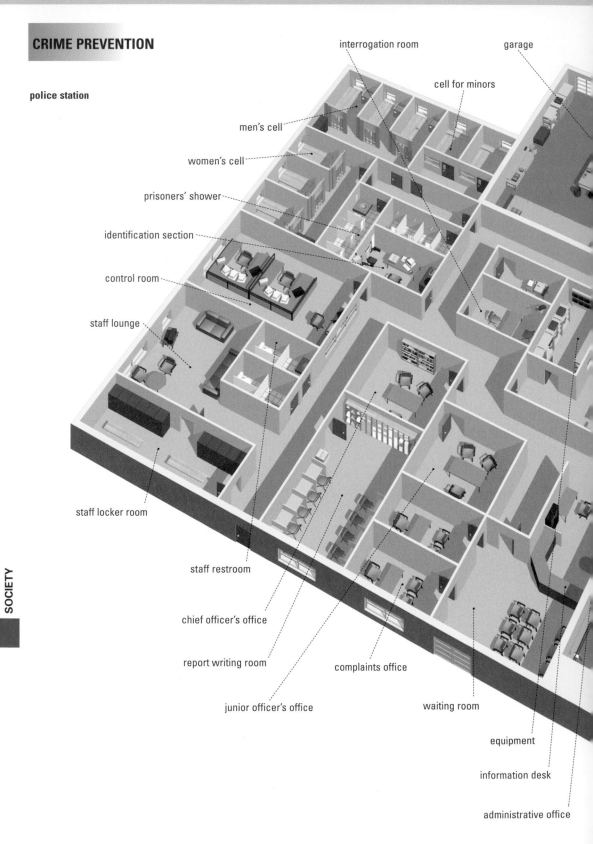

interrogation room

garage

cell for minors

men's cell

women's cell

prisoners' shower

identification section

control room

staff lounge

staff locker room

staff restroom

chief officer's office

report writing room

complaints office

junior officer's office

waiting room

equipment

information desk

administrative office

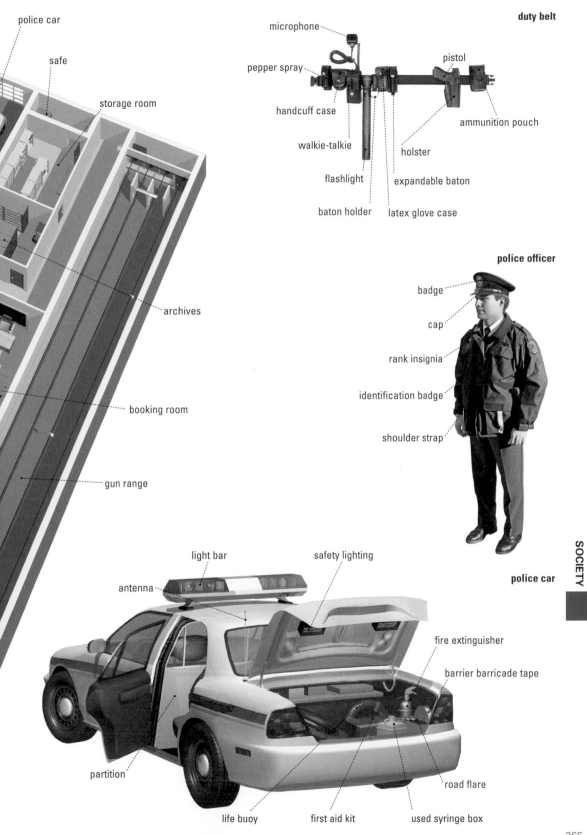

police car

safe

storage room

archives

booking room

gun range

duty belt

microphone

pepper spray

pistol

handcuff case

ammunition pouch

walkie-talkie

holster

flashlight

expandable baton

baton holder

latex glove case

police officer

badge

cap

rank insignia

identification badge

shoulder strap

police car

light bar

safety lighting

antenna

fire extinguisher

barrier barricade tape

partition

road flare

life buoy

first aid kit

used syringe box

SOCIETY

Among the different establishments that provide health services to the public, hospitals are the most complete and offer the widest range of services. In large cities, health institutions have become immense medical centers with staff specializing in every field of medicine. Hospitals provide quality care to the sick and wounded around the clock.

patient room

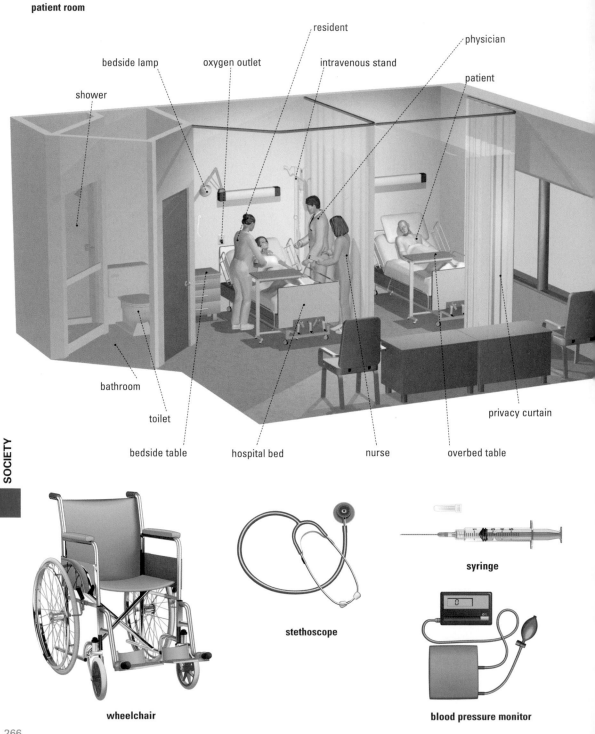

resident

physician

bedside lamp

oxygen outlet

intravenous stand

patient

shower

bathroom

toilet

bedside table

hospital bed

nurse

overbed table

privacy curtain

wheelchair

stethoscope

syringe

blood pressure monitor

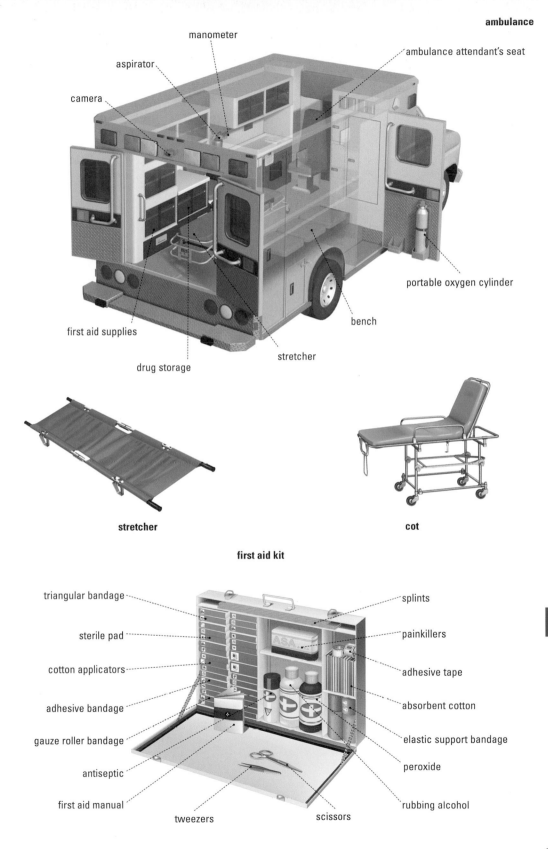

ambulance

manometer

aspirator

camera

ambulance attendant's seat

portable oxygen cylinder

bench

first aid supplies

stretcher

drug storage

stretcher

cot

first aid kit

triangular bandage

sterile pad

cotton applicators

adhesive bandage

gauze roller bandage

antiseptic

first aid manual

tweezers

scissors

splints

painkillers

adhesive tape

absorbent cotton

elastic support bandage

peroxide

rubbing alcohol

ASA

EDUCATION

In most developed countries, school is obligatory up to a certain age. Primary education, which begins around the ages of four to seven, is generally offered at no cost. As school children improve their skills in reading, writing and counting, they also develop their moral, intellectual and physical abilities. Many children in developing countries, however, do not receive any formal education because of a lack of resources.

SCHOOL

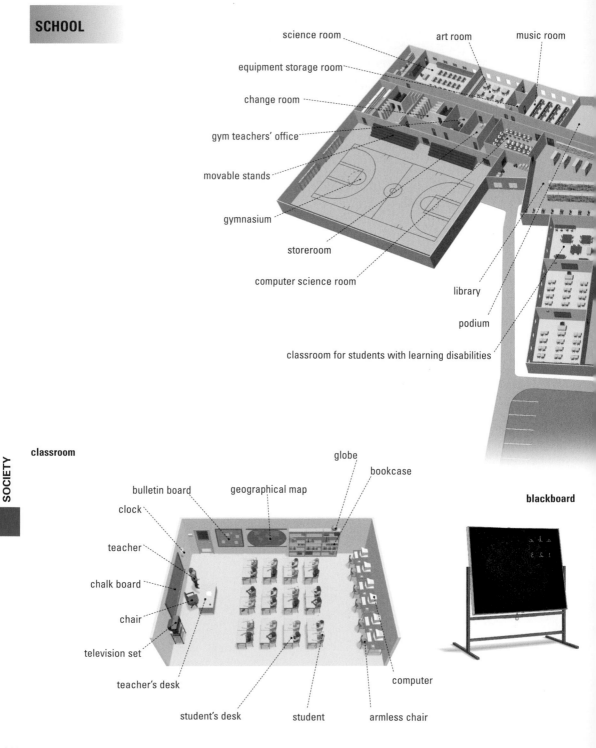

science room

art room

music room

equipment storage room

change room

gym teachers' office

movable stands

gymnasium

storeroom

computer science room

library

podium

classroom for students with learning disabilities

classroom

globe

bulletin board

geographical map

bookcase

clock

blackboard

teacher

chalk board

chair

television set

teacher's desk

computer

student's desk

student

armless chair

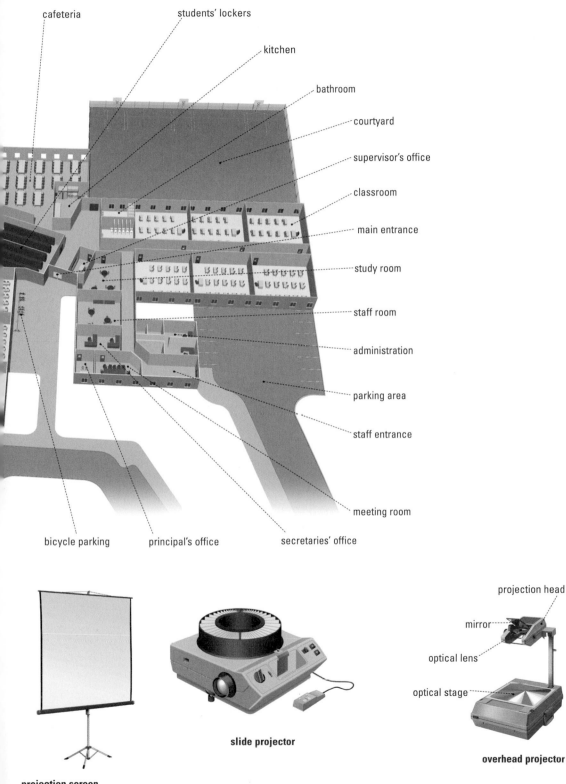

cafeteria

students' lockers

kitchen

bathroom

courtyard

supervisor's office

classroom

main entrance

study room

staff room

administration

parking area

staff entrance

meeting room

bicycle parking

principal's office

secretaries' office

projection screen

slide projector

projection head

mirror

optical lens

optical stage

overhead projector

school supplies

ballpoint pen

spring · cartridge · joint · clip · push-button · point · thrust device · thrust tube

clip

nib · **fountain pen** · air hole · barrel · cap

memo pad

staples

stapler

staple remover

glue stick

paper clips

pencil sharpener

thumb tacks

tape dispenser

eraser

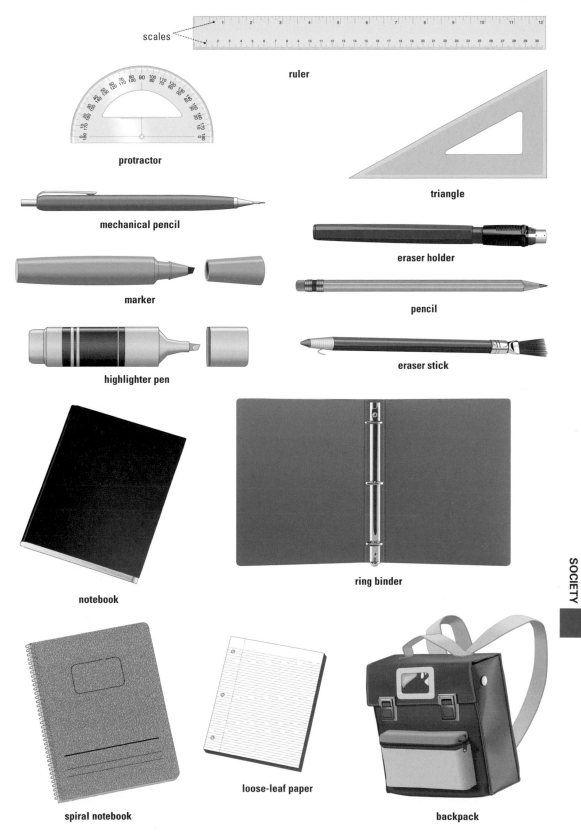

scales

ruler

protractor

triangle

mechanical pencil

eraser holder

marker

pencil

highlighter pen

eraser stick

notebook

ring binder

spiral notebook

loose-leaf paper

backpack

Whether they work on a movie set where scenes are shot or go to the movie theater to see the finished product, fans of motion pictures are found all over the world. For many, movies are much more than entertainment or a process of photographing and projecting moving images. Movies allow people to experience powerful emotions and live great adventures while sitting comfortably in their seats.

MOVIE THEATER

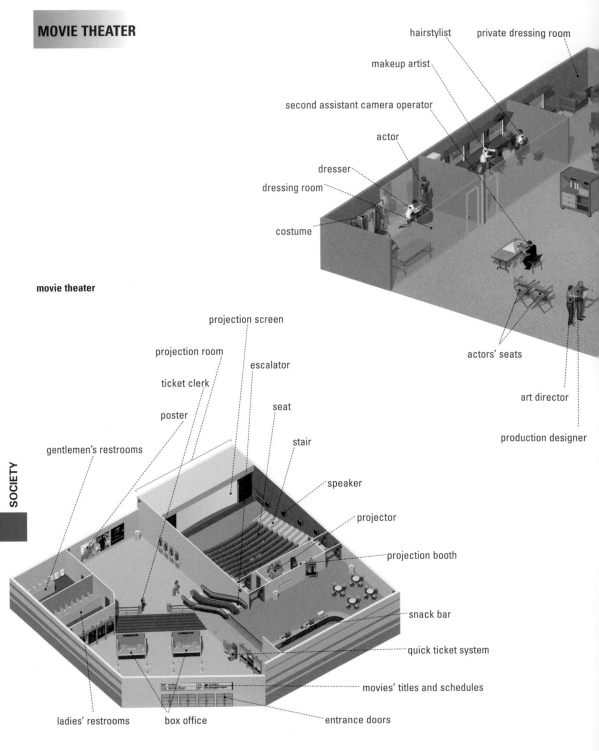

hairstylist

private dressing room

makeup artist

second assistant camera operator

actor

dresser

dressing room

costume

movie theater

projection screen

projection room

escalator

ticket clerk

seat

poster

stair

gentlemen's restrooms

actors' seats

art director

production designer

speaker

projector

projection booth

snack bar

quick ticket system

movies' titles and schedules

ladies' restrooms

box office

entrance doors

sound stage

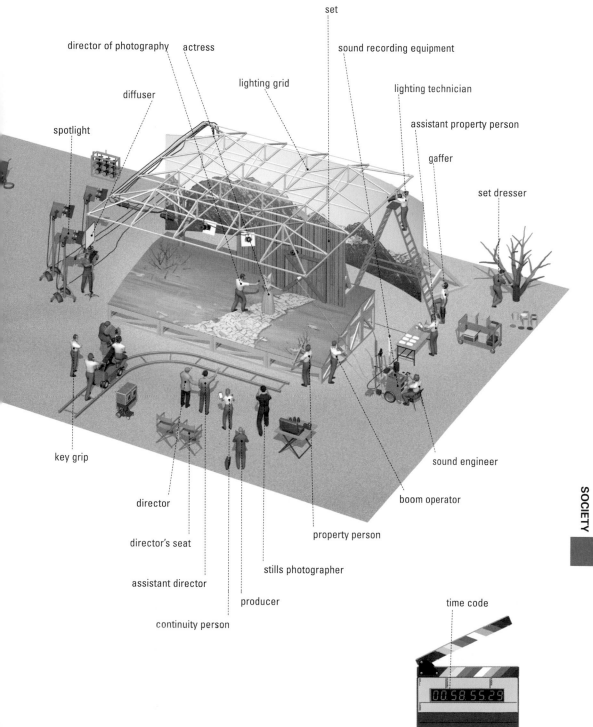

set

director of photography   actress

diffuser

lighting grid

sound recording equipment

lighting technician

assistant property person

spotlight

gaffer

set dresser

key grip

sound engineer

director

boom operator

director's seat

property person

assistant director

stills photographer

producer

continuity person

time code

00:58:55:29

clapper/the slate

GYMNASTICS

The goal in gymnastics is to perform movements as perfectly as possible. Artistic gymnastics requires agility, strength and flexibility. Rhythmic gymnasts must also have a good sense of choreography. Artistic and rhythmic gymnastics include events performed by both men and women, and some for one or the other. Gymnasts who specialize in trampoline perform complicated acrobatic figures in the air.

GYMNASTICS

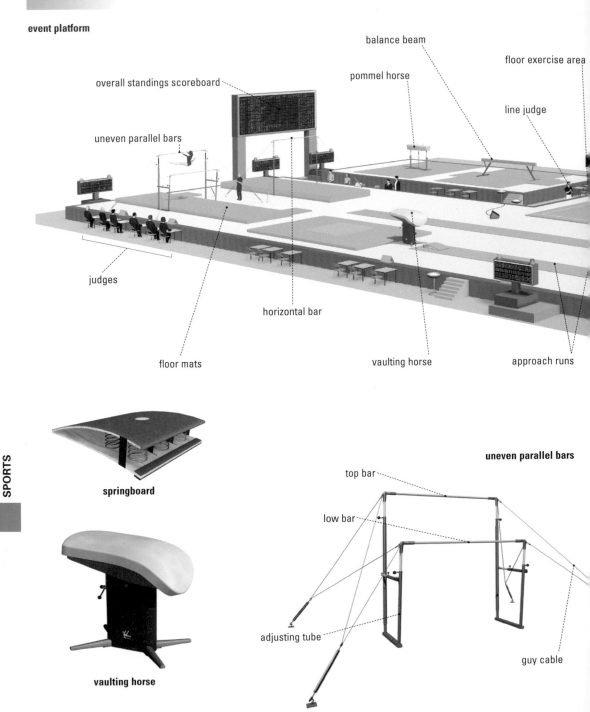

event platform

balance beam

floor exercise area

overall standings scoreboard

pommel horse

line judge

uneven parallel bars

judges

horizontal bar

floor mats

vaulting horse

approach runs

springboard

uneven parallel bars

top bar

low bar

adjusting tube

guy cable

vaulting horse

balance beam

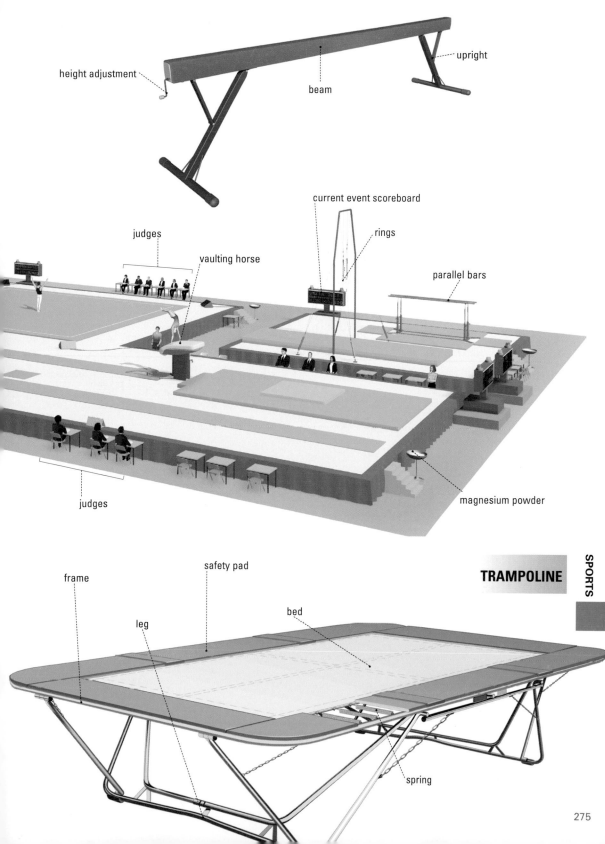

upright

height adjustment

beam

current event scoreboard

rings

judges

vaulting horse

parallel bars

magnesium powder

judges

safety pad

TRAMPOLINE

frame

bed

leg

spring

SWIMMING

The swimmer's goal is to glide through the water as quickly as possible with the least amount of effort. Swimmers must train constantly and intensively in order to perfect their technique. Athletes usually specialize in one of the four recognized styles of swimming: the front crawl (also called freestyle), butterfly, breaststroke or backstroke.

starting block

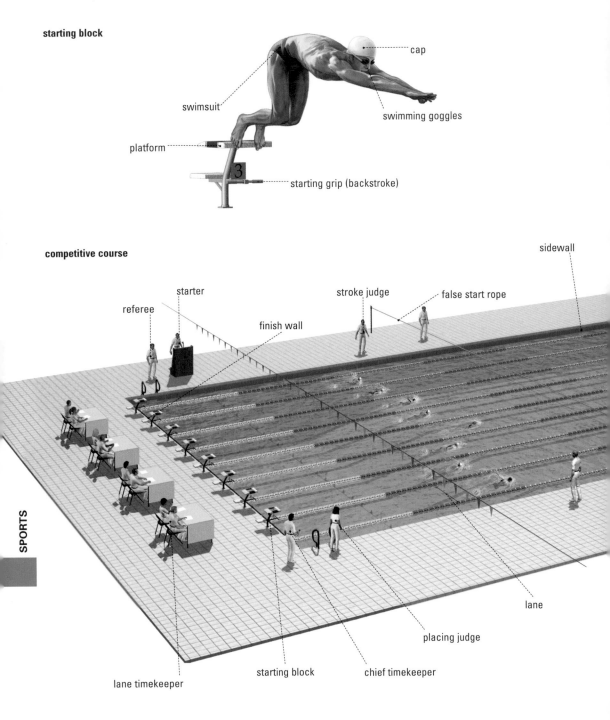

cap

swimsuit

swimming goggles

platform

starting grip (backstroke)

competitive course

sidewall

starter

stroke judge

false start rope

referee

finish wall

lane

placing judge

starting block

chief timekeeper

lane timekeeper

butterfly stroke

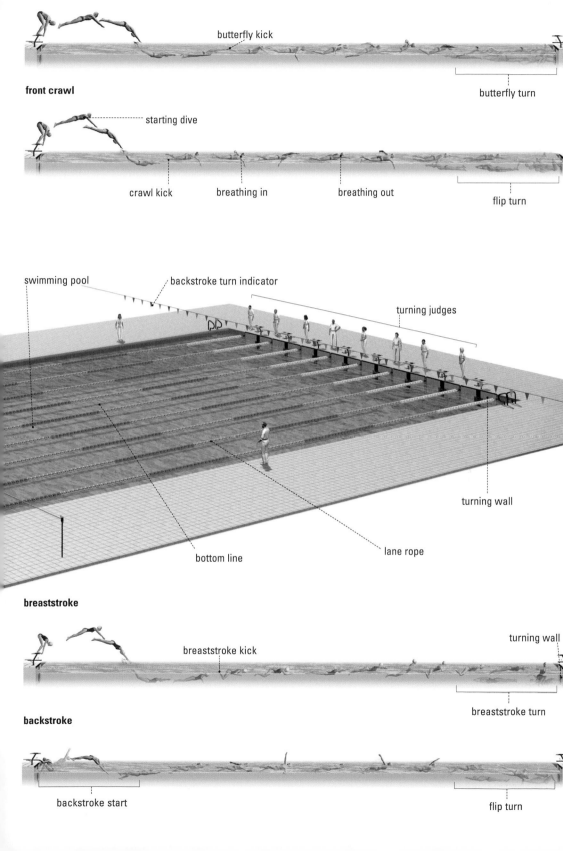

butterfly kick

butterfly turn

front crawl

starting dive

crawl kick

breathing in

breathing out

flip turn

swimming pool

backstroke turn indicator

turning judges

turning wall

bottom line

lane rope

breaststroke

breaststroke kick

turning wall

breaststroke turn

backstroke

backstroke start

flip turn

Among the sports practiced on water, some, like rowing, require the participation of a team. Several people must work together to synchronize their movements in order to cross the finish line. In other sports, like surfing, canoeing, kayaking or windsurfing, athletes perform as individuals. In almost all of these sports speed is a factor, and quick reflexes and an excellent sense of balance are necessary.

SAILBOARD

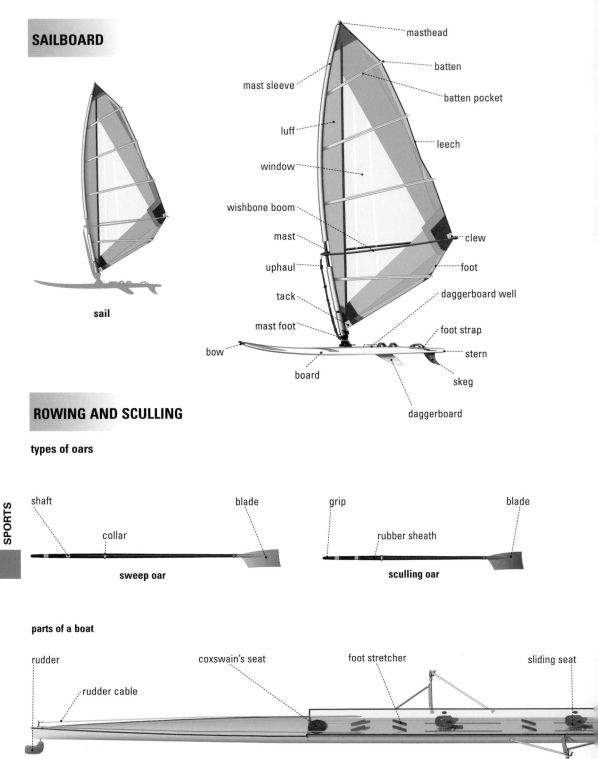

sail

masthead

batten

mast sleeve

batten pocket

luff

leech

window

wishbone boom

mast

clew

uphaul

foot

tack

daggerboard well

mast foot

foot strap

bow

stern

board

skeg

daggerboard

ROWING AND SCULLING

types of oars

shaft

blade

grip

blade

collar

rubber sheath

sweep oar

sculling oar

parts of a boat

rudder

coxswain's seat

foot stretcher

sliding seat

rudder cable

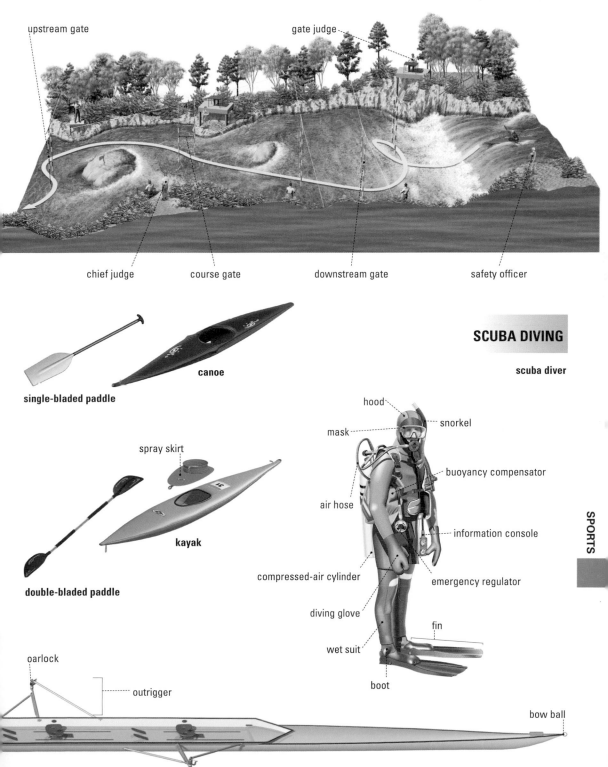

CANOE/KAYAK

whitewater

upstream gate

gate judge

chief judge

course gate

downstream gate

safety officer

single-bladed paddle

canoe

spray skirt

kayak

double-bladed paddle

oarlock

outrigger

SCUBA DIVING

scuba diver

hood

snorkel

mask

buoyancy compensator

air hose

information console

compressed-air cylinder

emergency regulator

diving glove

fin

wet suit

boot

bow ball

SPORTS

EQUESTRIAN SPORTS

Horse racing, like all other equestrian sports, requires that both the rider and horse make a good team. Both must strive for perfection in their quest to reach the finish line. It is the jockey, however, who makes all the decisions during a race. Jockeys mainly use their legs and hands to control and direct their horses.

HORSE RACING (TURF)

jockey and racehorse

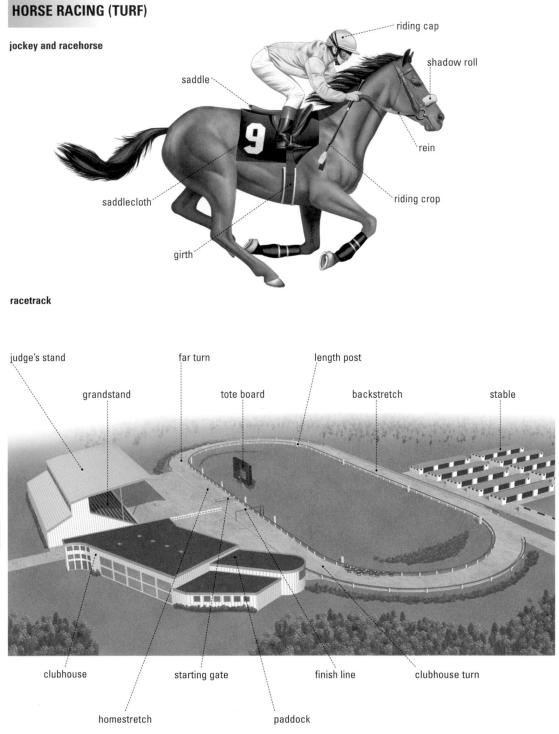

riding cap

shadow roll

saddle

rein

saddlecloth

riding crop

girth

racetrack

judge's stand

far turn

length post

grandstand

tote board

backstretch

stable

clubhouse

starting gate

finish line

clubhouse turn

homestretch

paddock

As the name suggests, precision and accuracy sports require a perfect mastery of one's movements and a high level of concentration. Whether the athlete is shooting an arrow, knocking down pins or hitting a golf ball, every action must be performed with great precision, since the object must hit a specific target, often located at a distance.

archer

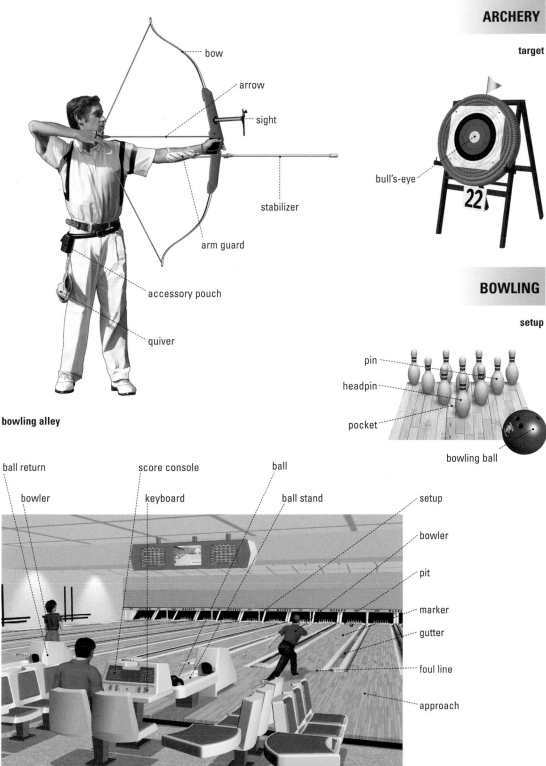

bow

arrow

sight

stabilizer

arm guard

accessory pouch

quiver

ARCHERY

target

bull's-eye

22

BOWLING

setup

pin

headpin

pocket

bowling ball

bowling alley

ball return

bowler

score console

keyboard

ball

ball stand

setup

bowler

pit

marker

gutter

foul line

approach

SPORTS

GOLF

course

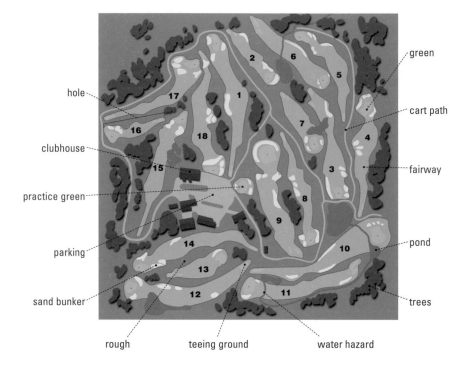

green

hole

cart path

clubhouse

fairway

practice green

parking

pond

sand bunker

trees

rough   teeing ground   water hazard

golf equipment and accessories

golf ball

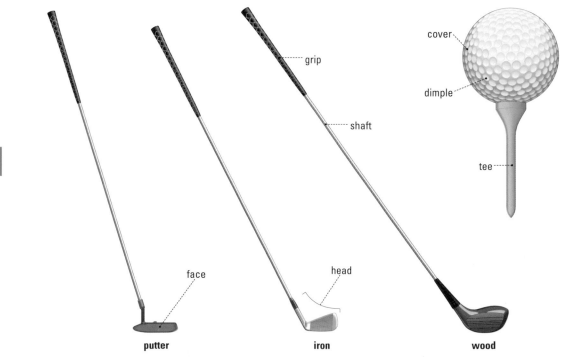

cover

dimple

grip

shaft

tee

face

head

putter

iron

wood

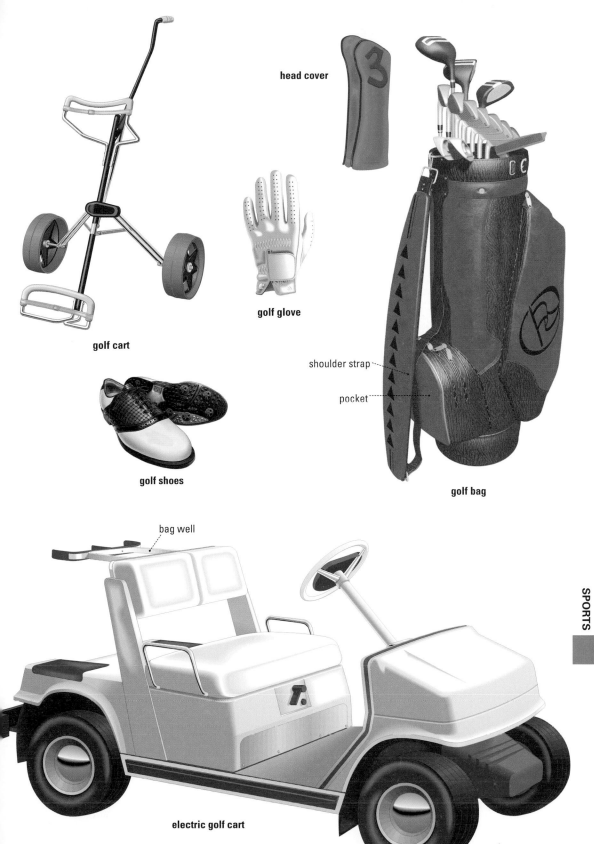

head cover

golf glove

golf cart

golf shoes

shoulder strap

pocket

golf bag

bag well

electric golf cart

WINTER SPORTS

Whether they take place on a skating rink, frozen track or snow-covered slope, winter sports are among the fastest non-motorized sports in the world.

Practiced as a team or individually, as recreation or in competition, these sports require specific equipment such as skis, skates, snowshoes or sleds.

ICE HOCKEY

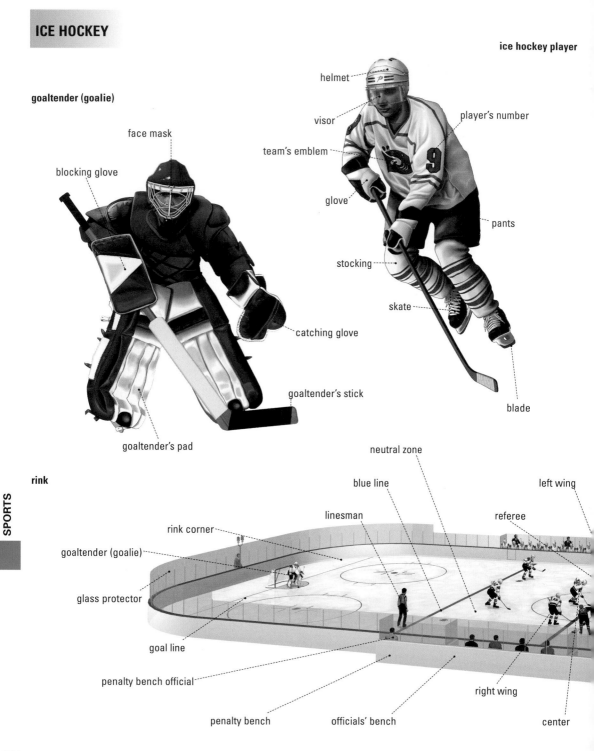

ice hockey player

helmet

visor

team's emblem

player's number

glove

pants

stocking

skate

blade

goaltender (goalie)

face mask

blocking glove

catching glove

goaltender's stick

goaltender's pad

rink

neutral zone

blue line

left wing

linesman

referee

rink corner

goaltender (goalie)

glass protector

goal line

penalty bench official

penalty bench

officials' bench

right wing

center

protective equipment

player's stick

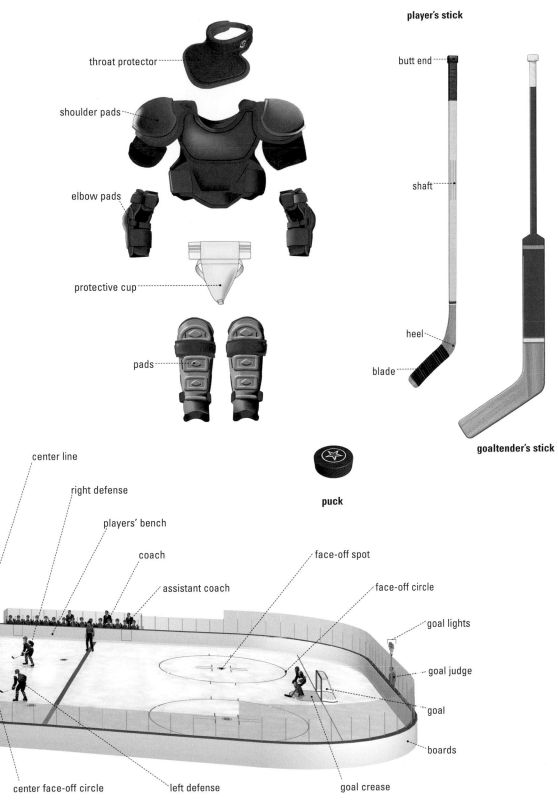

throat protector

shoulder pads

elbow pads

protective cup

pads

butt end

shaft

heel

blade

goaltender's stick

puck

center line

right defense

players' bench

coach

assistant coach

face-off spot

face-off circle

goal lights

goal judge

goal

boards

center face-off circle

left defense

goal crease

SKATING

hockey skate

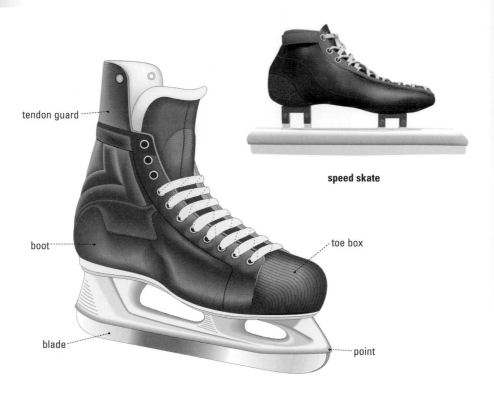

tendon guard

boot

blade

toe box

point

speed skate

figure skate

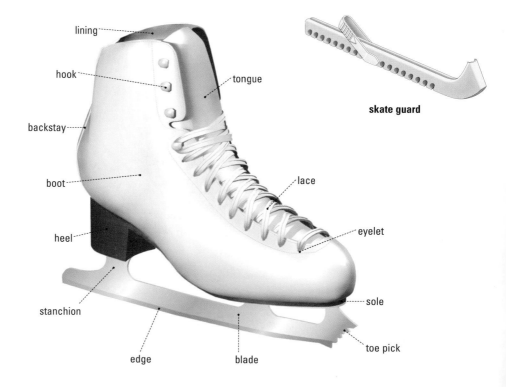

lining

hook

tongue

backstay

boot

lace

heel

eyelet

stanchion

sole

edge

blade

toe pick

skate guard

SNOWBOARDING

snowboarder

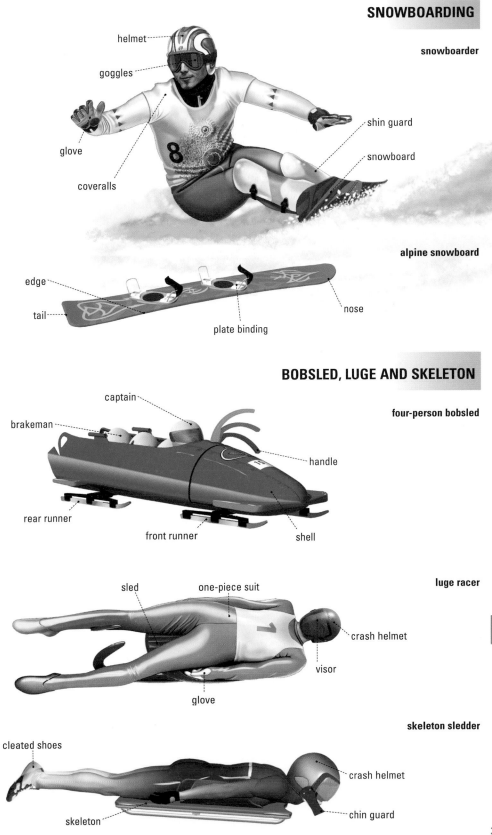

helmet

goggles

glove

coveralls

shin guard

snowboard

8

alpine snowboard

edge

tail

plate binding

nose

BOBSLED, LUGE AND SKELETON

four-person bobsled

captain

brakeman

handle

rear runner

front runner

shell

luge racer

sled

one-piece suit

crash helmet

visor

glove

skeleton sledder

cleated shoes

crash helmet

skeleton

chin guard

SPORTS

287

SNOWSHOES

Michigan snowshoe

elliptical snowshoe

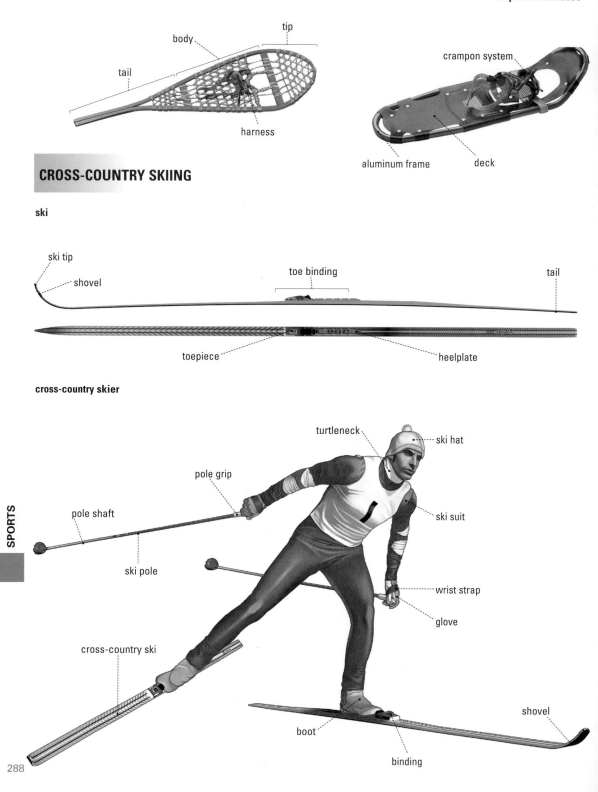

tip

body

tail

crampon system

harness

aluminum frame

deck

CROSS-COUNTRY SKIING

ski

ski tip

shovel

toe binding

tail

toepiece

heelplate

cross-country skier

turtleneck

ski hat

pole grip

ski suit

pole shaft

wrist strap

ski pole

glove

cross-country ski

shovel

boot

binding

safety binding

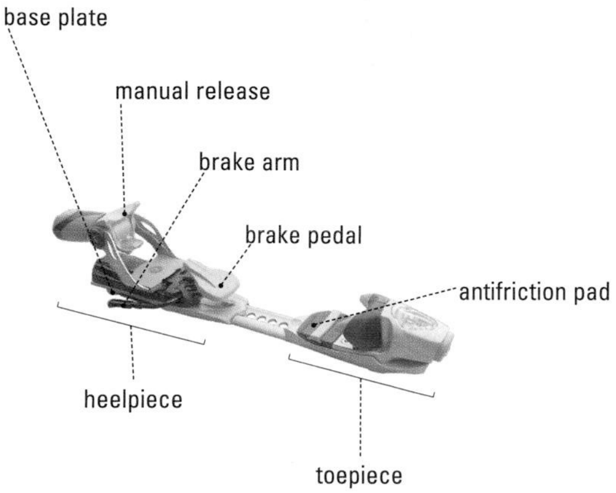

base plate

manual release

brake arm

brake pedal

antifriction pad

heelpiece

toepiece

ski boot

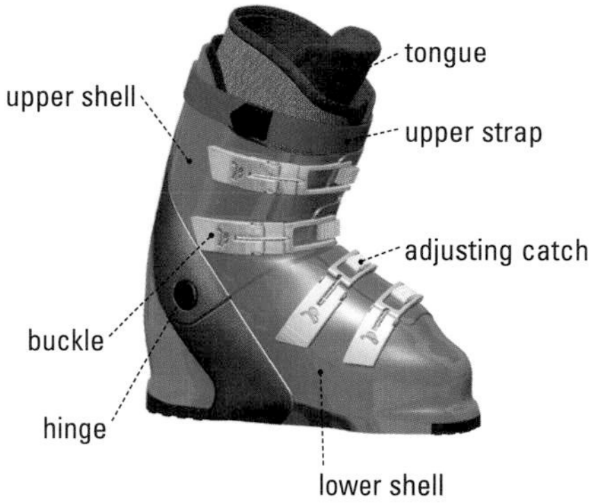

tongue

upper shell

upper strap

adjusting catch

buckle

hinge

lower shell

ski

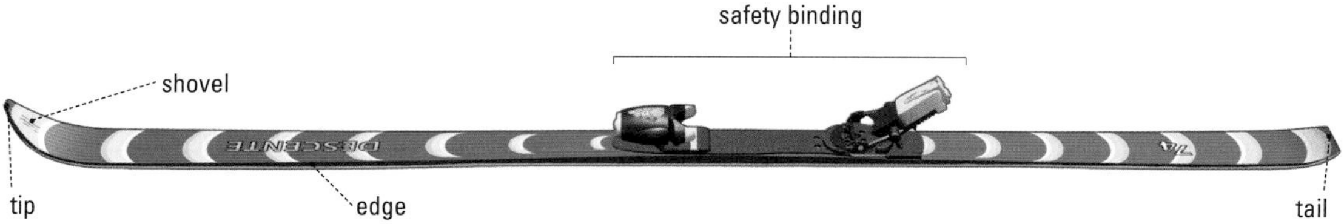

safety binding

shovel

tip

edge

tail

alpine skier

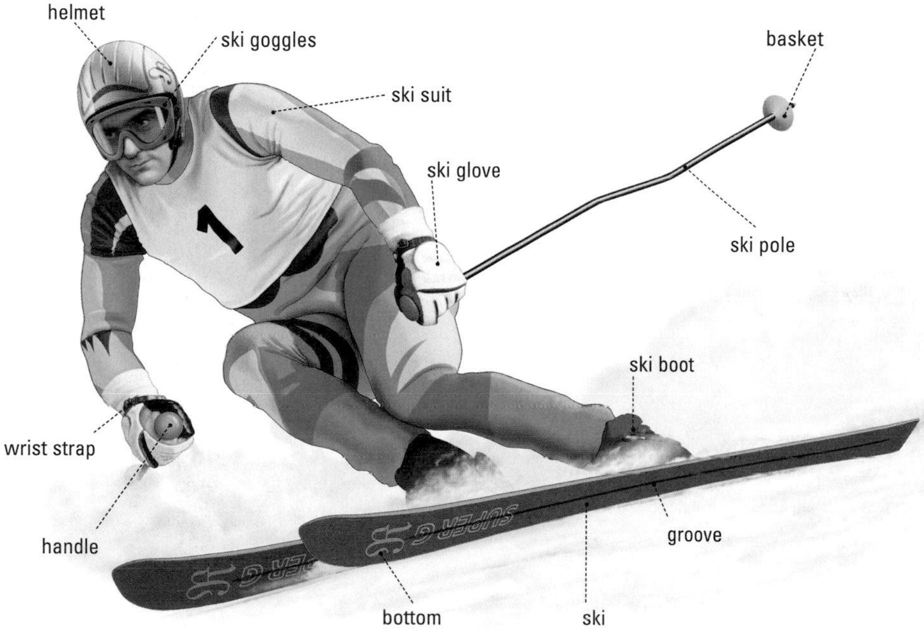

helmet

ski goggles

ski suit

basket

ski glove

ski pole

wrist strap

ski boot

handle

groove

bottom

ski

Ball sports are usually played in teams. Whether it is baseball, basketball, cricket, field hockey, football or volleyball, players must follow the rules of the game while trying to outmaneuver their opponents. The object in these types of sports is usually to move the ball into a goal as often as possible.

BASEBALL

player positions

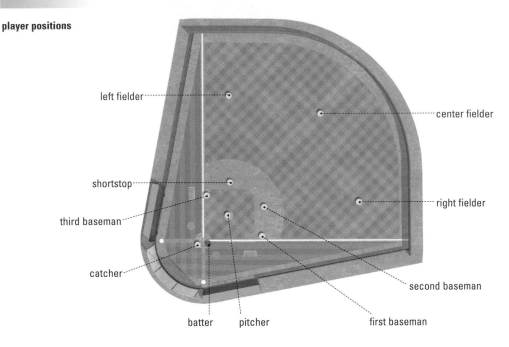

left fielder

center fielder

shortstop

right fielder

third baseman

catcher

second baseman

batter

pitcher

first baseman

field

left field

coach's box

foul line

dugout

on-deck circle

third base

backstop

home-plate umpire

pitcher's mound

first base

infield

second base

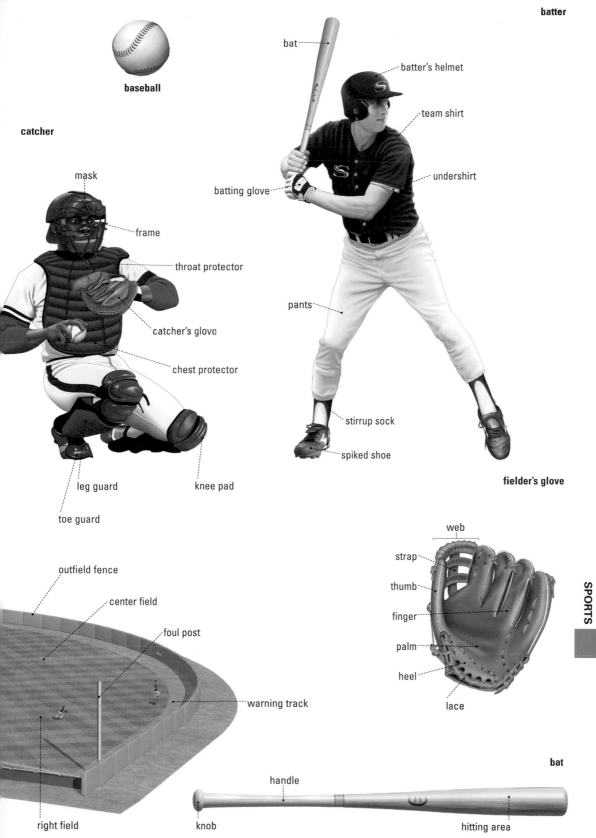

baseball

catcher

mask

frame

throat protector

catcher's glove

chest protector

leg guard

toe guard

knee pad

batter

bat

batter's helmet

team shirt

undershirt

batting glove

pants

stirrup sock

spiked shoe

fielder's glove

web

strap

thumb

finger

palm

heel

lace

outfield fence

center field

foul post

warning track

right field

bat

handle

knob

hitting area

CRICKET

cricket player (batsman)

bat

helmet

face mask

bat

glove

wicket

bail

stump

handle

willow

cricket ball

pad

cricket shoe

stud

pitch

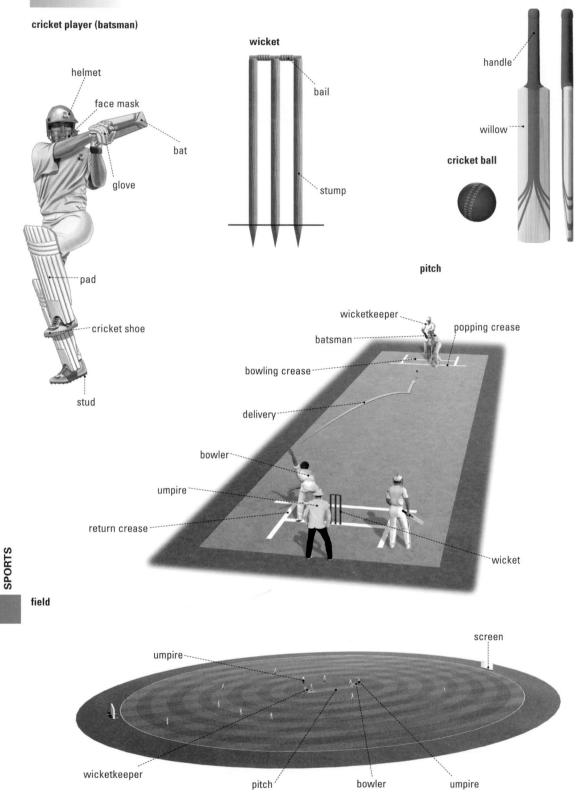

wicketkeeper

popping crease

batsman

bowling crease

delivery

bowler

umpire

return crease

wicket

field

umpire

screen

umpire

wicketkeeper

pitch

bowler

umpire

FIELD HOCKEY

field hockey player

stick

team shirt

shorts

stick

shin guard

shoe

handle

tape

blade

hockey ball

playing field

officials

right wing

center half

22 m line

right inside forward

right back

players' bench

right half

left half

coach

left back

corner flag

goalkeeper

referee

sideline

left wing

5 m line

left inside forward

striking circle

center forward

goal line

center line

goal

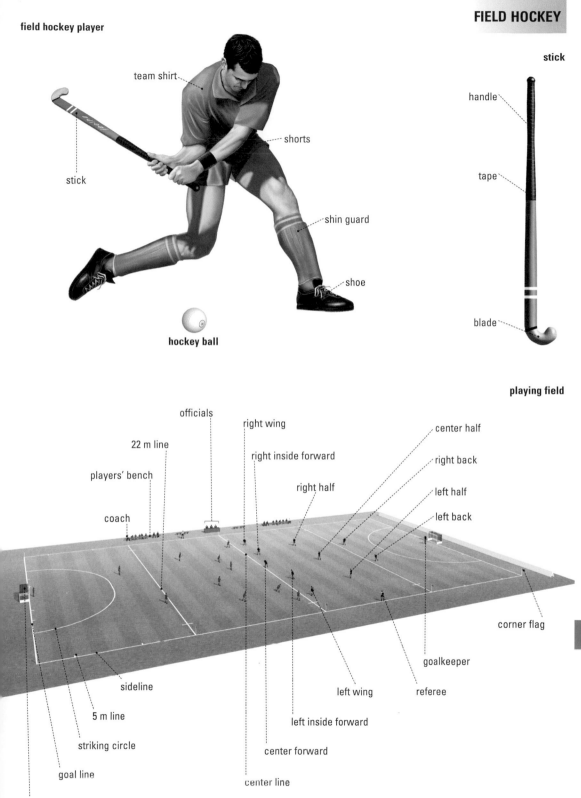

BASKETBALL

player positions

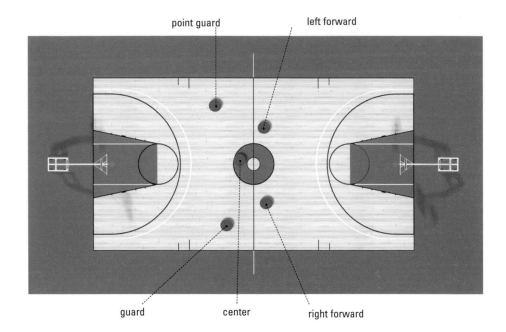

point guard

left forward

guard

center

right forward

court

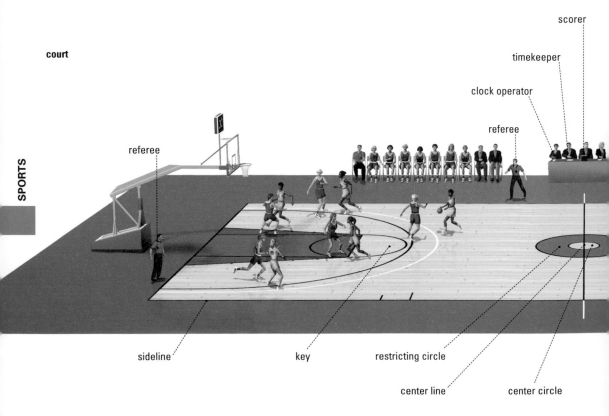

scorer

timekeeper

clock operator

referee

referee

sideline

key

restricting circle

center line

center circle

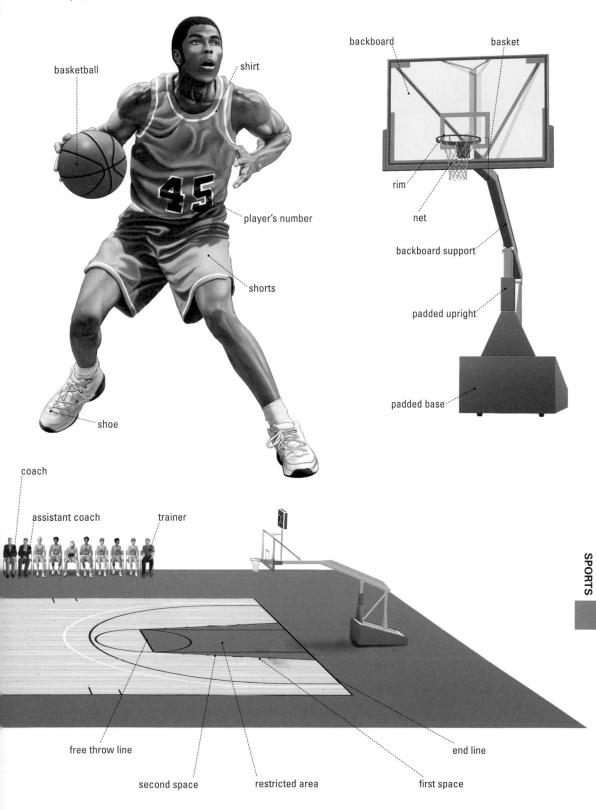

basketball player

backstop

basketball

shirt

player's number

shorts

shoe

backboard

basket

rim

net

backboard support

padded upright

padded base

coach

assistant coach

trainer

free throw line

second space

restricted area

first space

end line

AMERICAN FOOTBALL

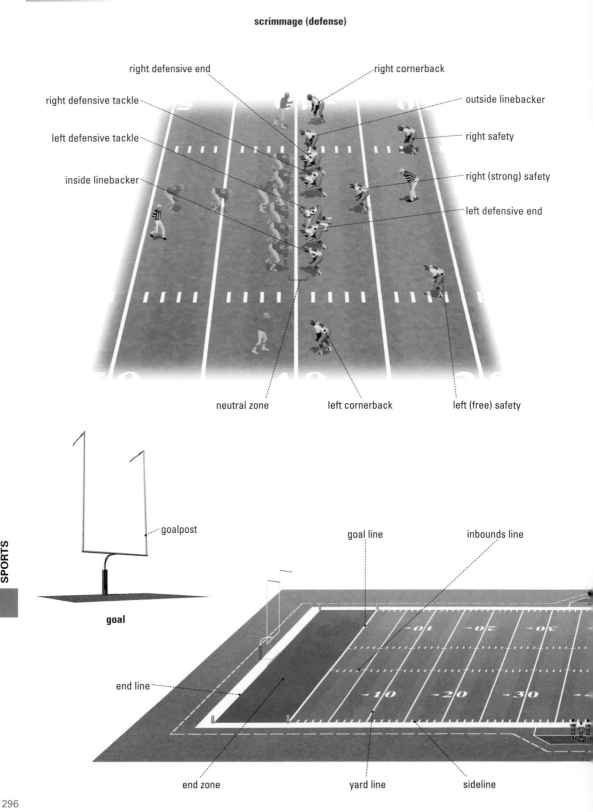

scrimmage (defense)

right defensive end

right cornerback

right defensive tackle

outside linebacker

left defensive tackle

right safety

inside linebacker

right (strong) safety

left defensive end

neutral zone

left cornerback

left (free) safety

goalpost

goal

goal line

inbounds line

end line

end zone

yard line

sideline

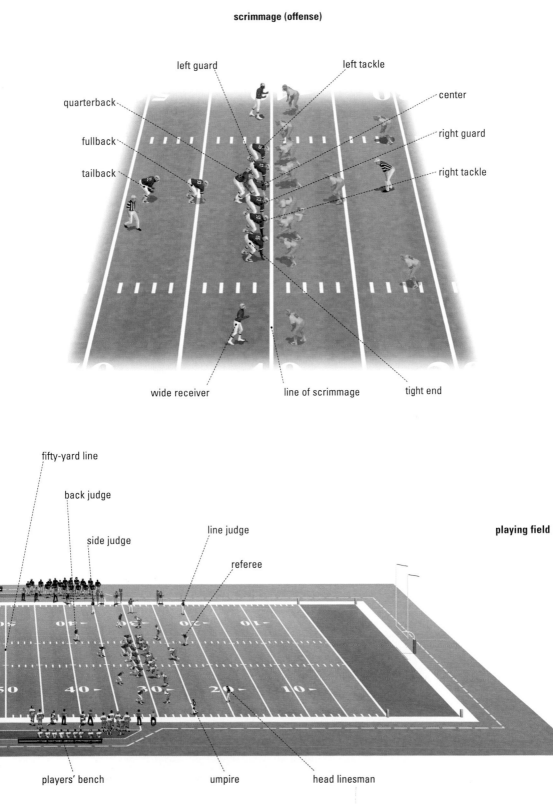

scrimmage (offense)

left guard

left tackle

quarterback

center

fullback

right guard

tailback

right tackle

wide receiver

line of scrimmage

tight end

fifty-yard line

back judge

side judge

line judge

referee

playing field

50 40 30 20 10

50 40 30 20 10

players' bench

umpire

head linesman

football player

protective equipment

helmet

chin strap

face mask

player's number

team jersey

wristband

pants

thigh pad

knee pad

sock

cleated shoe

shoulder pad

arm guard

chest protector

protective cup

rib pad

tooth guard

hip pad

football

forearm pad

neck pad

CANADIAN FOOTBALL

elbow pad

playing field

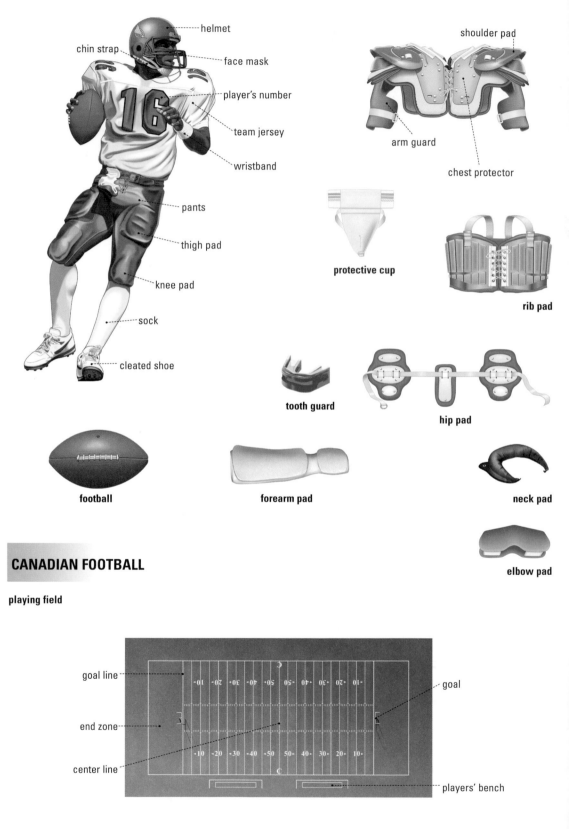

goal line

goal

end zone

center line

players' bench

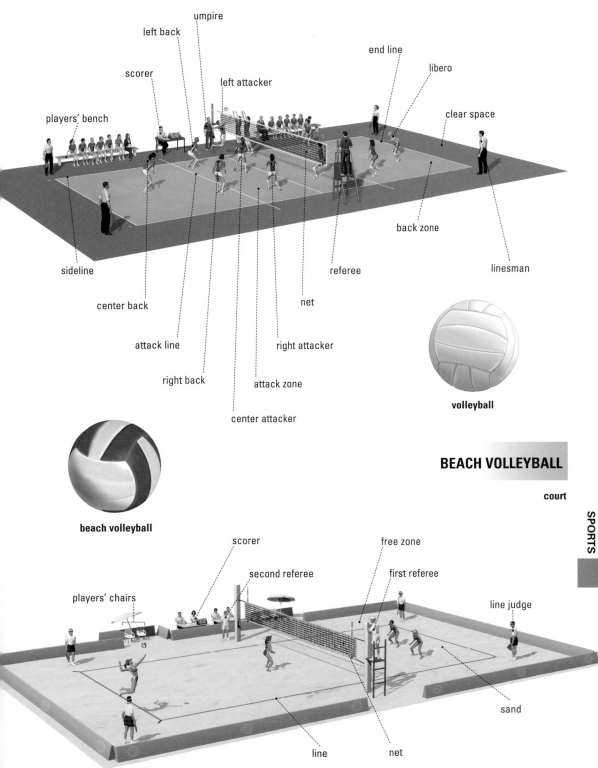

VOLLEYBALL

court

umpire

left back

scorer

left attacker

end line

libero

players' bench

clear space

sideline

back zone

linesman

center back

referee

net

attack line

right attacker

right back

attack zone

center attacker

volleyball

BEACH VOLLEYBALL

court

beach volleyball

scorer

free zone

second referee

first referee

players' chairs

line judge

sand

line

net

SOCCER

player positions

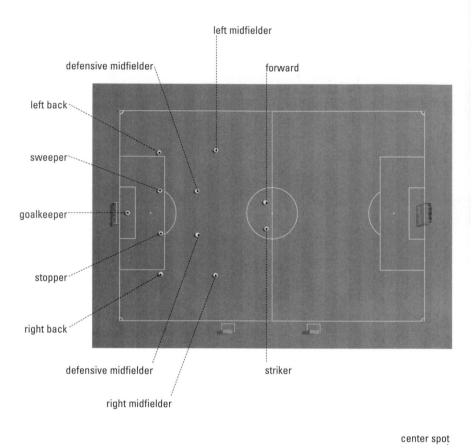

left midfielder

defensive midfielder

forward

left back

sweeper

goalkeeper

stopper

right back

defensive midfielder

striker

right midfielder

playing field

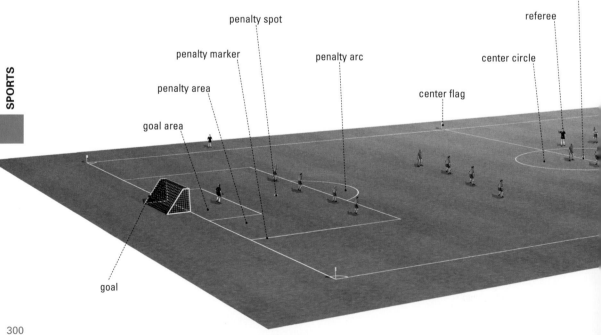

center spot

penalty spot

referee

penalty marker

penalty arc

center circle

penalty area

center flag

goal area

goal

soccer player

goalkeeper's gloves

team shirt

soccer shoe

shorts

shin guard

interchangeable studs

sock

soccer ball

corner flag

corner arc

touch line

halfway line

linesman

substitute's bench

Tennis is played in most countries. It is played by two people or by two teams of two on a clay court, grass court or artificial surface. Players hit the ball back and forth over a net. The ball may travel more than 120 mph (200 km/h). Several large tournaments draw many spectators each year. The oldest and most famous of these is Wimbledon, held in England.

TENNIS

tennis racket

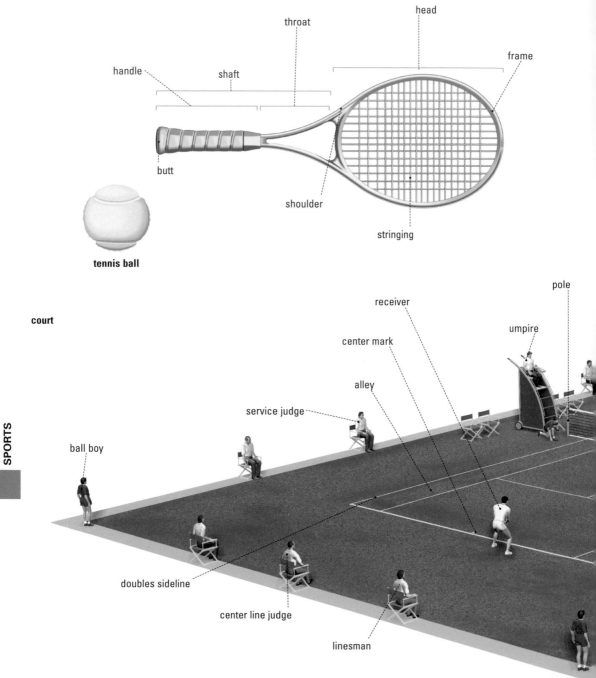

head

throat

frame

handle

shaft

butt

shoulder

stringing

tennis ball

court

pole

receiver

umpire

center mark

alley

service judge

ball boy

doubles sideline

center line judge

linesman

tennis player

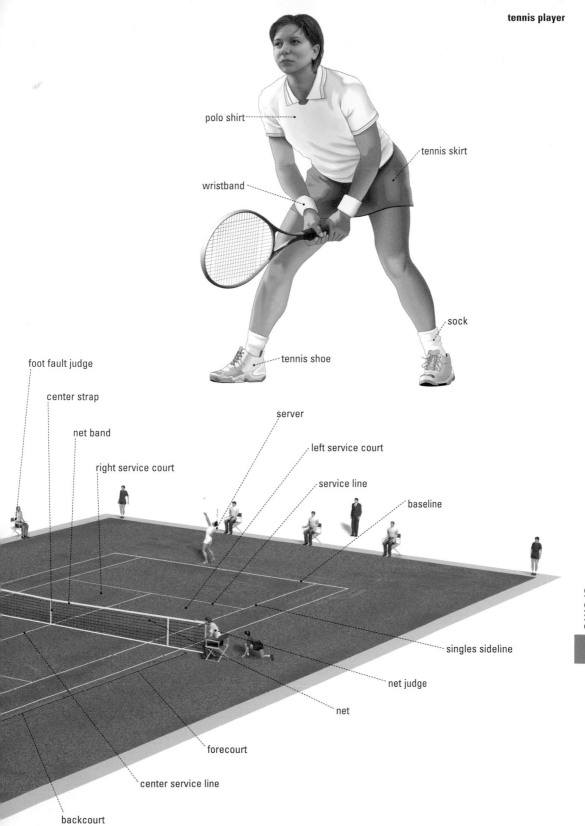

polo shirt

tennis skirt

wristband

sock

foot fault judge

tennis shoe

center strap

server

net band

left service court

right service court

service line

baseline

net judge

singles sideline

net

forecourt

center service line

backcourt

SPORTS

303

COMBAT SPORTS

Karate, boxing, wrestling and judo are combat sports in which two opponents of matching weight fight hand to hand. Top physical and mental conditioning is a requirement for the karateka, the athlete who practices karate, while the boxer needs dexterity and exceptional strength. To perform any martial art, combat or self-defense technique, athletes must completely master their level of force and their movements.

BOXING

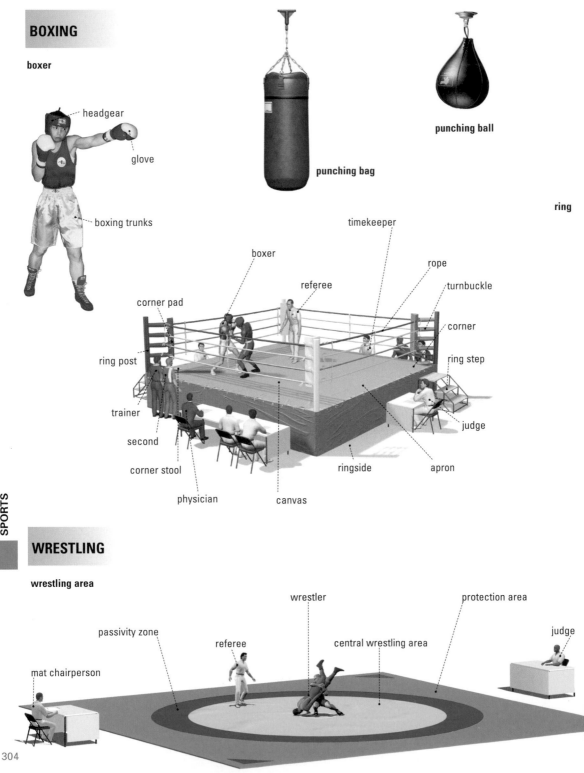

boxer

headgear

glove

boxing trunks

punching bag

punching ball

ring

timekeeper

boxer

referee

rope

turnbuckle

corner pad

corner

ring post

ring step

trainer

second

judge

corner stool

ringside

apron

physician

canvas

WRESTLING

wrestling area

wrestler

protection area

passivity zone

judge

referee

central wrestling area

mat chairperson

competition area

karateka

corner judge

timekeeper

arbitration committee

scorekeeper

referee

karate-gi

JUDO

judogi

obi

jacket

karateka

belt

trousers

mat

scorers and timekeepers

scoreboard

contestant

medical team

safety area

contest area

referee

danger area

judge

Car racing takes place on different kinds of tracks, where specially constructed high-speed vehicles race against one another. The drivers of these vehicles, as in other motor sports, need nerves of steel and extremely quick reflexes. They must be able to maintain complete control over their high-powered race-cars at all times.

CAR RACING

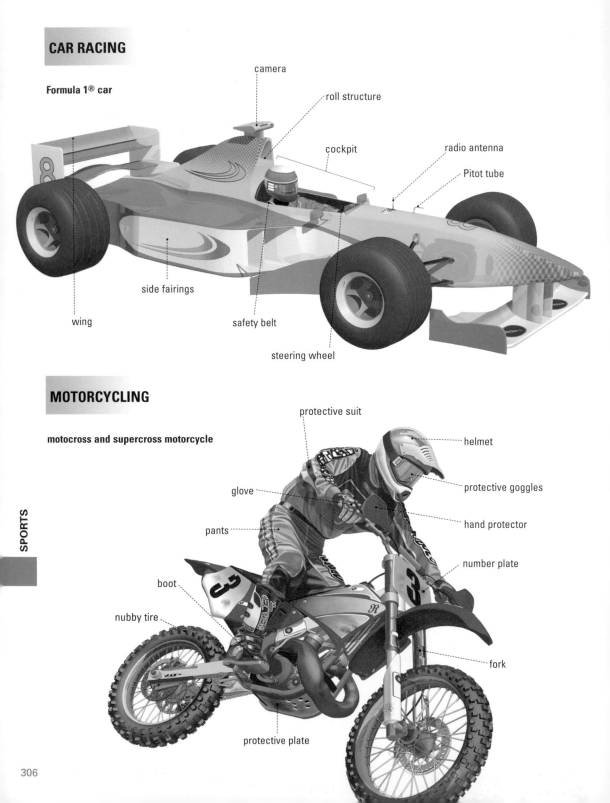

Formula 1® car

camera

roll structure

cockpit

radio antenna

Pitot tube

side fairings

wing

safety belt

steering wheel

MOTORCYCLING

motocross and supercross motorcycle

protective suit

helmet

glove

protective goggles

pants

hand protector

number plate

boot

nubby tire

fork

protective plate

Skateboarding and in-line skating are two sports that require excellent reflexes and coordination, as well as a good sense of balance. Skateboarders use creativity and technical skill to perform acrobatic figures on a variety of specially designed surfaces. In-line skating can take the form of acrobatics, speed skating or games such as hockey.

skateboarder

in-line skate

inner boot

upper shell

adjusting buckle

boot

axle

heel stop

truck

wheel

skater

skateboard

helmet

grip tape

wheel

elbow pad

wrist guard

knee pad

ramp

guard rail

platform

coping

vertical section

flat

SPORTS

CYCLING

Whether they practice on uneven terrain or a smooth track, cyclists must have a good sense of balance, excellent reflexes and great endurance. The various bicycles used in each of the cycling sports are made for specific events. The racing bike, for example, is designed to reach high speeds, while the cross-country bike is made for jumping over obstacles and riding on rough trails.

ROAD RACING

road-racing bicycle and cyclist

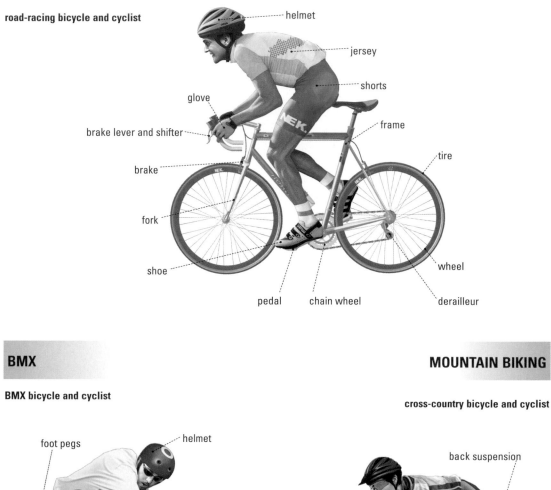

helmet

jersey

shorts

glove

brake lever and shifter

frame

brake

tire

fork

shoe

wheel

pedal   chain wheel

derailleur

BMX

BMX bicycle and cyclist

foot pegs

helmet

handlebars

glove

single chain wheel

foot pegs

single sprocket

MOUNTAIN BIKING

cross-country bicycle and cyclist

back suspension

goggles

front fork

clipless pedal

Camping is the ideal activity for travelers on a budget who want to enjoy the great outdoors. A sleeping bag and a few utensils are all one requires. Complete camping gear would include a tent, mattress and cooler to make the activity more comfortable. Reduced to its simplest expression, wilderness camping makes it possible to explore regions that are inaccessible by road.

family tent

TENTS

frame

living room

bedroom

window canopy

guy line

screen window

elastic strainer

canvas divider

sewn-in floor

wall

stake loop

wall tent

two-person tent

one-person tent

wagon tent

pup tent

dome tent

pop-up tent

SLEEPING BAGS

rectangular

semi-mummy

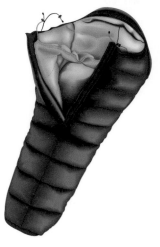

mummy

BED AND MATTRESS

air mattress

self-inflating mattress

foam pad

inflator

inflator-deflator

folding cot

CAMPING EQUIPMENT

Swiss Army knife

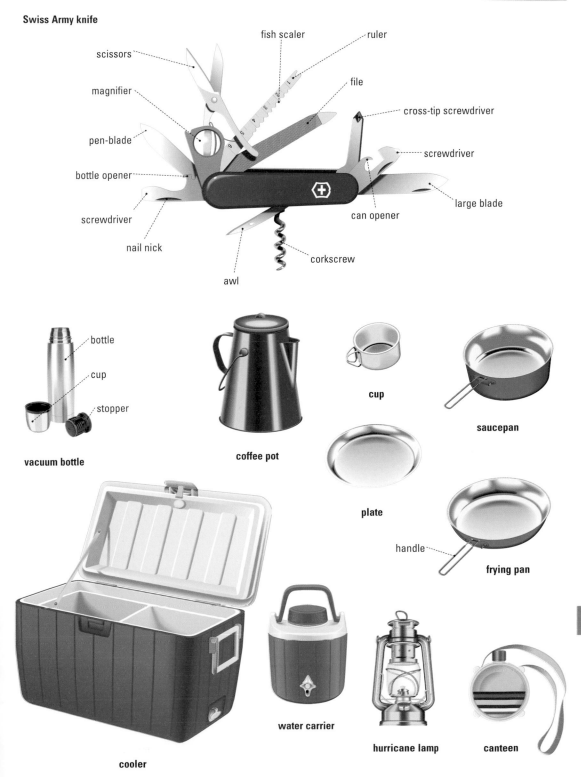

scissors

fish scaler

ruler

magnifier

file

cross-tip screwdriver

pen-blade

screwdriver

bottle opener

large blade

screwdriver

can opener

nail nick

corkscrew

awl

bottle

cup

stopper

vacuum bottle

coffee pot

cup

saucepan

plate

handle

frying pan

cooler

water carrier

hurricane lamp

canteen

backpack

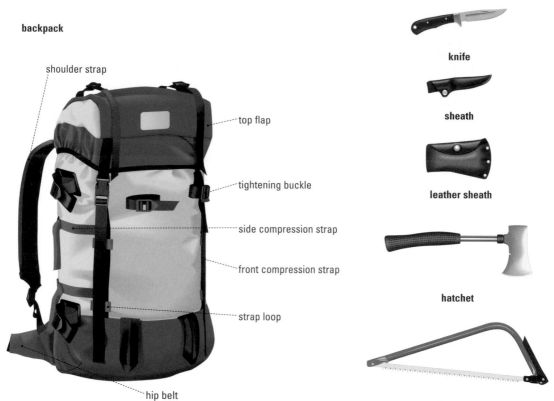

shoulder strap

top flap

tightening buckle

side compression strap

front compression strap

strap loop

hip belt

knife

sheath

leather sheath

hatchet

bow saw

magnetic compass

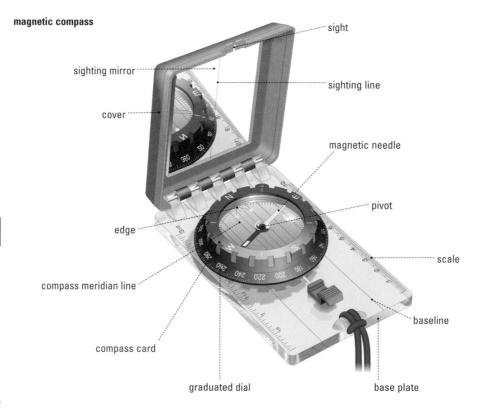

sight

sighting mirror

sighting line

cover

magnetic needle

pivot

edge

scale

compass meridian line

baseline

compass card

graduated dial

base plate

Table games have probably been around as long as people have enjoyed play. Dice were discovered in ancient Egyptian tombs and the game of chess dates back to the Middle Ages. Today indoor games are quite varied, and they include dominoes, cards, backgammon, darts and video games, to name a few. Whether individually or in a group, games are usually played for pleasure.

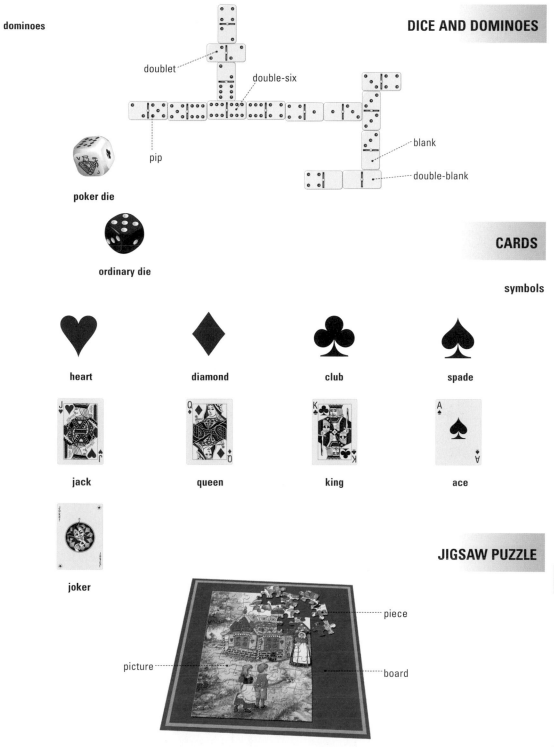

DICE AND DOMINOES

dominoes

doublet

double-six

blank

double-blank

pip

poker die

ordinary die

CARDS

symbols

heart

diamond

club

spade

jack

queen

king

ace

joker

JIGSAW PUZZLE

piece

picture

board

CHESS

chessboard

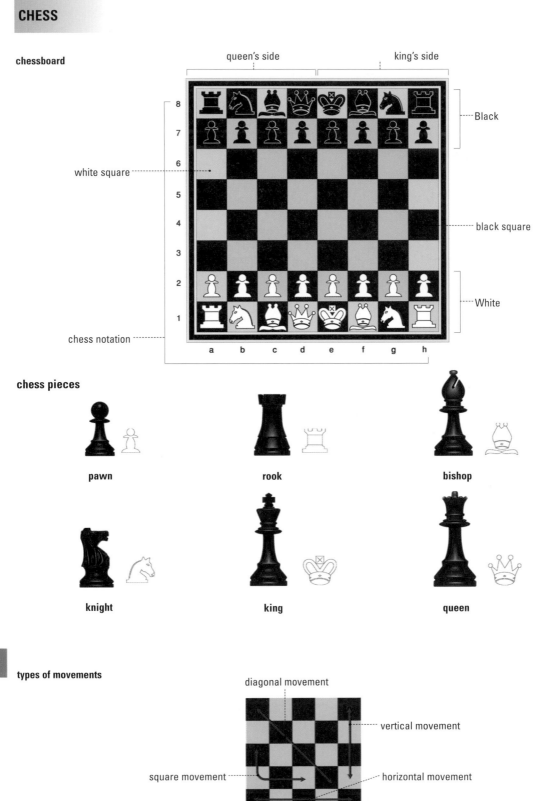

queen's side

king's side

White square

chess notation

Black

black square

White

a b c d e f g h

chess pieces

pawn

rook

bishop

knight

king

queen

types of movements

diagonal movement

vertical movement

square movement

horizontal movement

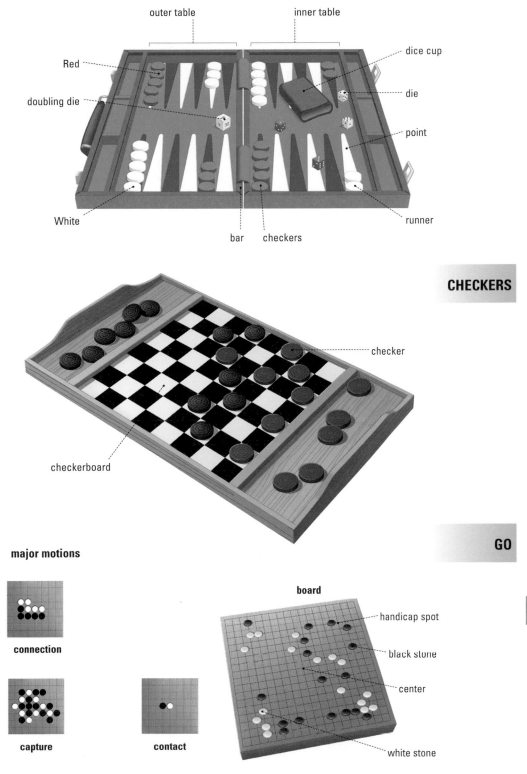

BACKGAMMON

outer table

inner table

Red

dice cup

doubling die

die

point

White

runner

bar checkers

CHECKERS

checker

checkerboard

GO

major motions

board

handicap spot

black stone

center

connection

white stone

capture **contact**

DARTS

dartboard

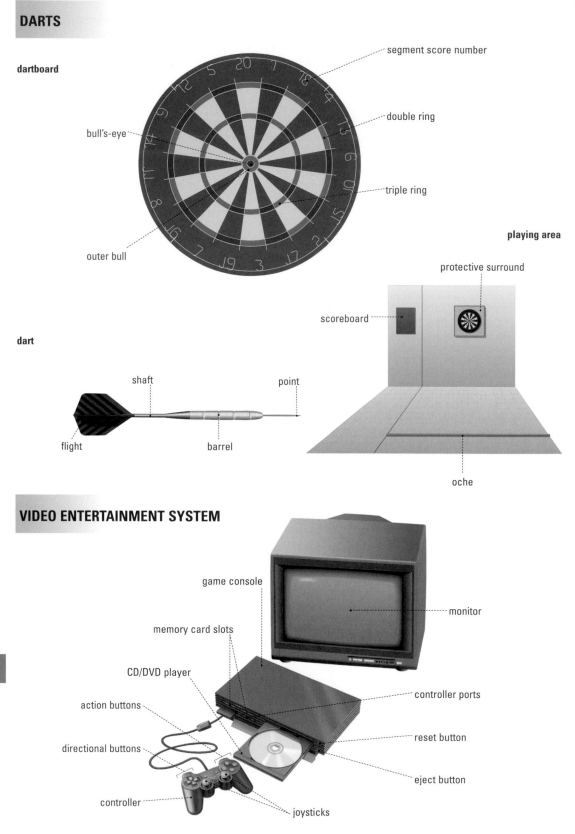

segment score number

double ring

bull's-eye

triple ring

outer bull

playing area

protective surround

scoreboard

dart

shaft

point

flight

barrel

oche

VIDEO ENTERTAINMENT SYSTEM

game console

monitor

memory card slots

CD/DVD player

controller ports

action buttons

reset button

directional buttons

eject button

controller

joysticks

Most major roads are marked with signs to guide drivers. Many of these signs are international, which means that no matter where drivers come from they can understand a road's particular code, such as the direction it is taking and where obligatory stops are located. Other road signs can be specific to a given region, while still taking their inspiration from international road signs.

MAJOR INTERNATIONAL ROAD SIGNS

stop at intersection

no entry

yield

signal ahead

direction to be followed

direction to be followed

direction to be followed

closed to pedestrians

falling rocks

deer crossing

closed to motorcycles

closed to trucks

school zone

pedestrian crossing

roadwork ahead

slippery road

SYMBOLS

317

MAJOR NORTH AMERICAN ROAD SIGNS

stop at intersection

no entry

yield

closed to motorcycles

closed to pedestrians

closed to bicycles

no U-turn

closed to trucks

direction to be followed

direction to be followed

direction to be followed

direction to be followed

school zone

pedestrian crossing

slippery road

signal ahead

falling rocks

roadwork ahead

SYMBOLS

We are surrounded by many different kinds of symbols. Common symbols are usually simple pictures that provide a variety of information in the blink of an eye. These signs are easy to understand, and they can even tell a person who cannot read where a hospital is located or where to find the closest information center. The messages conveyed by these symbols are universal and are not hampered by language barriers.

men's restroom

women's restroom

currency exchange

wheelchair access

camping (trailer and tent)

picnic area

coffee shop

camping (tent)

service station

fire extinguisher

camping (trailer)

hospital

telephone

restaurant

pharmacy

police

first aid

information

information

lost and found articles

no wheelchair access

picnics prohibited

camping prohibited

taxi transportation

SAFETY SYMBOLS

Safety symbols are essential. They alert people to possible dangers, label hazardous ingredients in products, and advise people to use certain protective equipment to avoid accidents. On a construction site, for example, a sign showing a head covered in a helmet reminds people to wear a safety helmet.

HAZARDOUS MATERIALS

corrosive

electrical hazard

explosive

flammable

radioactive

poison

PROTECTION

eye protection

ear protection

head protection

hand protection

foot protection

respiratory system protection

atmosphere 32, 41
atoll 31
atrium 218
attaché case 126
attack line 299
attack zone 299
attitude control thrusters 14
audio console 237
audio monitor 237
audio system 188
auditory meatus, external 93
auditory ossicles 100
auger bit, solid center 162
auricle 100
authorized landfill site 44
auto-reverse button 243
automatic dialer index 244
automatic drip coffee maker 151
automatically controlled door 252
automobile 184
automobile car 197
autumn 33
autumn squash 107
autumnal equinox 33
auxiliary handle 162
avocado 107
awl 311
axillary artery 99
axillary bud 48
axillary vein 99
axle 196, 307
azimuth clamp 12
azimuth fine adjustment 12
Aztec temple 219

B

B 222
baboon 83
baby food 115
back 73, 78, 84, 91, 101, 140, 141, 146, 161
back brush 132
back judge 297
back of a glove 123
back suspension 308
back zone 299
backboard 295
backboard support 295
backcourt 303
backgammon 315
backguard 153, 160
backhoe 209
backhoe controls 209
backpack 271, 312
backstay 286
backstop 290, 295
backstretch 280
backstroke 277
backstroke start 277
backstroke turn indicator 277
backward bucket 209

bactrian camel 87
badge 265
badger 80
bag well 283
bagel 114
baggage cart 253
baggage check-in counter 252
baggage claim area 252
baggage compartment 198, 203
baggage conveyor 205
baggage room 253
baggage trailer 205
bagger 257
bagpipes 224
baguette 114
bail 292
bailey 220
bakery 257
balaclava 124
balalaika 225
balance beam 274, 275
balancer 229
balcony 139
balcony door 139
baling 46
ball 281
ball boy 302
ball return 281
ball sports 290
ball stand 281
ballerina slipper 125
ballpoint pen 270
bamboo shoot 105
banana 113
band ring 129
bangle 129
banjo 224
bank 259
bar 128, 258, 260, 315
bar counter 260
bar line 222
bar stool 140, 260
barber comb 130
bargraph-type peak meter 237
bark 53
barograph 39
barrel 130, 131, 270, 316
barrel vault 218
barrette 130
barrier 141
barrier barricade tape 265
barrier beach 31
bartender 260
basalt 25
basaltic layer 24
base 103, 156, 157, 158, 166, 167, 170, 179, 198, 247
base cabinet 143
base plate 162, 289, 312
baseball 290, 291
baseline 303, 312
basement 138
basement window 135

basic source of food 41
basilic vein 99
basket 151, 289, 295
basketball 294, 295
basketball player 295
bass bridge 226
bass clarinet 234
bass clef 222
bass drum 232, 234
bass guitar 229
bass keyboard 224
bass pickup 228
bass register 224
bass tone control 229, 242
bassoon 231
bassoons 234
baster 148
bat 291, 292
bat, morphology 82
bath sheet 132
bath towel 132
bathrobe 119
bathroom 138, 139, 154, 266, 269
bathroom scale 170
bathroom skylight 139
bathtub 139, 154
baton holder 265
bats, examples 82
batsman 292
batten 278
batten pocket 278
batter 290, 291
batter head 232
batter's helmet 291
battery 173, 175, 196
batting glove 291
battlement 220
bay 9, 22
bayonet base 156
beach 31
beach volleyball 299
beak 88
beaker 166
beam 170, 215, 275
beam bridge 183
bean bag chair 140
beans 108
beauty care 257
beaver 77
bed 142, 275, 310
bed chamber 218
bedrock 26, 53
bedroom 139, 309
bedside lamp 266
bedside table 266
beech 54
beer 256
beer mug 144
beet 104
begonia 51
Belgian endive 106
bell 230, 231
bell brace 231
bell tower 221

bellows 224
bells 232
belly 84
belt 116, 305
belt highway 23
belt loop 116
beluga whale 89
bench 140, 255, 259, 267
bend 128
beret 124
bergamot 112
Bering Sea 19
berries 109
berries, examples 109
bezel 129
bib 121
biceps brachii 95
bicycle 194
bicycle bag (pannier) 194
bicycle parking 269
bicycle, accessories 194
bicycles, examples 195
bidet 154
bilberries 109
bill 72
bills, examples 73
binding 124, 288
binocular microscope 167
biosphere 40
biosphere, structure 41
birch 54
bird 72
bird feeder 72
bird of prey 73
bird, morphology 72
birdhouse 72
birds 72
bishop 314
bison 86
bitter melon 107
Black 314
black beans 108
black bear 81
black currants 109
black flying fox 82
black gram beans 108
black radishes 104
black salsify 104
Black Sea 19
black square 314
black stone 315
black-eyed peas 108
blackberries 109
blackboard 268
blade 47, 49, 150, 155, 161, 162, 163, 179, 210, 214, 278, 284, 285, 286, 293
blade injector 131
blade lift cylinder 210
blade tilting mechanism 162
blank 313
blanket 142
blasting charge 180
blastodisc 72
blender 150
blending attachment 150

C

E

INDEX

M

INDEX

muffler felt 226
muffler pedal 226
multigrain bread 114
mummy 310
mung beans 108
muntin 137
muscles 95
museum 251
mushroom 47
mushroom, structure 47
music 222
music room 268
music stand 233
music store 258
musical instruments 224
musical instruments, traditional 224
musical notation 222
muskmelon 113
mute 230
muzzle 78, 79, 85
mycelium 47

N

nacelle 179
nail 161
nail cleaner 132
nail clippers 132
nail nick 311
nail scissors 132
naos 217
nape 72, 91
narwhal 89
nasal bone 93
nasal cavity 97
national park 23
natural 223
natural arch 31
natural greenhouse effect 43
natural sponge 132
nautical sports 278
navel 90
navigation light 207
NEAR 13
near/far dial 240
neck 67, 85, 91, 94, 146, 227, 228, 229
neck end 116
neck guard 263
neck pad 298
neck roll 142
necktie 116
nectarine 110
needle 29
negative contact 173
negative pole 175
Neptune 7
nerve 101
nerve fiber 101
nerve termination 101
nervous system 97
nervous system, central 97

nest 72
net 295, 299, 303
net band 303
net judge 303
nettle 106
neutral zone 284, 296
new crescent 10
new moon 10
newspaper shop 259
newt 66
next call 245
nib 270
nictitating membrane 79
nightshot switch 240
nimbostratus 35
no entry 317, 318
no U-turn 318
no wheelchair access 319
nonagon 172
nonbiodegradable pollutants 44
nonreusable residue waste 46
North 23
North America 18
North American road signs 318
North Pole 0, 20
North Sea 19
North-Northeast 23
North-Northwest 23
Northeast 23
Northern hemisphere 20
Northern leopard frog 66
northern right whale 88
Northwest 23
nose 77, 85, 90, 102, 206, 287
nose landing gear 206
nose leaf 82
nose leather 79
nose of the quarter 125
nostril 64, 65, 66, 67, 72, 85, 102
notation, musical 222
notch 170
note symbols 223
notebook 271
nozzle 14, 16
nubby tire 306
nuclear energy 177
nuclear energy, production of electricity 178
nuclear envelope 56
nuclear power plant 177
nuclear waste 45
nucleolus 56
nucleus 10, 11, 56
number of tracks sign 198
number plate 306
numeric keyboard 170
nurse 266
nut 227, 228, 229
nutcracker 147

O

oak 54
oarlock 279
oars, types 278
oasis 29
Oberon 7
obi 305
objective 167
objective lens 12, 235
oboe 231
oboes 234
observation deck 253
observation window 15
obtuse angle 171
occipital bone 93
ocean 9, 22, 42
ocean weather station 38
Ocean, Arctic 19
Oceania 19
oche 316
octave 222
octave mechanism 231
octopus 57
odometer 188
off-road motorcycle (dirtbike) 191
office 253, 260, 261
office building 200, 251
office tower 250
officers' dormitory 262
officers' washrooms and showers 262
officials 293
officials' bench 284
offshore prospecting 180
oil 180
oil paint 212
oil pastels 212
oil pollution 45
oil spill 45
oil terminal 200
okapi 87
okra 107
old crescent 10
olives 107
on-air warning light 237
on-board computer 188
on-deck circle 290
on-off button 243
on-off indicator 130
on-off light 244
on-off switch 130, 131, 151, 157
on-off/volume 242
one-person tent 309
one-piece suit 287
one-storey house 216
one-toed hoof 85
onion 103
online game 249
opal 129
operating instructions 261
operculum 65
opossum 76

opposable thumb 83
optic chiasm 97
optical lens 269
optical scanner 247, 257
optical sorting 46
optical stage 269
optician 259
oral cavity 96, 97
orange 112, 211
orange, section 112
orange-red 211
orange-yellow 211
orangutan 83
orbicularis oculi 95
orbiculate 49
orbiter 14, 15
orbits of the planets 6
orchestra 234
orchid 50
ordinary die 313
organ 226
oriental cockroach 63
ornamental kale 106
ornamental tree 134
ornaments 223
oscillating light 263
ostrich 75
other signs 223
ottoman 140
outer bull 316
outer core 24
outer table 315
outer toe 72
outfield fence 291
outgoing announcement cassette 244
output jack 228
outrigger 209, 263, 279
outside counter 125
outside linebacker 296
outside mirror 184
outsole 122, 125
outwash plain 29
ovary 50
ovate 49
oven 143, 153
oven control knobs 153
overall standings scoreboard 274
overalls 121
overbed table 266
overcoat 119
overflow 154
overhead connection 176
overhead projector 269
overpass 182
ovule 50
owl 74
oxygen cylinder, portable 267
oxygen outlet 266
oxygen pressure actuator 17
oystercatcher 75
ozone layer 32

P

Q

INDEX

INDEX